EXPERT WITNESSING IN FORENSIC ACCOUNTING

A Handbook for Lawyers and Accountants

ZEPH TELPNER
MICHAEL MOSTEK

CRC PRESS

Boca Raton   London   New York   Washington, D.C.

Library of Congress Cataloging-in-Publication Data

Telpner, Zeph
 Expert witnessing in forensic accounting : a handbook for lawyers and accountants /
Zeph Telpner and Michael S. Mostek
   p.   cm.--(Expert witnessing)
 Includes bibliographical references and index.
 ISBN 0-8493-0898-4 (alk. paper)
 1. Forensic accounting--United States. 2. Evidence, Expert--United States. I. Mostek,
Michael S. II. Title. III. Series
KF8968.15 .T45 2002
657—dc21   2002017497
                                                                      CIP

Visit the CRC Press Web site at www.crcpress.com

© 2003 by CRC Press LLC

No claim to original U.S. Government works
International Standard Book Number 0-8493-0898-4
Library of Congress Card Number 2002017497
Printed in the United States of America 1 2 3 4 5 6 7 8 9 0
Printed on acid-free paper

Preface

Part One

Forensic accounting–expert witnessing is not a new discipline, but few accounting textbooks exist to present a broad view of the profession of forensic accounting–expert witnessing. Books do exist on special subparts of it, including the determination of damages, business valuations, general discussions of fraud investigations, or other limited areas of forensic accounting. Books devoted to the expert witness in court are designed to assist all experts to become more valuable to the court, and to the attorneys who must work with them.

Much of this book is written in the first person, with the authors' experiences used as examples. All cases used as illustrations are from actual disputes worked on by the authors. We believed that actual cases with the insight of those who worked on them would be more helpful than if we had analyzed disputes that were resolved by others.

We also wanted this book to differ from other textbooks. We did not want to tell a reader what to do; we wanted to show the reader how to do it.

The authors have devoted many professional years to litigated matters or tax disputes short of litigation. I have practiced public accounting either as an employee, partner or proprietor since 1956. My co-author, Michael ("Mike") Mostek, J.D., has been a trial attorney since 1985 and is a partner in a 17-attorney law firm.

My first forensic engagement occurred in 1961 when I was assigned to the Sister Elizabeth Kenney embezzlement in Minneapolis. Later, I discovered falsified records and inventory theft by the manager of a gas distribution subsidiary of a natural gas company. In 1964 and 1965, I was engaged to reconstruct the accounting records for a multistate bankruptcy estate. I did not testify as an expert until 1966, when I was appointed to serve as Master in Chancery by the Iowa District Court. The appointment authorized me to take testimony under oath, and to have the U.S. Marshall enforce summons for me.

For many years, CPAs and other accountants have been called upon to testify in court. CPAs were rarely sued for malpractice until the 1960s, when malpractice charges against CPAs began to mount. With an explosion in litigation and malpractice charges, accounting expert witnesses more frequently have been hired to assist with tax, accounting, financial litigation and fraud when money is involved.

In 1979, I wrote a continuing professional education (CPE) seminar for CPAs entitled "The Practical Aspects of Forensic Accounting and Litigation Support." The seminar was presented five times by state CPA societies. The average attendance was eight students, so the course died.

For many years, each accountant who was interested in forensics and expert witnessing was self-taught. Often, he was a bad teacher. Now, large accounting firms have departments that are dedicated to forensics. The American Institute of Certified Public Accountants (AICPA) and related state associations now present a few forensic courses each year. Usually these focus on fraud. Two organizations feature many forensic accounting seminars. One is the American Board of Forensic Accountants (a division of the American College of Forensic Examiners). Only recently has it begun to present many relevant courses annually. Most of its seminars are prepared by college professors who also have practical forensic experience, and experienced forensic CPAs from local, national, and Big Five accounting firms. The other is the Association of Certified Fraud Examiners, which offers many fine courses on fraud.

In 1999, I was presenting a program on forensic accounting at the Waldorf Astoria and later wandered into the room of one the exhibitors, where I met Becky McEldowney, senior acquisitions editor for CRC Press. I proposed to write a handbook on forensic accounting and accounting expert witnessing for attorneys so they would know when and how to work with accountants. Becky asked me to address it to accountants also. Later, Becky accepted my proposal to co-write it with Mike, directing our comments to both accountants and lawyers. Mike and I are compatible and work well together on trials. I have learned much from Mike, as I have from other lawyers with whom I have worked.

We have tried to show some successes and failures of experts — including our own imbecilities when they occurred. Some of our examples expose a local accountant, some expose a Big Five or national firm. Some expose my mistakes. The purpose of such examples is to remind an attorney to always match the accounting expert with the job to be done. An example from my own career demonstrates how the arena in which one learns a trade or profession can make all the difference. After working for very large firms — Arthur Andersen then Peat Marwick — I opened my own practice in Iowa, where I suddenly was called upon to prepare farm returns. When the first return I prepared for a cattle rancher was reviewed, the Internal Revenue agent removed six steers from the depreciation schedule. Being a city boy, I didn't know steers were castrated bulls and couldn't reproduce. Therefore, they were not subject to depreciation. Both the rancher and the agent laughed at me. The rancher said he knew I was making a mistake when I depreciated them, but, he thought, "more power to me," if the depreciation deduction passed an IRS examination. Later, when I tried to convince the agent that the steers were for display purposes, he refused to accept my argument, but he said that I deserved an "A" for trying.

To speed the reading of this book, we have not used the phrases, "he or she," or "him or her." We have used the masculine pronouns: "he, his or him." My niece is a successful trial lawyer and I would never slight her. So please, women lawyers and accountants, substitute "she," or "her," at any time or place.

Zeph Telpner

Part Two

Whenever Zeph and I worked together, we realized that the laws of civil procedure, evidence, expert opinions, trial procedure and the presentation of expert testimony were a mystery to many accountants and even some lawyers. And, we both knew that not all lawyers take the time to provide the information or explain the adversary process in a way that would truly help the forensic accounting expert do the best job in preparing and presenting his opinions. Our goal here is to write a handbook that pulls together all the essential information on this topic, useful to both the lawyer and the expert.

This is not a scholarly book written from the ivory towers of the law schools or business schools. You can pick any topic in this handbook and probably find published volumes of detailed material that you could spend many hours studying. And, there may be times when an important issue in your case demands that an exhaustive study be undertaken. But, in our estimation, this is more often the exception than the rule. This is a book conceived and written in the trenches, for professionals pitched in the adversarial process. We hope it will serve as a fitting reference guide for lawyers who are helping their experts prepare testimony, and for forensic accountants who are preparing to testify. We hope that you will be able to pick up this book and find, if not all the answers, then the succinct explanation you need in short order. It is intended to provide a framework within which the lawyer and the forensic accountant can build their working relationship by providing some common ground and a common rudimentary base of knowledge.

This handbook is a valuable addition to any legal or accounting library. We hope the lawyers who purchase this book will share it with their accounting experts, and use it as an aid in preparing them to assist with the case. We hope the accountants who acquire this book will share it with their lawyers and use it to learn more about or refresh their understanding of the legal process whenever they may be called upon to develop an opinion and provide testimony in legal proceedings.

We offer this handbook to serve as a useful tool for both the lawyer and accountant in meeting these objectives. If you are a lawyer, we hope you will receive our methods and advice as tools you can use to help you fulfill all of these responsibilities. With so many demands on your time and attention in preparing your case, we urge you to turn to this handbook and even share it with your forensic accounting expert as a means of building that all-important relationship. And we urge you to do it early in your case. We intend this handbook to make at least this aspect of your work more effective and efficient, relieving some of the burden and allowing you to focus more energy on other details of the case.

This handbook is designed to offer accountants a better understanding of the process in which they have become involved. Accountants will be armed with a working knowledge of the adversary process. They will be confident in asking the lawyer for the information needed to develop and present their opinions. In summary, our essential argument — that lawyers and expert accountants must work together closely and early in preparing a case — forms the premise for this handbook. We believe it will help provide the tools you need to work closely and effectively in preparing your current case and those that follow. It is up to you to decide when you will start working together, but we believe the earlier the better.

Of necessity, this book discusses the procedural and evidentiary rules that most often affect the forensic accounting specialist in his work. When doing so, we will refer to the federal civil rules in effect and customs prevailing in our locality at the time of this writing. Readers, of course, should be aware that the requirements and customs of the federal courts in their locality might differ. Also, the rules of criminal procedure will apply in a criminal case. And certainly, the rules and customs, whether civil or criminal, vary from state to state, sometimes significantly. A detailed review of all potentially applicable criminal and civil rules in both federal and state courts is unworkable and would probably make this handbook difficult to use. Referring to the uniform federal civil rules is both useful and efficient in pursuing the goal of creating a common working knowledge of these matters, upon which the lawyer and accounting expert can expand and simplify as needed for purposes of their work.

Good luck with your case, and work early and often with your experts.

Mike Mostek

The Authors

Zeph Telpner, CPA, limits his practice to forensic accounting and tax consulting provided nationally from his offices in Council Bluffs, Iowa. Formerly with the firms now known as Arthur Andersen LLP, and KPMG Peat Marwick LLP, he is self-employed. He received his BSBA degree from Creighton University in 1958, and earned his CPA designation from Nebraska and Iowa in 1962. His public accounting career began in 1956, and he completed his 41st year in forensic accounting in 2001.

His federal and state court forensic engagements as an expert accounting witness and consultant include disputes in accounting malpractice, criminal tax fraud, corporation breach of contract, business valuations, trademark infringement, murder liability, injury damages, divorce, and bankruptcy. He also has served as Special Master, Master in Chancery, and bankruptcy examiner.

Zeph has written and presented 18 continuing education seminars for CPA and trade associations, the Internal Revenue Service and businesses in 26 states. In 1985, he wrote an industry training and reference guide, *Accounting and Tax for the Trucking Industry,* for Arthur Andersen LLP. About 250 of his human interest essays and business profiles have been featured in newspapers and magazines.

Zeph is recognized nationally as an expert in truck transportation and providing continuing professional education to CPAs. In 1981, he sold his ongoing trucking industry practice to Arthur Andersen LLP. He has served on the boards of directors and committees of national and local accounting associations.

Michael S. Mostek, J.D., is a shareholder with the law firm of Koley, Jessen, P.C., in Omaha, Nebraska. He has practiced environmental law, real estate, business law and civil litigation for the past 16 years. He advises clients nationally on due diligence, liability and compliance issues under both state and federal environmental laws and regulations.

Mike received his J.D. degree from Creighton University School of Law (1985), and his B.A. degree from Kearney State College (1982). He was admitted to the Nebraska Supreme Court in 1985, the U.S. Court of Appeals, Eighth Circuit, in 1989 and to the U.S. Supreme Court in 1990.

Mike frequently speaks and writes about real estate and environmental topics and participates in several specialized interest law associations as a member or as a section chairman.

Table of Contents

7   The Effect of the Attorney–Client Privilege and Work Product Doctrine   209

The Forensic Accountant

1

1.1 A Forensic Accountant as Expert Witness or Consultant

1.1.1 Expert Witness

Lawyers, judges, and forensic accountants often view expert witnessing through different eyes. A lawyer would like his client's expert witness to rebut the opposing expert, and to arrive at a conclusion favorable to his client. Judges often want the expert to arrive at a conclusion when the judge cannot reach one without the expert's assistance. There are times when more than one conclusion can be reached from the forensic facts available to the expert, but the judge wants the expert's facts and logic without a conclusion. This allows the judge to arrive at his own conclusion uncolored by opinions of the expert witness.

A forensic accountant is one who has mastered the science of accounting and is able to assist lawyers and the courts to understand and apply accounting issues to the law and to disputed matters. Forensic accounting experts have extensive experience in investigations to determine solutions to disputed accounting matters, to write expert reports on their investigation, and to appear in court as expert witnesses. The expert may be hired solely as a consultant to an attorney and his client during litigation, or as one who provides opinion evidence as an expert. Often, the roles of expert witness and expert consultant merge if so requested and arranged by the attorney on behalf of his client. The accounting expert witness should reach conclusions independent of the attorney and client who hired him even though they may arrive at similar conclusions. He must direct his written reports and oral testimony under oath to assist the trier of fact to arrive at valid conclusions in light of the accounting matters as applied to the law.

Expert witness accounting can be somewhat like politics. While the expert witness accountant must be independent of the parties to the dispute, he may conclude from the facts, and his interpretation of them, that his engaging attorney is correct and that the opposition is wrong. If he can demonstrate the proof of his conclusions, he is a strong expert witness.

Accounting often baffles nonaccountants, and, in its advanced theory, it also can baffle long-time accountants. Even the most skillful and experienced lawyer can misunderstand what the accountant is telling him. The accountant seems to speak in a different language. Even lawyers who are also certified public accountants (CPAs) but have not practiced public accounting, or have minimal accounting experience, often misunderstand accountants. Of course, judges and juries are not immune to confusion relative to accounting. The attorney must help the accounting expert witness to state his conclusions in terms that the attorney, the judge and the jury can understand.

The differences in thinking between the legal and accounting professions require that the attorney understands how to choose the right forensic accountant for the disputed matters.

Forensic accountants are not equal, regardless of their years of professional accounting experience. Some may be computer experts and others computer novices. Some may have limited their work to specialization. Some may be tax experts, auditing experts or experts in assisting public corporations with the ponderous accounting requirements of the Securities and Exchange Commission. Within a tax specialty, many subspecialties can exist: income tax return preparation, tax disputes at the appeals office level or in tax court, or both. Some specialize in estate and gift taxes, others in state income and sales taxes. There are specialties by type of tax entities, such as Domestic International Sales Corporations, Subchapter S Corporations, Partnerships, Limited Liability Companies, and by transactions such as corporate reorganizations, liquidations and incorporations.

Industry specialization is also common. There are forensic accounting experts on taverns, entertainment, clothing, furniture, airlines, banks and a myriad of other industries. Industries, too, often have many subdivisions. Clothing manufacturers, for example, might include manufacturing, wholesaling, or retailing within their corporate conglomerate. Truck and automobile manufacturers often have finance company parents or subsidiaries and captive insurance companies.

1.1.2   Consultant

The role of a forensic accountant as a consultant is not limited to litigation support or expert witnessing. A forensic accountant might be hired to review and strengthen internal controls, to determine if assets are missing, or to discover if tax laws or accounting rules have been applied correctly to company transactions. Forensic accountants are often hired to determine if an embezzlement has occurred or, if so, how much is missing and how it was done.

1.2   When the Forensic Accountant Should Be Hired for Litigation Matters

When litigation revolves around facts that require interpretation and discovery of accounting matters, development of accounting issues, accounting opinions, or expert witnessing, the lawyer should convince his client to hire a forensic accountant before a petition or complaint is filed or answered. The accountant will be able to develop accounting issues for the complaint or answer, assist with interrogatories and requests for records, and reduce the volume of unneeded accounting information that a lay person might request.

By hiring a forensic accountant early, an attorney may save time for himself and money for his client. The accountant can assist with deposition questions and accounting interpretations of statements made by the deposed expert or lay witnesses in general business, finance, and accounting matters, or specific matters of a specialized industry. The expert can make discovery suggestions or bring relevant transactions to the attorney's attention.

Early contact with the expert gives both the accountant and the lawyer time to prepare or review the expert's proposed job engagement contract and negotiate time, fees and costs. It also allows the lawyer time to determine whether the expert is the proper one for the current facts in dispute, or if a different expert would be better.

1.3   Where to Find an Expert Forensic Accountant

Before searching for an expert forensic accountant, review the available facts to determine whether you need one. If you need one to determine the value of a business, should you hire a CPA or a member of the appraisal institute (MAI)? Many CPAs have received a certified valuation analyst (CVA) designation from the American Institute of Certified Public Accountants (AICPA). An MAI's experience would ordinarily give him an opportunity to prepare more evaluations than an accountant who has a complete accounting practice in addition to sporadic business valuations. If the accountant is an expert in the type of business or industry to be valued, he may have an edge over an MAI who is not an industry expert.

Assume that you must value a large, less-than-truckload, over-the-road motor carrier. Will you hire an MAI or a CPA who is a CVA or an economist? You will not hire any of them if they have not had trucking experience. Instead, you can hire a CPA who is an expert on trucking, a non-CPA who may be an expert on sales of trucking companies, a trucking company executive, or a motor carrier attorney. Professional appraisers with no experience in the industry may not be as qualified as an industry expert who is not a professional appraiser.

1.4   Must the Accounting Expert Witness Be a CPA?

To determine whether a high-volume tax return preparer has followed the Internal Revenue Service (IRS) Rules of Practice, an enrolled agent or an accounting practitioner who prepares hundreds of individual income tax returns might be a better witness than a CPA who prepares ten returns. For most tax and accounting matters, a CPA is more likely to satisfy the expert witness requirements of *Daubert* than is a non-CPA. (See *Daubert v. Merrell Dow Pharmaceuticals, Inc.,* 509 U.S. 579 (1993) in Chapter 2 for its application to an accounting expert witness.) In accounting and tax matters, a CPA's credentials usually are thought to be more acceptable than non-CPA accountants. However, a mediocre CPA will not do better work than an outstanding accountant without a CPA certificate. It is up to the engaging attorney to qualify the expert witness in court even if he is not a CPA. Many experienced accountants who have not passed the CPA examination often supervise inexperienced CPAs. Deciding what type of expert witness is needed for financial, business, accounting or tax disputes depends on all facts and circumstances when the decision to hire is made.

Lawyers often believe that they require the services of a Big Five or a national or regional accounting firm for forensic accounting and expert witness work. Sometimes, a case does require a large firm. A violation of the federal or state securities laws is best served by accounting firms that have considerable experience with public offerings.

Most litigation can be resolved with highly experienced local accountants. Trucking companies are best served by an expert with hands-on experience in the trucking industry if the matter does not involve securities violations. A partnership of cardiologists involved in litigation among themselves could be served by an accountant for a partnership of physicians who may not be cardiologists.

Accounting or international taxation malpractice by an international or national accounting firm might require an expert accounting witness from another international or national accounting firm as the expert if the issues arise from international taxation or an audit engagement for a publicly traded company. Other types of malpractice by any firm, regardless of size, can often be resolved by a local CPA.

Some law firms have found excellent experts by hiring a CPA to review the issues and help determine what kind of accounting expert is needed. Once the determination is made to hire a forensic accounting expert witness, many sources are available. A few of the sources are:

- Local industry. If you have a trucking company dispute, ask in-house counsel of similar size and type of trucking companies for recommendations.
- Trade association. State motor carrier associations exist in most states.
- A local state society of CPAs and the state board of public accountancy.
- The Teamsters Union.
- Review continuing accounting education courses to determine who is teaching and writing accounting and tax courses on the particular specialty in which you are interested.
- Legal research will discover similar cases and you can ask those attorneys which expert witness they used.

Trade magazines for lawyers contain ads for expert witnesses placed by individuals and by business organizations who refer experts to lawyers. Referral organizations often have an add-on to the expert's hourly rate that can almost equal the expert's rate. If the expert's normal rate is $150 an hour, the add-on could bring the rate to $225 an hour or more. The expert's agreement with the referring service usually prohibits him from disclosing the add-on. Lawyers should ask the referring organization if it has an add-on, the amount of the add-on, and if it is willing to negotiate a lower rate. They often are willing to share a *pro rata* write-down of the fee with the expert.

1.5 How to Determine Whether the Right Forensic Accountant Has Been Selected

After selecting one or more accountants, interview each briefly by telephone to determine whether he is interested and if he is qualified. Relate a brief synopsis of the issues to each and request a *curriculum vitae* (CV). If the CV appears promising, ask for a job proposal. If the expert asks for copies of the complaint, interrogatories and answers, requests for records and answers, summaries of depositions, the lawyer's summary of the case, the estimated date of trial, the identities and firm affiliation of the opposing expert accountants, an interview with the hiring attorney, and who will pay for the expert's work, the hiring attorney can begin to believe that his expert has been located.

The attorney should make an appointment to interview the expert in the expert's office. The lawyer should ask to review the accounting, tax and specialized industries library of the expert. If he has a sparse library, then ask how he proposes to research. If he is a member of that industry's trade association, he can use the specialized industry library. Some have been allowed to use the IRS district library, and others have arranged to use the library of a larger firm, including the libraries of Big Five firms. You can find out about their library sharing capabilities.

Ask for copies of expert witness reports that he has issued to the court. These will provide an idea of his investigative and research skills, and of his ability to write about a technical matter in lay language so that judges, jurors and lawyers will understand the issues. His report also will give you an idea of his ability to reason and to convince others of his conclusions.

Determine from the CV and from the interview whether the expert engages in non-accounting activities. If he gives several speeches annually about his work, if he has taught continuing professional education courses to other CPAs and to business executives, if he has taught college level courses, then he has signaled his ability to communicate ably from the witness stand.

If the expert satisfies the attorney during this interview that he is the expert to hire, then the attorney should review the documents he requested from the expert and, if satisfied, should ask the expert to send a job engagement letter.

1.6   How the Expert Prepares for and Responds to the Initial Interview by the Lawyer

Before the expert meets with the hiring lawyer, he should read and make notes of the complaint, interrogatories and answers, requests for records and answers, summaries of depositions, the lawyer's summary of the case, the estimated date of trial, the identities and firm affiliation and of the opposing experts.

He should make copies of his expert reports for the lawyer, but he should blank out the names on those reports that did not become part of the public records of a court proceeding.

The expert should ask the lawyer what is expected of him and explain whether he can meet those expectations. He may suggest a change in strategy in certain accounting matters. The lawyer might, for example, expect the expert to review a roomful of invoices, but the expert may have determined from a deposition or other documents that the review of the invoices will not be relevant to the issues.

The accountant can obtain information on the lawyer from Martindale and Hubbell. This multi-volume set, available in most law libraries, contains information on the law firm, its representative clients, brief biographies of its members, and a rating of the lawyer's professional skills. This can help determine compatibility between the lawyer and the expert.

1.7 What a *Curriculum Vitae* Should Contain

A CV is a short account of an expert's career and professional qualifications. It is not a biography to introduce him, but is designed to give a lawyer an idea of what the expert can do and to help him qualify the expert professionally so he can give expert testimony. The following excerpts from a CV do not contain rules cast in iron, and most CVs are prepared according to an expert's individual preference and style.

The first page of a CV should be on the expert's letterhead for easy identification. That ensures that the mailing and office address and telephone, fax and e-mail numbers are always included in the CV.

The first page should contain a table of contents so a lawyer can turn quickly to any specific section that is of special interest to him. A helpful first page might look like this:

Zeph Telpner, CPA

Curriculum Vitae

Table of Contents

Each of the pages following the table of contents will have the header:

Zeph Telpner, CPA
Curriculum Vitae

The header on each page is followed by the contents description. A sample of the body text of a CV follows:

Representative Engagements in Forensic Accounting, Expert Witnessing and Litigation Support

(The forensic engagements and other litigation experiences are listed first, as this is the core experience of an expert witness. The list of engagements should contain the name of the case, the court, who hired you, what you were hired to do, and whether you testified, were deposed, or issued an expert report. The following are a few cases that I believe to be of particular interest. Some forensic accountants list all of their cases by title only and without commentary.)

Business Termination

In the Matter of Arbitration Between: McNicholas Transportation Co. and Central States Southeast and Southwest Areas Pension Fund, American Arbitration Association Case, Chicago, Illinois and Cleveland, Ohio. Engaged by Central States to determine if McNicholas had terminated or diminished its business. Testified.

Bankruptcy

In re the Mason and Dixon Lines, Inc., Chapter 11 Reorganization, United States Bankruptcy Court for the Middle District of North Carolina. Engaged by Central States Pension Fund to challenge the Multi-Employer Pension Plan Act Withdrawal Liability. Testified.

In the Matter of Best Refrigerated Express, Inc., debtor, U.S. Bankruptcy Court for the District of Nebraska. Appointed examiner in the interests of the creditors and of the estate *in re* Chapter 11 filing of debtor. Issued examiner's report.

Loss of Earnings

Knoer v. Future Foam, Inc., Iowa District Court. Engaged by plaintiff to establish loss of earnings for an owner-operator who was run over by a truck from a private fleet. Testified.

Accounting for Assets

Wings Trans. Inc. v. Arnold H. Delancey, et al. and Wings Trans. Inc., et al. v. Harry Hahn and Debra Merritt, Iowa District Court. Appointed Special Master to make an accounting of the trucking company. Settled out of court.

Antitrust Price Fixing Conviction, Petition of Appeal

Lewis Service Center, Inc., a Corporation v. Mack Truck, Inc., a Corporation, and Mack Financial Corporation, U.S. District Court, Nebraska. Engaged by defendant for antitrust appeal to U.S. Court of Appeals for the 8th Circuit, and later appealed by Plaintiff to U.S. Supreme Court. CA8 reversed District Court and U.S. Supreme Court upheld CA8. Issued explanatory letter to attorneys.

Water Utility Rate Dispute

City of Pacific Junction, Iowa v. Glenwood Sewer and Water Department (Board of Waterworks Trustees of the City of Glenwood, Iowa), Iowa District Court of Mills County. Engaged by defendant to interpret ratemaking accounting contract, and to determine proper rate increases under the contract. Issued report. Settled out of court.

Trademark Infringement Profits

Dakota Industries, Inc., v. Dakota Sportswear, Inc., U.S. District Court (SD). Engaged by defendant to determine whether it earned profits from manufacture and sale of merchandise alleged to have been an infringement of trademark. Issued report and testified.

Independent Contractor or Employee

Boles Trucking, Inc., a Corporation, v. United States of America, U.S. District Court of the District of Nebraska. Engaged by plaintiff as an expert witness to determine and give testimony that plaintiff's drivers were independent contractors and not employees, and that payroll taxes should not have been assessed by the Internal Revenue Service. Issued report and testified.

Breach of Contract

Reo Distribution Services, Inc., v. Fisher Controls International, Inc., et al., U.S. District Court, Western District of Virginia, Harrisonburg Division. Hired by defendants to rebut damages and allegation that agreement to purchase transportation was wrongfully abrogated by defendants. Issued expert's report. Settled out of court.

Miscellaneous Other Litigation

Master in Chancery in partnership dissolution; accounting for a multistate bankruptcy, accounting for estate distribution among beneficiaries, breach of contract, various business valuations in dissolution disputes and divorces, malpractice litigation against CPAs.

Representative Work in Tax Non-Litigation Matters

Taxpayers' lawyers or accountants have engaged me to assist them before the IRS Appeals Office, or before the U.S. Tax Court with criminal fraud cases in Arizona, Colorado, Missouri, Nebraska and Iowa; non-criminal protests to appeals office re: income, excise property, estate and gift tax assessments, and in matters of disallowance of exempt status.

Books and Articles Written

(Any textbooks and articles you have written on forensics, expert witnessing, and other accounting topics that have been published in professional publications have special significance to the user of your CV. These give an indication of the broad range of your technical knowledge and its acceptance by others in your profession. The non-technical columns illustrate your ability to write.)

Continuing Professional Education Textbooks Published by the AICPA, IRS, California and New York Accounting Education and Corporate Business Clients, etc.:

The Practical Aspects of Litigation Support and Forensic Accounting
The Substance of Examinations (for Internal Revenue Agents)
Accounting and Taxation for the Trucking Industry (for Arthur Andersen & Co.)
Creative Tax Research
Accounting for the Trucking Industry
The Trucking Industry — Contract Carriers (AICPA)
Purchase, Sale or Liquidation of Partnerships and Proprietorships
Sec. 351 Incorporations and Related Record Keeping Requirements
How to Borrow from the IRS

Articles and Columns

The Journal of Accountancy

Nebraska Trucker
Grit
Feature writer and columnist for the *Midlands Business Journal* and *The Daily Nonpareil*

Teaching Experience

(Teaching experience alerts the lawyers to your ability to explain technical accounting topics to an audience in an easily understood manner. Judges and jurors are an audience.)

My Own Courses

I have taught all of the seminars that I have written for state CPA associations, the IRS, trade associations, or private industry in 23 states and the District of Columbia.

College Courses

I have taught college level income tax, accounting and auditing courses in the following capacities:

- Lecturer in accounting and taxation — University of Nebraska at Omaha
- Adjunct Professor of Taxation — Buena Vista University at Council Bluffs
- Adjunct Professor in Accounting — Iowa Western Community College at Council Bluffs, Iowa

Other

Many professional groups have invited me as guest speaker on the topics of revenue agent's examinations, income taxes, trucking accounting, miscellaneous management and accounting matters, and forensic accounting. A few of these are:

- National Accounting and Finance Council of the American Trucking Associations, Inc. — annual conventions in San Francisco, CA and St. Louis, MO
- Georgia Society Of CPAs — Practioners' Forum, Macon, GA
- New York-New Jersey Motor Carrier Association Accounting Council — Conference in Paramus, NJ

- Land Improvement Contractors Association — Annual Meeting in Orlando, FL
- Deloitte & Touche — Firm training in Des Moines, IA
- A&S Building Systems, Inc. — Management seminar for closely held businesses in Reno, NV

Experience

(Professional work experience provides the lawyer with knowledge of who trained you originally and what you have accomplished. These credentials are important to some lawyers.)

Employment

March 1989 to present: Self-employed.

October 1987 to March 1989: Sold most of ongoing tax practice to regional CPA firm and maintained my own office to continue my forensic accounting and litigation support practice.

December 1985: Sold half of my ongoing income tax practice to regional CPA firm and continued as self-employed.

December 1980: Sold my ongoing trucking practice to Arthur Andersen & Co.

September 1978 to September 1980: Tax partner of Miller & Moore (now Baird, Kurtz & Dobson).

December 1965 to September 1978: Self-employed.

1964 to 1965: Managing CPA of Peat, Marwick, Mitchell & Co, Council Bluffs, IA.

1963 to 1964: Tax Partner of Telpner, Bernstein, Friedman & Tighe. (My partners merged with the former Elmer Fox & Co. and I merged with the former Peat, Marwick, Mitchell.)

1958 to 1963: Arthur Andersen & Co., audit senior, then supervisor in tax department.

Education, Awards, etc.

(Much of this information is only to illustrate that you can complete the commitments that you make.)

Education

Bachelor of Science Business Administration, major in accounting (1958), Creighton University, Omaha, NE.

Licenses and Certificates

> Certified Public Accountant: Nebraska No. 605 (1962), Iowa No. 874 (1963)
> Certified Forensic Accountant (2001–among the first 18 awarded)

Professional Memberships:

> American Institute of Certified Public Accountants (1962)
> Iowa Society of CPAs (1963)
> Nebraska Society of CPAs (1962)

Accounting Honors and Awards:

> Diplomate American Board of Forensic Accountants
> Diplomate American Board of Forensic Examiners
> Meritorious Service Award — National Accounting and Finance Council of the American Trucking Associations, Inc.
> Outstanding Accountant Award — Nebraska Motor Carriers Assoc.
> Professional Service Award — Nebraska Motor Carriers Assoc.
> Outstanding Committee Chairman Award — Iowa Society of CPAs

Attorney References

(The authors have not listed references here. References change, lawyers retire, or you might not have worked with one for years. This is merely a reminder to review your CV before you send it out and revise it. Always ask your references for permission to list them on your CV. Otherwise, you may list one who might not give you a glowing reference.)

The Accounting Expert Witness

2

2.1 Introducing the Attorney to an Accounting Expert Witness

2.1.1 Why Hire a Forensic Accountant

To prevail at trial, all trial lawyers know they must be able prove the *prima facie* elements of their claim or defense. Certain claims, such as accounting malpractice, require the opinion of an expert in the field to prove the occurrence of a breach of the standard of care. In this instance, the attorney has no choice but to find a well qualified accounting expert to help meet this element of the claim. To support a claim of malpractice, the attorney will need an expert to opine as to the prevailing standard of care and whether the defendant breached the standard. The forensic accountant will be required to review the record, determine what happened and render an opinion that the defendant accountant or accounting firm breached the standard of care prevailing in their community at the time the error occurred. Without this opinion, the case is doomed to failure, because the expert's testimony is part of the attorney's *prima facie* case.

In other cases, the forensic accounting expert will serve the roles of investigator, counselor and educator to the attorney, the court and the jury. The subjects of expert testimony and the standards for admitted expert opinions and other testimony are discussed later in this chapter.

In fulfilling any of these roles, forensic accountants offer many skills to assist the attorney. Forensic accountants have specialized education and experience in working with trial attorneys and in uncovering accounting, tax and financial facts and issues in the discovery process. They also have the skills

15

and know-how necessary to issue an expert's report that will assist the engaging attorney and the trier of fact to understand the accounting, tax, and financial issues, and to reach logical conclusions and testify on them. An attorney may try to address all these matters without the assistance of a qualified accounting expert, but, even if he has the technical skills to do this work himself, the time and effort required to conduct these activities will limit his ability to properly prepare the case. By assigning the accounting investigation and related tasks to the accounting expert, the attorney can devote his attention to overseeing the entire case.

The forensic accounting expert should know that if he has been hired to assist with a case, it is because the attorney either must have an expert opinion to prove an essential element of his case — such as breach of an accountant's standard of care — or to bring the accountant's knowledge and training to bear on some other important aspect of the case. Attorneys do not generally hire and prepare expert witnesses unless it is essential to the case. Their testimony is not always viewed with favor and there is some sense that juries tend to view their testimony with some skepticism. Experts are viewed as "hired guns" who testify only because they are being paid to do so. If an expert is hired, it is because they have some important information. It is essential that they understand their precise role in the preparation or the presentation of the case. The expert witness must be thoroughly and completely devoted to assisting the attorney in this effort.

The amount of work, time involved, and cost of the forensic accountant will depend on the needs of the hiring attorney. Accountants are hired for many reasons and their work will be determined by the facts, issues and results required by the client if they can achieve those results in accordance with the needs of the client and the requirements of the trier of fact. The times at which an accountant might be hired are as follows:

- Before litigation begins to determine whether allegations of either a prospective plaintiff or defendant contain valid accounting or financial issues that may support a basis for a complaint, or defense against a complaint
- Shortly after litigation begins to serve as an accounting consultant to advise the client on accounting matters in dispute
- Shortly after litigation begins to serve as both an expert witness and consultant
- Shortly before the trial date to serve both as an expert witness and consultant during the trial

It is not advisable to hire the expert witness shortly before the trial date. In the long run, it probably costs the client more, either directly or indirectly, if the expert is hired late in the process. The best results are obtained when the accounting expert and the attorney establish a working relationship early in the case.

2.2   The Relationship between the Attorney and the Accounting Expert Witness

2.2.1   The Importance of Providing All Information to the Expert

The accounting expert witness must determine facts and issues and answer the issues within his area of expert knowledge. He must always begin by conferring with the engaging attorney to receive initial direction and understanding of what the attorney's goals are for the accountant. The attorney should ensure that the accounting expert witness is provided with all documents he requests and with those the attorney believes the expert will need even if not requested. Obviously, these documents include all of the financial, accounting and tax information that may be relevant to the case. These are the documents of the accounting expert's trade. However, the attorney should not overlook the information associated with the attorney's trade. These documents would include but not be limited to the complaint, depositions, interrogatories, answers, requests for production of records, motions, orders, and all related documents filed with the court. The attorney should readily provide all of this primary information, that is, the official court papers and other public documents, to the accounting expert. If the attorney is confident that the accounting expert understands the rules and risks associated with the use of confidential attorney memoranda and other work products, the attorney may choose to provide this information to the expert. In some circumstances, the expert may be unable to reach valid conclusions without this information, or efficiency may demand that summaries of documents and records be provided to the expert. In that case, the attorney should take special care to educate the expert on the work product doctrine and what must be done to preserve the protections afforded by that doctrine. The rules and pitfalls associated with the expert's use of confidential memoranda and other work product are discussed in Chapter 7. If he chooses to withhold vital information from the accounting expert, the attorney must accept that the accountant is handicapped in his pursuit of the facts and issues and in his ability to reach conclusions useful to both the trier of fact and the client.

Attorneys are sometimes reluctant to provide the expert witness with complete copies of the depositions that have been taken in the case. Usually, this is out of concern for the costs that will be incurred by having the expert review all of this information in detail. However, we believe the attorney should always provide actual and complete depositions to the expert, and not the lawyer's summary of them. At a minimum, the attorney should provide the complete depositions of all of the witnesses whose testimony will have direct bearing on the expert's work. The accounting expert witness will read the depositions with the eyes of an accountant and may reach conclusions and develop issues on accounting testimony that differ from an attorney's conclusions. Then the accountant and the attorney will discuss the differences. Also, to the extent that deposition summaries are provided to the expert and relied upon by him in formulating his opinions, the attorney's summaries will become discoverable by the opposition. Again, the attorney's summaries may contain the attorney's mental impressions regarding the witnesses and the case. If so, this is attorney work product that should be protected as discussed in Chapter 7.

2.2.2   The Importance of the Engagement Letter

The attorney–expert relationship should be described and governed by a written agreement between them. After the expert makes a preliminary brief review of this data, he will prepare a *job engagement letter* (JE letter), also known by accountants as job arrangement letter, or job engagement contract, that explains his understanding of what the attorney and mutual client would like the expert to accomplish. The JE letter should include a comment as to whether the expert can meet the expectations of favorable results within the expert's responsibilities to both the client and the trier of fact. The engagement letter should set forth the scope of the expert's work, how he expects the attorney to work with him on his preparation of the expert report, and to prepare him for testimony at depositions and trials. It will also set forth what he intends to testify on and his fee range and out-of-pocket costs for the work. A complete discussion and examples of the JE letter is presented in Chapter 3.

An attorney who hires a forensic accountant as an expert witness should review the JE letter thoroughly to be certain the expert has a complete understanding of what may be expected of him. Also, the attorney needs to understand what the expert can reasonably deliver, given the circumstances under which he was hired. Perhaps the attorney has been involved in and working on the dispute for a year or more. The expert may need hours, days or weeks to develop and understand sufficient facts and issues in order to resolve them as successfully as the engaging attorney hopes to have them resolved. The JE letter will include the estimated hours needed to complete the work. Obtaining a $500 opinion may be possible, and even probable, but it will not be valuable. It would not be any more valuable than a $500 opinion rendered by the attorney to the client on his chances of prevailing in the case. Litigation is expensive and the attorney should not expect a well qualified expert to work under substantial time or financial constraints and do his best work. If the client cannot afford the expert's fee, the attorney should discuss it with the expert. Perhaps he will reduce it for good cause. He may be receptive to *pro bono* work, or at least to working for a substantial discount if believes that it will bring justice to someone who otherwise could not pay for it. The experts who agree to do this must understand that, even if the fee is discounted, the expert will still be morally and ethically obligated to give what ordinarily might be a $30,000 opinion, even if only for the $500 fee he negotiated.

2.2.3 The Expert's Determination of Where to Begin

The attorney should not try to substitute his judgment for that of the forensic expert in deciding how he should begin his work. Many attorneys do this, at least indirectly, by delivering partial information to the expert. However, the attorney and the client are best served by providing complete financial and trial records to the accountant. Usually, the attorney should avoid making the determination as to what documents may be relevant to the accountant's examination. If the attorney makes this judgment without letting the expert know what other information might be available, important information may be unintentionally withheld from the expert. The attorney should give his expert access to everything and let him decide what is relevant, or at least assist the attorney in making the determination.

Likewise, the attorney should allow the expert witness to decide where to begin his examination. After the accountant reviews the initial court documents and other records, he may wish to begin his work with accounting records. There are many instances where the accounting expert will rationally choose to begin with other types of records.

- If the client is suing an accounting firm for malpractice for erroneous financial statements, the witness will usually begin with the financial statements, the defendant's working papers and the client's accounting records.
- If the issue is tax malpractice, he may wish to begin with the tax returns.
- If the attorney is seeking to pierce the corporate veil, the witness may wish to review the income tax returns before reviewing accounting records and financial statements.
- A case on partnership dissolution may cause the accountant to begin with the income tax returns and the partnership agreement.
- If the issue is one of a business valuation, he may wish to begin with a tour of the plant.
- For a corporate reorganization or liquidation, the accountant may wish to begin with the corporate minutes, capital stock records,

income tax returns, and any private rulings requested on the transactions by the Internal Revenue Service.

In all of these examples, the accountant would be proceeding directly to the records that provide the quickest and possibly the easiest solution to his examination. If the attorney does not understand why the accountant wants to examine the documents and is reluctant to provide them, the attorney should ask the accountant why he needs them. He usually has solid reasons for seeking the information.

2.2.4   The General Responsibility of the Attorney to the Expert Witness

This section could be subtitled "don't treat your expert as if he were your junior attorney." Lawyers are busy professionals who many times believe they do not have to assist the expert with guidance. However, the attorney must remember that the rules and tactics of litigation are not second nature to the expert witness. Take time to explain things such as the work product doctrine, the tools of discovery, the importance of the expert's report, the way expert testimony must be presented and what to expect on cross-examination. For example, when the expert delivers a draft of the report, the lawyer must review it thoroughly, discuss it with the expert and give reasons for any suggested changes. If the attorney does not agree with any part of the report, or believes that it does not meet the requirements of the court, then he must tell the accountant. He must explain the court rules on expert's reports and the importance of conforming to the rules. If the attorney does not understand the accountant's explanations of the accounting transactions, then he must seek further clarification and keep discussing it with the expert until he does understand. It is imperative for the attorney to become an instant accountant; if the report doesn't make him one with his knowledge and understanding of the facts of the case, then the expert will have little chance of educating or persuading the trier of fact. The attorney must instruct the expert to present his opinions so that the layperson will understand it. This is the essence of the expert's mission.

The attorney must understand the importance of independence to accounting experts — and to experts in general. An expert who is forthright and honest in his testimony will be more persuasive and look less like a hired gun. The concept of independence is well established in the accounting profession, especially among accountants who have worked in the audit field and are regularly charged with rendering independent third-party opinions on financial issues. Although the expert's opinions must be independent, an attorney should explore the reasons for preliminary opinions that are adverse to his client's cause. The attorney should ask the expert about any assumptions he made and whether there may be other information that would help the expert render an opinion more favorable to the client. If the accountant appears to have overlooked any important facts, the attorney should ask why certain items that he believed to be important were not considered in the expert's report. If appropriate, the attorney might also ask whether the expert might have reached a different conclusion if he had provided certain further information that had not previously been available. An expert's report may not always satisfy an attorney and his client, and there may be no way for the expert to render a favorable opinion. If so, the attorney should consider using the expert as a consultant rather than a testifying expert.

Attorneys must diligently assist the expert accountant to ensure that he has all the information he needs, follows the law, and fulfills his responsibility to the attorney, the client and the court. The expert accounting witness does not practice law and needs the legal guidance of the engaging attorney.

2.2.5   The Attorney's Responsibility to the Testimony of the Accounting Expert Witness

Sometimes the accounting expert witness gives outstanding testimony for a deposition or in the trial court. Sometimes the same expert is like the little girl in the nursery rhyme. When she was good, she was very, very good, and when she was bad she was horrid. Why the inconsistencies? We believe that much of the problem lies with the engaging attorney.

Our experience has shown that whenever the expert's testimony has been either exceptionally good or exceptionally bad, the credit —or blame — goes to the attorney. When a trial attorney takes the time required to prepare the expert, perhaps over 1 to 3 or more days, the expert is more credible and does a better job in his deposition or in court. This is not because the attorney tells the expert what to say or what opinions he should render. It is because the expert understands how his testimony and opinions fit into the complexity of the case as a whole. During preparation of the witness, the attorney should inform him about the elements of the case and what is needed from the expert to be certain his opinions are thoroughly understood, admissible in evidence and otherwise acceptable to the trier of fact. When the attorney takes this time to prepare the expert, his performance will be above average. When the attorney spends only an hour or two to prepare the expert, the attorney may witness greatness in his expert, in spite of the attorney's lack of care in preparing the expert, or may witness great mediocrity. In either case, assuming the expert is well qualified and possesses good communications skills, the credit for the greatness or mediocrity that ensues usually goes to the attorney.

2.3 Legal Qualification of the Accounting Expert Witness

2.3.1 General Requirements for All Witnesses

Up to this point, we have concentrated on the subjective aspects of the expert's qualifications, such as his technical skills as an accountant, his ability to communicate and educate his audience on complicated accounting aspects of a case and, ultimately, his power to persuade the trier of fact of the truth of his opinions. We now turn to the technical rules that must be satisfied by all experts, regardless of their skills in these subject areas of expert witnessing.

2.3.2 The General Requirement of Competency

Before he can be qualified as an expert, the forensic accountant must first meet the same general requirements as any witness in a court proceeding. While these requirements usually are not difficult to meet, they are fundamental to an understanding of the role and qualifications of a witness as one who should be allowed to provide opinion evidence in court. Rule 601 of the Federal Rules of Evidence states the general rule of competency by providing that:

> "[e]very person is competent to be a witness except as otherwise provided in these rules." *Fed. R. Evid. 601.*

Therefore, the rule is one of general inclusion with certain limited exceptions.

It should be noted that similar rules of competency are provided for in all of the state courts. As with other procedural and evidentiary rules, the state court versions must be compared to determine whether there are any differences. This can be important in cases that are pending in federal court because, in certain federal cases, state law will provide the "rule of decision" and, in those cases, state rules must be followed to determine the competency of a witness. *Fed. R. Evid. 601.* These are generally cases in which the parties are pursuing state law claims (for example, contract claims or tort cases such as malpractice), but have been allowed into federal court because the case is between citizens of different states. Generally, these technical rules should not concern the expert accounting witness; it is up to the attorney to recognize and manage these issues. We mention the issue here as a reminder to the attorney of his obligations in this regard.

2.3.3 Lack of Personal Knowledge

The lack of personal knowledge is the most general basis for concluding that a witness is not competent to testify. This rule is stated in Rule 602 of the Federal Rules of Evidence, which provides:

"A witness may not testify to a matter unless evidence is introduced sufficient to support a finding that the witness has personal knowledge of the
matter. Evidence to prove personal knowledge may, but need not consist of
the witness' own testimony. This rule is subject to the provisions of Rule
703, relating to opinion testimony by expert witnesses." *Fed. R. Evid. 602.*

Therefore, the witness is generally not competent unless he has "personal
knowledge" of the matter under consideration. Essentially, this means that
the witness has personally experienced the matter through one of his five
human senses; he has *seen, heard, felt, tasted* or *smelled* something that is
relevant to the case at hand and can describe his experience in court. This
concept is critical to understanding the basis for many of the evidence rules
and requirements for court testimony. In our everyday affairs, we may believe
we have knowledge of some matter based upon what some other person has
experienced with his senses and reported to us. This is the kind of knowledge
we obtain from newspapers and television reports. But this is not personal
knowledge; it is hearsay.

Before a witness can testify as to the facts he personally experienced, the
court must be satisfied that the witness was in a position to personally
experience and did, in fact, experience these facts. For example, a witness to
an automobile collision will not be allowed to testify whether the light was
green or red until he first testifies that he was present at the location of the
accident on the day and at the time in question. He would also need to state
his position in relation to the traffic light and indicate that he has good
eyesight and could see the light while the accident was happening. The court
rules and lawyers call this "laying the foundation" for the real testimony they
want from the witness. Only after sufficient foundation is laid will the court
allow the witness to state what he saw: whether the light was red or green
when the collision occurred.

Rule 602 also provides that the requirement of personal knowledge is
"subject to the provisions of Rule 703," which is the rule that describes the
allowable bases for expert testimony. Rule 703 is discussed in detail below,
but generally provides, among other things, that the expert is allowed to base
his opinions on facts that have been reported or "made known" to the expert.
In other words, the expert is not strictly required to have "personal knowledge" of the facts or data on which he is basing his opinion.

2.3.4   The Oath or Affirmation

The rules on competency also imply that a witness who would refuse to give
an oath or affirmation before testifying is not competent to testify. Rule 603
of the Federal Rules of Evidence provides:

"Before testifying, every witness shall be required to declare that the witness will testify truthfully, by oath or affirmation administered in a form calculated to awaken the witness' conscience and impress the witness' mind with the duty to do so." *Fed. R. Evid.* 603.

If a witness refuses to make such a declaration, the court would refuse his testimony, probably on the grounds that he lacks competency.

2.3.5   Other Grounds for Disqualifying Lay Witnesses

The rules also provide two other general categories of "persons" who are not competent to testify: judges and members of the jury. *See Fed. R. Evid.* 605 and 606. Because of the general rule of competency stated in Rule 602, that "all persons" are competent to testify unless otherwise provided in these rules, questions concerning the age, mental capacity and other similar qualifications of the witness are generally not considered grounds for disqualification. Only those persons who refuse to declare an oath or affirmation, judges and jurors are disqualified by the rules.

2.3.6   Opinions from Lay Witnesses

On occasion, it is necessary to allow a lay witness (someone who is not qualified as an expert) to express opinions, conclusions or inferences based on facts that the person has observed. Rule 701 of the Federal Rules of Evidence provides as follows:

"If the witness is not testifying as an expert, the witness' testimony in the form of opinions or inferences is limited to those opinions or inferences which are (a) rationally based on the perception of the witness, (b) helpful to a clear understanding of the witness' testimony or the determination of a fact in issue, and (c) not based on scientific, technical, or other specialized knowledge within the scope of Rule 702 [concerning testimony by experts]." *Fed. R. Evid.* 701.

For example, the lay witness may be allowed to express an opinion concerning the mental state of a person they had personally observed. The witness, although not qualified as a mental health professional, may be allowed to testify that the person "looked sad." This would be allowed only if the court found that all of the requirements stated in the rule were satisfied: the conclusion is rationally based on the witness' perceptions, meaning personal knowledge; the opinion is helpful to a clear understanding or determination of an issue, and the witness is not actually testifying as an expert witness. It should be noted that, although the witness is presenting an opinion, saying that a person "looked sad," is still an opinion based on the personal observations of the witness. It may have been based on the look on the person's face, the way she walked or the words she spoke. The conclusion is not and cannot be based on facts perceived by other persons that are then made known to the witness. Only the expert witness can base his opinion on facts perceived by others and made known to the expert.

The last requirement, that the lay opinion is "not based on scientific, technical or other specialized knowledge within the scope of Rule 702" was added with the December 2000 amendments to the Federal Rules of Evidence. This is intended to prevent the circumvention of the discovery rules, which require the disclosure and advance notice of expert witnesses and their opinions (see Chapter 7). Generally, a party is required to disclose to all other parties the identity and opinions held by witnesses who may be called to provide expert testimony at trial. *Fed. R. Civ. P.* 26(a)(2). However, lay opinions are not subject to the same disclosure requirements. Controversy arose because parties and their lawyers would try to have expert testimony admitted as lay opinions to avoid the disclosure requirements. The rule was changed so that now the court will focus its attention on the subject matter of the testimony. If it is based on "scientific, technical or other specialized knowledge," it will be considered expert testimony and subject to the pretrial disclosure requirements.

2.3.7   Mixed Expert and Lay Opinions

In considering the topic of lay opinions — and lay testimony in general — it should be noted that experts may be called upon to provide testimony concerning facts that they have perceived themselves. For example, in the case of a business valuation, the expert may tour the plant and other facilities owned by the company. He may testify as to fact what he has personally perceived while on his tour. In doing so, he is functioning as a fact witness. He may also testify that, given all he observed while on his tour, the plant and other facilities were generally in a "rundown" condition. This is a conclusion that does not necessarily require any sort of specialized knowledge but is based on the personal knowledge of the expert and is helpful to the fact finder in determining the value of the enterprise. The conclusion would probably be allowed as a lay opinion, and most likely would be intermingled with actual expert opinions regarding the value of the business, such as proper capitalization rates and other conclusions based on specialized knowledge. The important point to remember concerning the general rule of competency is the requirement for personal knowledge and the exception to this requirement for expert witnesses.

2.4   *Daubert*

What's the fuss about *Daubert v. Merrell Dow Pharmaceuticals, Inc.*, 509 U.S. 579 (1993)? Although it applies to all experts, the effect upon accounting expert witness is less pronounced. Generally, *Daubert* requires all expert accounting witnesses to express opinions that are supported by professional credentials, by facts and substance and authoritative pronouncements as appropriate. Substantive authority will depend upon the facts and issues. Testimony on certified financial statements will be supported by official accounting pronouncements by the Financial Accounting Standards Board, State Boards of Accountancy, the Securities and Exchange Commission and other agencies that set accounting standards and principles. The Internal Revenue Code, related regulations, rulings, and court decisions can support tax issues. Whatever our testimony, we must have authoritative support.

Our opinions must be dependable. Can the trier of fact rely upon it? Is it related and of use when deciding on the facts and issues in dispute? *Daubert* insists only that we live up to the standards of our profession.

Our opinions and our evidence must be generally acceptable by our profession. They must be reliable and relevant, and must have authoritative support. And we must be genuine experts in the area of our testimony.

Many forensic accountants with whom I battled in the courts many years ago were not competent. Today, so many accounting forensic experts are honest and knowledgeable that they long ago surpassed the past in competence. Appearing as an expert in court is more difficult each day, as the opposing experts keep each other alert and involved in constant learning.

The Expert's Job Engagement Letter

3

3.1 The Importance of a Job Engagement Letter

The first time I testified in court was to satisfy a Master in Chancery appointment by an Iowa District Court to compute net income of a joint venture. The litigation occurred in 1966. I had many questions for the judge because I had never before testified or been a Master. The judge told me that he didn't know much about accounting and that I should ask the attorneys for each of the plaintiffs and for the defendant for legal interpretations and instructions.

Because generally accepted accounting principles (GAAP), common sense, and the rule of law will allow several acceptable methods to determine net income, I computed four possible net income amounts in my report. I explained the strengths and weaknesses of each method so that the court could reach a conclusion. During a preliminary review of my report, the attorneys instructed me to reach a conclusion in my report and recommend the most appropriate net income of the four. I suggested an arithmetic average of two of the net income methods that I believed to be the most appropriate. The sitting judge was satisfied with this resolution.

Before I issued my Master's report to the court, the judge withdrew from the case. A replacement judge received my report and conducted the trial. During the trial, the judge reprimanded me severely and warned me that a Master must not arrive at a conclusion in his court. He said that I should limit my role to fact finding only, and that he would reach any conclusions from my report that he deemed appropriate.

Whenever you are appointed to be a Master of any kind for the court, you must discuss the form of your report with the judge, ask him whether

you should reach a conclusion and include this information in a job arrangement letter to the court. I had done this, and the judge told me to get that
information from the attorneys. Unfortunately, when the new judge took
over the case, I did not anticipate that he might issue new instructions.

After the replacement judge reviewed my report and listened to the
testimony, he awarded $1,000 to the plaintiffs as their share of the net income
from the construction instead of two-thirds of the $30,000 (a large sum in
1966) of profit that the plaintiffs had anticipated. Because the fees for my
services exceeded the award that the court had made, the judge once more
reprimanded me and set a hearing to determine how much of my fee should
be paid, and by whom. I was forced to hire an attorney to represent me at
the hearing. I was awarded the entire fee, but my attorney received one-third
of it, and I did not receive it until 15 months after I had billed it.

My later job arrangement letters specified that, among other work, I
would reach and report my conclusions. Had I done that in 1966, the court
would have accepted or rejected my intent to reach and report conclusions
and it would have included the terms for paying me in an order to the
litigants. Further, the court would have enforced payment of my fee. In 1966,
a preliminary report to the court wasn't required. After this case, I always
injected what I would testify on, what I would base my testimony on, and
the conclusions I would reach. In 1966, I was young and trusting. Now, I am
not young, but unfortunately, I am still trusting — but always issue a job
engagement letter (JE letter).

In later years, I was appointed a Special Master in a trucking lawsuit. An
order from the district court judge specified my billing rate, whom I should
bill, and who was to pay me. It also ordered that I would not return records
to the litigants until I was paid. When we work with the judge, the judge will
work with us for court appointed work.

3.2   Examples of Job Engagement Letters

The following letters are presented in this chapter because they are a depar-
ture from traditional JE letters:

In re: The Marriage of HENRY LOUIS BECHER and MARY ANN BECHER
("BECHER vs. BECHER")

Gentlemen:

General Discussion

Mr. Jay J. Jackson contacted me to obtain my services as an expert witness
on behalf of your client, Respondent, Mary Ann Becher ("Mary" or "Mrs.

Becher") in the matter of Becher vs. Becher. (The individuals are collectively referred to as "the Bechers"). I have read documents that Mr. Jackson had sent to me. Also, Mrs. Becher phoned me for information and advice.

After negotiations and considering Mrs. Becher's limited financial circumstances, I agreed to reduce the hourly rate for my services to $100 plus expenses. Travel time after 5 P.M. will be billed at one-half the rate or $50 hourly plus expenses. If I am required to travel during my regular working hours, my hourly rate will be $100. (*Mrs. Becher's husband had not been generous with support for Mrs. Becher and their children. Her finances were slim. For the sake of justice, a forensic accountant must at times reduce fees. The fee for this work was reduced to the nub before the work was finished.*)

On January 7, 1994, I sent Mr. Jackson a draft for discussion purposes of an estimate of fees. I had agreed not to charge for preliminary discussions and reading of materials, so my draft estimate did not include charges for preliminary work. (*My first few paragraphs discuss how I was introduced to the client and some work and fee information. Often this information is sought in cross-examination. The cross usually asks when you first talked with your engaging attorney about these matters.*) On January 28, 1994, Mr. Jackson discussed these matters with me and requested this formal job engagement letter. The following information is submitted in compliance with your request for expert witness services.

Specific Discussion

You have asked me to testify as an expert on the value of Missouri HDT Repair, Inc. ("HDT"), a business in Any City, Iowa owned one-half each by the Bechers.

If necessary, I shall prepare a written summary of my findings and shall be available to be deposed if required, and, if possible, for depositions of other experts, and for an appearance in court.

The following statements are provided on the understanding that Petitioner and Respondent have not completed discovery in this case, and as such are still in the process of discovering true facts. As an accounting expert witness, I am still in the process of discovering true facts that relate to my conclusions and testimony. (*This information is almost always required by the litigants far in advance of the report, deposition, or trial date. It is not possible for the expert to deliver a completed report until he completes his work. This informs the parties that more work is yet to be done, but the expert doesn't know precisely what it will be.*) I have determined the existence and significance of certain documentary evidence, and the identity of some of the witnesses

and some of the evidence that such witnesses possess. The following statements are the best statements that I can make at this time:

Name and Address: Zeph Telpner, CPA, [Street, City, State, Zip].

Subject Matter: I expect to testify regarding the value of HDT. I will also
testify about the accounting records, procedures and controls of HDT, and
of its business viability and going-concern basis.

Facts and Opinions: I expect to testify:

That in my opinion HDT had value in excess of value proposed by Petitioner. (*How can an expert express this type of opinion when he has done little
more than review the Petition and a brief history of the case? This is not a
problem. He has been hired to prove that the value set by the other expert is
too low, and that the value is actually higher. He states only "I expect to testify"
to that conclusion. He may not be able to reach that opinion when his work
is completed.*)

That the accounting records, procedures, and controls of HDT are not
adequate by themselves to determine the value of HDT. (*The preliminary
documents provided to this expert included the report of the Petitioner's expert.
That expert relied only upon the accounting records, procedures and controls.
He did not visit the plant, observe operations or make sufficient analyses.*)

Summary of Grounds:

Aside from my general background and extensive experience in the truck
transportation and truck sales, service and repair industry; accounting and
gathering factual information, the testimony of witnesses at trial and such
documentary evidence as may be presented by the parties at trial, the following paragraph presents the general grounds for each of my opinions
stated in the corresponding paragraphs under Facts and Opinions, above.

The general grounds for my opinions that HDT had value in excess of the
value submitted by Petitioner, and that the accounting records, procedures,
and controls of HDT are not adequate alone, to determine the value of HDT
will be: the accounting books, records, source documents, income tax
returns and analyses of these data as I consider necessary; the relevant
computations and tax returns and other related working papers of Harrod,
Dale & Co., PC ("Harrod"), Gold City, Iowa, the outside certified public
accountants of HDT. Also, I will review the 1993 working papers of Swagman & Billabong P.C., Big Sioux, IA, who prepared HDT's 1993 income tax
returns. Additional grounds will be the testimony of Petitioner and Respondent, and the testimony of the Petitioner's expert witnesses; verification by

outside sources when I consider it necessary; and the general practices of other companies in the truck sales and services and repairs industry; and such books, periodicals, studies, and other references as may be generally relied upon by expert witnesses. (*Today,* Daubert *will require the expert to base his opinion on such relevant information. Yesterday, the ethics of the profession, the Rules of Civil Procedure and knowledge of expert testimony accepted by most courts would compel us to follow* Daubert *long before it existed. Under the following "Summary and Proposal," the expert provides information to the parties that his work will be based upon acceptable accounting standards and court requirements.*)

Summary and Proposal

To arrive at my conclusions, I must review, verify, analyze and inquire of certain documents in your possession, and certain information, accounting and inventory records in the possession of HDT, Harrod, Swagman & Billabong, the Petitioner, and the Respondent. This will require me to visit the physical facilities of HDT and to interview its employees. Also, I must interview certain other persons who possess information relevant to a conclusion by an expert.

I will also prepare questions as my work progresses in order to acquire sufficient additional information to allow me to reach valid and rational conclusions.

I will not charge for my preliminary services performed between October 5, 1993 and February 2, 1994.

Fees for my services are $150 an hour plus expenses, and $75 an hour for travel plus expenses. I have agreed to reduce my fees to $100 hourly, and $50 hourly for travel due to the soft financial position of the Respondent. I estimate that my total fees for the work required to allow me to testify on behalf of Mrs. Becher will amount to between $6,920 and $9,080 plus expenses for research, preparation, analyses, reporting, depositions, travel to Any City, Iowa, time spent with your representatives to prepare me for direct and cross-examination; and court appearances. If these services amount to less than $6,920 based on the hourly rate of $100, I shall bill you for the lesser amount. If, for example, the total time amounts to 10 hours, then the total fee would be $1,000. There is no minimum fee. If it appears that these services will exceed $9,080, I will stop work to discuss it with you as soon as the total amount can be estimated with greater precision. I require an advance cash deposit of $3,000 payable to Zeph Telpner, CPA, and mailed to me at [Address]. A stamped, addressed envelope is enclosed for your convenience. Please signify your acceptance of this proposal in the space provided below and on the enclosed copy of this letter. Mrs. Becker should also sign and date it. Return a signed and dated copy together with a check to me in the amount of $3,000. I will submit biweekly progress billings to you.

Sincerely,

Zeph Telpner

Accepted:

Firm Name and Address

By: (Name of receiver)

Date: 2/4/94

cc: Mary Ann Becher, Respondent

(*In the above example, the final fees were lower, and out-of-pocket costs were waive to help the respondent and her two children survive with their diminished income. This is a job that may not give an expert adequate fees, but might give us lessons in new skills and techniques. Plus, we could forge a valuable contact with a grateful attorney. Aside from that, the JE letter will explain itself after you have read it.*)

Each JE letter must be tailored to the facts and issues. Most jobs should be full-fee engagements. The following letter was a proposal to assist a regional CPA firm that had been sued for $100 million. I did not charge for the preliminary work to respond to their request for a professional courtesy discount to another CPA firm. The firm's managing partner had attended my CPE seminar on forensic accounting.

The preliminary work arose because they wanted to determine if I could help them, or if they had no defense. The $100 million was settled out of court for $70,000. The insurance company believed that to be less than the cost of a trial. The petitioner's expert was incompetent and unfortunately worked for a Big Five accounting firm. I mention this only to stress that expert witness work often places small-firm experts as opponents against giant-firm experts. Each expert has his own areas of specialization.

I have often testified in trucking litigation on the opposite side of a partner from a Big Five firm who served as the expert witness for the opposing party. If the issue had to do with Security and Exchange Act violations, I would be incompetent, and the Big Five, or other national firms would be competent.

I have not prepared a financial statement of any kind since 1974 and would be incompetent to testify as to whether a financial statement was "presented fairly" regardless of the size of the firm providing the expert witness.

Every expert witness who is a genuine expert in the area of his testimony will succeed and do a good and honorable service for the litigants, their attorneys, the jurors, and the trier of fact. The key words are "genuine expert." Nothing can substitute for authoritative and substantive knowledge of your field.

The following JE letter will explain itself:

RE: Samuel X. Xerxes and Alice Y. Xerxes vs. Herbert T. Robinson

Gentlemen:

Your letter to me of December 3, 1992 from D. Gene Pritchard ("Request") briefly summarized *Xerxes v. Robinson*, and transmitted the following documents:

"Stillwages Deposition Exhibit 4/Exhibit O Xerxes' 1983-1991 Tax Returns

General Ledgers for the Robot: 1987–June, 1992

S.X. Xerxes Handyman Tax Returns (1984–1988)

Robot News Advertisement

Pages 98–154 of Xerxes' March 27, 1990 Deposition

Xerxes Deposition Exhibits 13–16

Pages 210–220 of Stillwages Deposition

Velvel Simulcast Deposition Outline

Velvel Simulcast Deposition Transcript with Exhibits

The Request states that "this case basically consists of two" complaints against Herbert Robinson.

Page 1 of the Request provides that I have agreed to assist you "in handling the second claim, the claim against Herbert Robinson," and that you have asked for my assistance in evaluating the testimony of Velvel Simulcast, the economics expert for the Xerxes.

Page 7 of the Request directs me to assume that State Center for Business Assistance ("SCBA") failed to provide the $5,000 investment described in the Request. I am asked, therefore, "to determine the effects of this failure on the Xerxes' business venture, also known as "*The Robot*" (the trade name of the tool).

Page 16 of the Request states "we are requesting that you review these materials, provide us with an informal letter report of your initial impressions, and inform us if you are willing and able to act as an expert witness on our behalf in this matter."

During my conversation with D. Gene Pritchard on the Request, I agreed to scan the information that was sent to me with the Request, and to send you a response of my initial impressions. I have agreed to do this without charge in order to determine if I would be willing and able to act as an expert witness on your behalf in this matter. I further agreed to submit an estimate of my fees.

Preliminary Impression:

Velvel Simulcast testimony:

The opinion expressed by Velvel Simulcast in his deposition is based almost solely on speculation and hypothetical facts. Even so, his hypothetical conclusions cannot be reached logically from his speculation and hypotheses, nor can factual conclusions be reached.

Effect of failure by SCBA to provide $5,000:

From the information transmitted to me in and with the Request, I can reach two rational conclusions: (1), either the failure to provide $5,000 has absolutely no effect on the Xerxes' business venture, or (2), the information provided is not sufficient for an expert to arrive at a conclusion as to the effect that failure to provide $5,000 has on the business venture of the Xerxes.

Willingness and ability to act as expert witness on your behalf:

I am willing and have the ability to act as an expert witness on your behalf to rebut, where appropriate, the opinions and calculations of the plaintiffs and to provide the proper substantive alternatives.

Preliminary discussion based only on scanning the documents identified under "enclosures" on the request:

Stillwages Deposition pages 210–220:

These deposition pages actually support a position that the Xerxes can succeed without outside investment and would not need an investment by SCBA or anyone else. His deposition is mere speculation, hyperbole and nonsense based on no facts or on unsubstantiated facts. An expert must examine the underlying factual basis to support his testimony.

Stillwages Deposition Exhibit 4/Exhibit 0:

These exhibits are an SCBA mishmash of informality, unsubstantiated claims, incomplete plans, projections and cost estimates that lack basic cost accounting and business planning to carry out a far-reaching manufacturing and sales plan. The bases for the computations are seemingly pulled out of the air. An expert must examine the underlying factual data that supports the computations and projections.

Xerxes' 1983–1991 Tax Returns:

Xerxes' returns report an average annual income of about $4,300 for the 8 years. When capital gains are subtracted from income and the gross selling prices of the capital assets are added to the income, the average annual income is about $7,000. The returns reported five exemptions in 1983, four in 1984 through 1987, three in 1988 and 1989 and two for 1990 and 1991. The Xerxes are either outstanding money managers or have receipts that have not been identified. The returns broadcast warning signals that should be investigated because the history of plaintiffs does not indicate outstanding money management ability, and the plaintiff's Petition seems to indicate impoverishment.

General Ledgers for the Robot:

The information identified as general ledgers are sales journals and cash disbursements journals and are not sufficient in disclosures, or complete in details to determine the income. These journals show substantial withdrawals recorded as salaries to the Xerxes. The income does not appear adequate to support the withdrawals. There seems to be a source of cash other than operations and SCBA investments. There may have been sufficient additional cash to eliminate the need for any outside investments. The records and cash sources must be specifically substantiated and identified.

S. X. Xerxes Handyman Tax Returns:

These corporate tax returns are for the 5 years ending October 31, 1985 through 1989. They report a capital deficit of about $29,000 as of October

31, 1984, and about $6,000 as of October 31, 1989. None of the balance sheets show cash balances. Until October 31, 1986, the balance sheet reported a receivable of $53,350 from officers. In the year ended October 31, 1987, the receivable was removed from the balance sheet together with a building that was reported as sold. These records might reveal that the building was transferred to the Xerxes. Also, the Xerxes' 1983 individual income tax return reports a dividend from their corporation. This may have been paid out of capital. The returns indicate a disregard for complying with a corporate structure.

Robot News Advertisement:

I could find no evidence of advertising or marketing study made to determine the best method of advertising. Why was this semi-annual news magazine chosen instead of those robot magazines with a larger circulation?

Pages 98–154 of Xerxes' March 27, 1990 Deposition and Xerxes' Deposition Exhibits 13–16:

After a quick reading of this deposition and related exhibits, I believe that the testimony is unsupported wishful thinking without substantive research and support for Xerxes' conclusions. As for the exhibits, many of the usual overheads, selling, operating costs and studies supporting the costs, selling prices and marketing decisions have not been accounted for nor supported in a substantive manner.

Velvel Simulcast Deposition Outline:

I have not reviewed this outline, as I did not wish to be influenced by it for my preliminary comments.

Velvel Simulcast Deposition Transcript with Exhibits:

Mr. Simulcast has testified that he has no experience in many of the areas needed by an expert to evaluate the ability of Xerxes, the value of the Robot, the costs to manufacture and sell it, the methods to sell it, and whether or not it will sell. He has done no research, or analyses. He has merely applied simple arithmetic to numbers supplied by his client.

Even his own assumptions have no substantiated bases. A patent may have a 17-year life, but the invention may have a life that is shorter or nonexistent. He does not know the average useful life of such products nor how often SCBA clients achieve success. He does not even know if the staff of SCBA has prepared evaluations with substance.

His comments on correlation between advertising and sales are not correct, and he did not visit the facilities of the Robot, review its production, nor discuss it with the Xerxes.

He presents no acceptable basis to confirm the number of bowlers who will buy the product, and no reliable calculation of the inflation factor of 5%. He provides no evidence that the 18% discount rate he has used is valid.

In short, his opinion is speculation based on lack of facts, and his calculations are mere number gyrations based on unsubstantiated amounts and instructions provided to him by the plaintiffs or representatives of the plaintiffs.

Summary and Proposal:

The depositions, exhibits, records, tax returns and summaries that you sent to me indicate that the plaintiffs have not demonstrated the facts, the research or the knowledge to prove that they were injured by SCBA's failure to invest $5,000.

I must perform sufficient additional research and investigations to rebut with certainty the financial, accounting, marketing and other business conclusions and arguments of the plaintiffs; and to provide the appropriate facts and information that the court requires from an expert so that it can evaluate and reach a logical conclusion on the factual information, explanations and experience supplied to it by the expert.

As I promised, I have not charged for my services to date. My billing rate for additional services will be billed at $150 an hour plus out-of-pocket costs. I estimate that the work required to allow me to testify on your behalf will require between 100 and 250 hours for research, preparation, depositions and court appearances. If it takes less than 100 hours, I shall bill you for the lesser amount. If it appears that the time will exceed 250 hours, I will stop work to discuss it with you as soon as the total time can be estimated with a greater precision.

A space to accept this proposal is printed below. Please signify your acceptance of this proposal in the space provided below and on the enclosed copy of this letter. Return an accepted copy together with a check to me in the amount of $6,500 for my retainer. I will submit weekly progress billings for the work.

Sincerely,

Zeph Telpner

A job engagement letter offers protection to the expert witness and his client and engaging attorney. A letter is a tool to create a meeting of minds between an expert and those who seek to hire him.

A good letter will:

- Be addressed to the right party. Should it be the attorney, his client, or a judge?
- Recite the facts provided to the expert and what he has been asked to do.
- Explain what he expects to testify on, and what authoritative and substantive support he will base his scope of work and opinions on.
- Provide a statement of the work he must perform to reach a conclusion.
- Explain what he will charge and when he expects payment of his fees and costs.
- Ask for a retainer.

If the expert discusses the JE letter with the attorneys before he issues it, resistance to the fees or the scope of work can be lessened.

Where to Begin

4

4.1 Begin with a Philosophy and Knowledge of Forensic Consulting and Expert Witnessing

When a forensic accountant is hired as a consultant in disputed matters, he will prepare an oral or written report of his conclusions. When the accountant is hired to be the expert witness, he will prepare a written report and testify during a deposition or in trial proceedings, or both. All require the expert witness to express his conclusions. The consultant and the witness have the same responsibilities to the engagement — to express opinions on the disputed facts. Each engagement, whether as consultant or expert, must be undertaken as if the consultant were also the expert witness. When an expert remembers his role to help others understand the facts and issues in disputed matters, he can begin to understand and develop a philosophy of expert witnessing. Above all, he must understand the facts and issues he has discovered.

To achieve success in forensic consulting or expert witnessing in engagement after engagement, a forensic accountant must become a superb investigator and researcher and adopt a creative investigation and research philosophy. How to investigate or research involves much more than examining accounting records or looking something up in a book.

A philosophy of forensic accounting or expert witnessing is a way of professional forensic life. It is a logical thinking process to stimulate the intellect and imagination to solve and explain litigation issues that revolve around accounting and legal matters. When our position is the correct one, we will always reach conclusions of substance. No one can be perfect, so we must be careful not to seek perfection — or our goal is impossible. Perfection is neither desirable nor beneficial to our expert witnessing. An expert must accept imperfection to complete his work in reasonable time and always in time for the trial.

To forgo perfection doesn't mean to reach for mediocrity. It means to master the concept of the ordinary or average person in everyday life. This is a most important expert-witnessing concept. To understand ourselves and others, we must realize that everyone is about the same. We all arise about the same time; wash, dress and eat about the same time; arrive at the office at about the same time; and leave for home about the same time. When we realize this, we can study ourselves and learn much about how our adversaries will react to what we say and do.

This is not an easy skill to master. Albert Einstein, for example, was ordinary. But he was merely an ordinary genius. Was he a greater genius than Edison? Ford? Steinmetz? Oppenheimer? When we understand that we must compare apples with apples, or prove that oranges are comparable to apples if that is our premise, then we master the concept of what it is to be ordinary or average or common. To be ordinary means to apply common sense to difficult problems. Common sense makes investigation and research easier. Examples in Chapters 5 and 6 will show how to apply this concept to seemingly complex issues and resolve them successfully.

An expert witness must arrive at conclusions based on facts, authoritative and generally accepted accounting and business principles and practices and substance and logic. An expert must avoid asserting personal dogmatic beliefs and be objective in reaching his opinions. He may, however, interpret the facts, issues and authority in a logical manner even though his interpretation may differ from others. If he can support his opinion to the satisfaction of the courts, juries, attorneys and clients, he will have succeeded.

This concept that interpretations may differ was expressed brilliantly in *Commissioner v. Newman, 159 Fed.2d 848.* In a dissenting opinion, Justice Learned Hand wrote:

"Over and over again, courts have said there is nothing sinister in so arranging one's affairs to keep taxes as low as possible. Everybody does so, rich or poor; and all do right, for nobody owes any public duty to pay more than the law demands; taxes are enforced exactions, not voluntary contributions. To demand more in the name of morals is mere cant."

Judge Hand has told us that a person is authorized to cast his transactions in any manner allowed by law. Even though an expert accounting witness usually is not also a practicing lawyer, he must understand objectively what the law and other rules that guide his opinion mean and ignore a mere belief of what he thinks they mean. Judge Hand's dissenting opinion has told us that, regardless of misinterpretation by others, if the law or other governing authorities allows us to carry out our business in a manner that others believe to be unfair, then it is normal, moral and allowable for us to do so. If we master Judge Hand's opinion, we will not reach erroneous conclusions and testify in court with an incorrect and rebuttable opinion.

Judge Hand's opinion is widely quoted and accepted. Many expert accounting witnesses who have heard of or read *Commissioner v. Newman* do not realize that Judge Hand was on the losing side. His dissenting opinion, however, lives on long after the opinions of the majority have been forgotten. If we keep Judge Hand's opinion in mind when our position is the correct one, then we will present expert opinions based on substance to a court.

The amount of work, time involved and cost of the forensic accountant will depend on the needs of the hiring attorney. Accountants are hired for many reasons, and the expert's scope of work initially will be determined by the results sought by the client. Once the attorney determines that litigation might be necessary, he may hire a forensic accountant to determine if valid accounting or financial issues exist that will support a basis for a petition. If the attorney believes that issues developed by his expert are not valid, he may either convince the expert of his viewpoint or seek a different expert. The expert may also refuse the engagement if he cannot be convinced of the attorney's viewpoint.

4.2   The Making of a Successful Accounting Expert Witness

4.2.1   Forensic Accounting and Law

Forensic accounting, consulting and expert witnessing are accounting guided by law. In tax matters, the internal revenue code is accounting expressed in terms of law. To be good, a forensic accountant must have a good knowledge of accounting — to be great, a great knowledge of accounting. But accounting alone is not enough. The forensic accountant must be able to read, understand and apply the law to the facts and issues. In matters of law, the engaging attorney or the judge will guide the expert when the court appoints the expert.

4.2.2   Continuing Education

A successful forensic accountant must read forensic accounting and tax periodicals, have a good accounting, tax and specialized industry library and read on his own time when necessary. He will attend and comprehend forensic accounting seminars and study new court decisions and forensic techniques in his field.

Reading technical accounting publications and attending continuing education classes alone are not adequate to train a professional mind to solve complicated forensic accounting problems. We must also expand our knowledge of liberal arts because we often find solutions to many forensic problems based on our liberal arts knowledge. We must read fiction. Fiction will stimulate our intellect and imagination to help us solve our forensic problems, reach logical conclusions and express ourselves comprehensibly when giving our opinions.

We will attend management courses and study philosophy and logic. A successful forensic accountant and expert witness will participate in community affairs, visit museums and learn about the routine daily lives of other people in order to master successful forensic techniques. Several examples in this chapter and following chapters will illustrate the value of liberal arts to the success of a forensic accounting and expert witnessing engagement.

In *Welch v. Helvering, 290 U.S. 111*, the U.S. Supreme Court explains clearly that everyday knowledge and common sense always apply to technical accounting and tax problems. The court also explained how it reached its conclusion on a complicated depreciation tax issue:

"Here, indeed, as so often in other branches of the law, the decisive distinctions are those of degree and not of kind. One struggles in vain for any verbal formula that will supply a ready touchstone. The standard set up by the statute is not a rule of law; it is rather a way of life. Life in all its fullness must supply the answer to the riddle."

When we master the concepts of Judge Hand's dissent in *Commissioner v. Newman* and of life and the law in *Welch v. Helvering*, we will not fool ourselves and give opinions that will be rebutted or rejected, nor will we overlook facts, issues and reasoning that could have been recognized but were not.

4.2.3   Expert Engaged before a Dispute Has Started through the Court System

When an experienced competent expert is hired before a dispute has started through the court system, he will discuss the facts and issues in depth with the attorney who engaged him. If that attorney has written a summary of the dispute, the accountant should read it. After he reads the summary, the expert will make a preliminary assessment and tell the attorney whether he believes valid accounting, financial or tax issues exist to support allegations of actions unfavorable to the client. He may believe that values or damages, for example, are under- or overstated. He may also realize that he has not identified any valid issues to dispute.

4.2.4   Expert Engaged after the Dispute Is in Court

When the expert is hired after litigation has begun, he will perform the same procedures as if he had been hired before. Initially, he will scan the original and any amended petitions, responses to the petition, counter claims, all depositions, interrogatories and responses, requests for production of records and responses, court orders, *vitae* and reports of opposing witnesses and all motions to be ruled upon or already decided by the court. The expert will discuss his preliminary needs with his engaging attorney, what records he will examine and with whom he will talk. The expert will briefly discuss the content of a proposed job engagement letter and his fees (see Chapter 3). If the attorney and his client decide to begin litigation and hire the expert, or if he is hired after litigation has begun, the expert will prepare a job engagement letter (JE letter) and a listing of issues, where necessary, for the attorney to consider for the original petition or for an amended petition. He also will submit a list to the lawyer of proposed interrogatories and the journals, records, documents and tax returns to request. He will list individuals he would like the lawyer to depose and the questions he would need to be asked. He should also ask his engaging attorney to arrange for the expert, if allowable, to attend all depositions where he can advise the lawyer on accounting-related questions and answers.

The expert will also need to review all answers and resistance to interrogatories and production of records. Finally, he will submit a written report of his findings and conclusions either to the client and his attorney or, if required, direct to the court, then will attend the trial and testify. The expert must arrange to attend the trial to listen to the testimony of all other witnesses so that he can base his expert testimony in part on the examinations of witnesses who precede him. His availability during the trial enables him to advise the trial attorney on certain accounting-related matters as the trial progresses. On occasion, a judge or an arbitrator may prohibit the attendance of an expert during testimony of the opposing expert. This will be resolved by the attorneys and the court, not by the expert witness.

4.4 Petition, Interrogatories, Requests for Production of Records, Motions, Orders and Depositions

The petition, interrogatories, requests for production of records, motions, orders and depositions begin the discovery process for the expert witness. When the litigation begins, each party has a general idea of the issues of the other. Each party also has information, unknown to the other party, which may be needed in order to attack or defend during the litigation. Finding this information is called "discovery" and the methods of obtaining this information is the "discovery process." Discovery assists the parties to prepare for the trial. It is a pretrial method used by one party to obtain facts, documents, records and other information about the case from the other party. This basic information is routinely omitted from accounting education seminars for beginners.

I attended a 2-day seminar on expert witnessing and litigation support for accountants that was sponsored by several state CPA associations. Promotional materials recommended advanced knowledge of the topic as a prerequisite to the seminar. Unfortunately, the seminar required the participants to begin with a review of the accounting records, tax returns and working papers of the opposing side. The instructor made no mention of complaints, petitions, interrogatories, requests for production of records, motions, depositions, orders, or any other documents generated for the trial. These legal documents are paramount to the discovery process and an expert cannot determine true facts and issues without them. Most CPAs are not lawyers and are not expected to be, but the expert witness must at least master legal terms such as *petition, interrogatories, depositions, orders* and other legal terms and concepts that are required by the engaging attorney. If you do not understand a term or concept, ask the engaging attorney. As a minimum, the forensic accountant, or any accountant who will testify as an expert, should buy a good law dictionary such as *Black's Law Dictionary*, or *Ballentine's Law Dictionary*. Court decisions are often cited in an expert's report as support for his position in tax or other litigated matters. A non-attorney forensic accountant should use a citation format that is familiar to or used by most attorneys and courts.

One valuable resource of citations is *A Uniform System of Citation*, which is published and distributed by The Harvard Law Review Association.

As you read documents you will learn their purposes. One Iowa trial attorney has explained that a petition, for example, is a pleading to a state court that contains the names of the plaintiff and the defendant, what the plaintiff claims the defendant has illegally or improperly done to him and what the plaintiff wants the court to do for him and do to the defendant. In the federal courts, the petition is called the complaint. An Arizona lawyer has explained that a petition is a document filed to request the court to grant relief from or take action with respect to a particular situation. A complaint is a document filed with the court to commence a cause of action against another party. Therefore, he says, a complaint is usually against an individual or a corporation. A petition, on the other hand, can be a request to be exempted from the applicability of a particular regulation. Depending on the jurisdiction, the counter party can be the governmental entity responsible for the regulation.

One law dictionary defines a complaint as the original or initial pleading by which an action is commenced under codes or the Rules of Civil Procedure. It sets forth a claim for relief. A petition is defined generally as a written request to the court or other ruling body, usually a government authority, to allow the petitioner to exercise a right, or to prohibit someone else from exercising one. These three differing definitions for two common documents indicate that the accounting expert witness must ask his engaging attorney to provide a definition in lay language to the expert if the expert does not know the purpose or meaning of a document. This will ensure that the lawyer and the expert understand one another.

Starting with the books and records is not a productive first step. The expert cannot know what to look for unless he first reads the petition and amendments, counterclaims, cross-petitions and similar documents that were filed with the court by the parties. Because the petition states the issues that are involved and the relief requested, it is the expert's entrance to getting the facts. Without facts, issues cannot be developed, and without issues, facts cannot be discovered, nor can an expert determine what to examine.

In general, interrogatories are formal questions from one party asked of the other party in the litigation to discover facts and issues. Answers to interrogatories alert you to the tactics of the other side and provide you with facts to check for accuracy and to develop issues. They also suggest other questions to ask for more inclusive discovery.

Requests for production of records and the answers to requests tell the expert what records will be available for investigation. They will also tell the expert what else to ask for.

Orders and motions provide information on what else should be investigated or what can be ignored.

Depositions provide additional facts, inform the expert of the other parties' agenda and beliefs and provide him with additional items to be evaluated. When the expert prepares cross-references among the various depositions, documents, facts and issues, this will help him to develop additional facts and issues.

After the expert has investigated, examined, or read all of these documents filed with the court and develops additional facts and issues, he can design a work program. A good program will guide an expert from the beginning of his investigation to the end of his opinions and his report.

Because of the specialized nature of accounting, the forensic accounting expert will submit a preliminary list of interrogatory suggestions to the lawyer. He will also prepare suggestions to include in a request for records. During depositions of other parties, the accountant should attend, make notes and advise the lawyer of additional questions to ask.

4.5 Basic Concepts and Techniques

Each expert has his own methods of investigation. However, certain basic concepts and techniques apply to all expert witnessing engagements. To resolve problems, common sense (reasoning, logic) is the most valuable asset we have to find answers. Business and life are not reducible merely to technical components. There are, however four basic questions that must be answered by every expert witness to arrive at an opinion that can be relied upon by courts, juries and attorneys for the plaintiff and the defendant:

1. What are the facts?
2. What are the issues?
3. Where and how do I resolve the issues?
4. How should I report my findings?

These four questions must guide every competent forensic accountant whether he is called upon to act as an expert witness or a consultant to resolve the dilemma his client must respond to. The dilemma is not unlike which came first — the chicken or the egg? Which comes first to the expert — the facts or the issues? Forensic accountants can agree that without facts there is no problem to solve. We do not always agree on issues, nor do we always recognize issues. Issues are the questions that we ask about facts. When we ask questions, the answers often tell us that we need more facts. Issues also tell us what we must do about facts — what approaches we will take to solve the problem. More importantly, issues will help us to decide if facts are, in reality, facts. Issues will help us to eliminate and cut through extraneous information that hinders a solution to a problem.

Some believe that the where and how to investigate a problem are the most important solutions to all conclusions. They want to know where and how far to look. Must they read everything on the subject or study each fact in minute detail? Is the problem so ordinary that a minimum of effort will resolve it? Some forensic accountants believe that reporting their findings takes precedent and that they must decide upon a solution before beginning their investigation.

When we look at the four basic questions of facts, issues, where and how to resolve the issues and how to report our findings as being arranged in a circle, they will appear to be interdependent. They are.

As the investigator becomes more experienced and successfully resolves forensic accounting problems, he will learn that number 2 of the four basic questions is supreme. Whenever we can determine the right issues, the development of facts, the where and how of investigation and the report become simple. How to determine correct issues will be covered in depth in Chapter 5 with analyses of several disputes. Following are simple illustrations of everyday incidents that happen to ordinary people not involved in litigation. These discussions will prepare us for Chapter 5.

4.5.1   What Are the Facts?

To begin an investigation for expert witnessing or consulting, all forensic accountants must obtain a few elemental facts. Eventually, we must determine the facts as completely as possible, but initially, only a few facts will come to our attention. The realization that other facts are needed arises when you discover issues in the petition, interrogatories, depositions, requests for records, trial transcripts, attorney's summary, motions, orders, transcripts of hearings on motions among other legal documents and court decisions provided by your engaging trial attorney.

The two most important concepts of forensic consulting or expert witnessing are: (1) the investigator must never assume that what he believes to be facts actually are facts unless he verifies them and (2) the investigator must be certain that the issues that he develops from facts are determined from right reason and not from a bad case of *post hoc ergo propter hoc* thinking. This phrase means, literally, "after this, therefore this." This results in a fallacy in thinking. We draw an erroneous conclusion from a fact. For example, assume that you walked out of your house and slipped on the steps and fell just as a cloud passed overhead. If you believed that the cloud caused your fall, you would be guilty of *post hoc, ergo propter* thinking This type of thinking caused an appeals officer to believe that an overly full briefcase contained documents that all pertained to the taxpayer, and that to review them would be a formidable job. An investigator may make logical assumptions about what facts mean, but not about whether they actually exist. If facts exist, they can always be verified. Over and over, an investigator must stress this to himself. It is a simple rule — never assume facts. Always investigate and determine if what you believe to be facts actually exist or if they are figments of your imagination. To determine facts properly, the forensic accountant must learn to know that he does not know. The following discussion will illustrate these concepts:

Assume that you are walking to lunch. A good friend is approaching from the other direction. She is walking fast and is not smiling. You intend to speak to her when she is close enough to hear you. Just as you start to speak, you notice that she is staring at her feet as she walks. She walks on without looking at you. You feel annoyed, hurt and angry. "What's wrong with her?" you think. "What did I do to her? If she's too good to speak to me, then to hell with her."

You have just imagined that your friend deliberately ignored you and you became angry. You have assumed the existence of facts that are only imagined. The only facts you actually have are that your friend walked toward you, but, when she was close enough to speak, she looked at her feet and walked on past. Based on this, you asked yourself, "What does this mean?" Then you answered, "It means that she doesn't like me, or that I did something wrong to her, or that she thinks she is too good for me."

If you had objectively answered your own question, your honest answer would have been that you did not know what it meant. To discover why your friend seemingly snubbed you, you would have to ask her why she walked on without speaking or looking. Because she is your friend, you would have been reasonable to assume that she was preoccupied and had not noticed you.

Our imaginations are needed to discover more facts, but, when we have facts, we must be careful not to make assumptions about them without proof. We must prove always that the facts are real and our conclusions about them are logical in order to arrive at a rational answer.

Facts will come to us from many sources, but often it takes an inordinate amount of work to discover facts. We must use good questioning techniques to pull them from the mouths of involved persons, who may not recognize what is important to the solution. We can get facts from our client, his attorney and from his employees, suppliers, customers, friends, relatives and newspaper clippings, and, of course, the legal documents already discussed. Facts will come from examination of records, notes, wills, tax returns, working papers, correspondence and many other documents. Ask questions of yourself and others to get facts.

As our investigation continues, we often discover that we need additional facts. We can either stop our investigation to obtain them, or make a note of the facts needed and work around them until we cannot investigate further without them.

When we obtain all the facts, many questions are completely resolved and other problems will be reduced. If your friend who walked past you without speaking had told you later that her father was terminally ill and that she had been preoccupied with concern for him and was on her way to the hospital, your self-centered problem would have been solved. You would lose your belief that she did not care for you.

When we learn to know that we do not know, we will discover the nature of a belief about unproven facts. A belief is the acceptance of a fact as truth when we are without certain proof. When you believed your friend had snubbed you, you were telling yourself that you did not know for sure, but had a suspicion that she had snubbed you. A belief must be recognized as lack of knowledge and verified. Eventually, with sufficient verification, we can arrive at an opinion about the situation. Our opinion, of course, is merely another belief, but it is based on more evidence than our original belief and will be stronger than a mere suspicion. To be good forensic accountants and expert witnesses, we must always ensure that our erroneous beliefs do not harden into convictions. Erroneous convictions are almost unchangeable.

A successful forensic accountant will not trust facts to his memory. Our working papers may wind up in the court record, so we should always write facts down in a complete and formal manner. Use as much detail as possible and try to arrange them in a logical sequence. This will organize them in our minds, serve as a basis for a logical beginning to our investigation and help organize and determine issues concerning the facts. Many of our detailed notes can be inserted into our consulting or expert witness reports without change.

4.5.2   What Are the Issues?

Issues are the specific questions or problems that can be determined from facts or, when appropriate, from imagination. If we cannot determine the issues from the facts, than we must improvise general questions such as, "Is the answer to our interrogatory about their installment sale procedures correct?" Then, we must read accounting and business literature about installment sales. We must also read the Internal Revenue code and regulations on installment sales. Our reading may suggest a specific issue about an answer to an interrogatory such as whether they have accounted correctly for their installment sales, or whether this is really an installment sale or a secured loan that should not be recorded as income.

Tax disputes would require the forensic expert to interpret the internal revenue code. If we are not familiar with the code section and related regulations, or with the issue, then we can use an index to tax or accounting articles. A good professional article about the problem will help us to understand it and will help us to discover issues. It may also solve the problem completely.

Issues should be written down in detail as they arise. Treat them as you treat facts and organize them in a logical and detailed manner.

4.5.3   Where and How Do I Resolve the Issues?

Issues will be resolved by investigation and research in the legal documents filed with the court; the attorney's memorandum; relevant correspondence; research in accounting, tax and specialized industry libraries; biographical clippings in a local public library; other public library reference sections; the Library of Congress; and research libraries available on the Internet. All forensic and expert witnessing issues must be approached as if the expert were responding to a rebuttal by the defendant of the plaintiff's allegations and a rebuttal by the plaintiff of the defendant's allegations. Unless we research both sides and determine who is right and who is wrong, there is no need to investigate and research at all. The opinions of both the plaintiff and the defendant would be equally correct. We know from experience that our opinions can always be challenged — and usually are.

When we reach expert witnesses reach their conclusions, they must always determine how an opposing expert would prove them to be wrong. Just knowing what the facts and issues are in the dispute is not enough to answer and resolve issues. The actual preparation for expert witnessing or accounting forensic consultation leads to three additional basic questions for the forensic accountant:

1. Where do I begin?
2. How do I proceed?
3. How do I know when I am done?

The answer to these three questions is the same whether the dispute involves general business or income tax matters such as damages, breach of contract, trademark infringement, business valuations or other tax issues. In all disputes, the expert must understand the facts, issues, industry or matter involved and the parties involved.

4.5.4 Where Do I Begin?

Whether engaged as expert accounting witnesses or expert accounting consultants your investigation and research will always begin with facts and issues. If the client, his attorney or the opposing side provides an issue, then that issue is a fact. Does the dispute, for example, involve the value of a trucking company, or whether the trucking company was a going concern? The expert must understand all facets of the trucking industry to accept this type of job. Did the dispute involve a price fixing allegation made by a truck retail dealer against a heavy-duty-truck manufacturer? The expert must understand heavy-duty-truck pricing and transactions among the manufacturer, its dealers and their over-the-road trucking company customers.

Is this a dissolution dispute among partners of a medical practice that specializes in cardiology? If so, the expert must be knowledgeable in medical partnerships that practice cardiology. Is the dispute a divorce that requires a division of assets and requires valuation of certain business assets? The expert must understand the emotions that are evident in many divorces and the expert must understand the assets to be valued and divided.

Tax matters will require research in the internal revenue code, state tax codes, related regulations, court decisions and other relevant sources. Because the internal revenue code is accounting expressed in terms of law, CPAs are authorized to interpret tax laws, testify as experts in tax disputes and issue tax opinions.

When a forensic accountant is engaged to determine non-tax matters such as damages, breach of contract, trademark infringement or business valuations, after he determines facts and issues, he must determine the answers to the issues. He must research. He can perform most of his research in tax libraries as well as accounting libraries. Damages, breach of contract, trademark infringement, business valuations or a myriad of seemingly non-tax disputes all revolve around income, expenses or taxable awards. In such disputes, a forensic accountant does well to seek answers in the internal revenue code that includes comprehensive coverage of taxable and deductible receipts and expenditures. All forensic investigations must be approached as if you were responding to adverse allegations, opinions, or arguments made against your client. It could be an internal revenue agent that takes an adverse position against the client's transactions. It could be a trial court, a federal or state arbitrator, an administrative law judge, a trial board of a regulatory agency or a professional association, individuals or other entities. Whenever we reach an opinion, we also must determine how another expert would prove us to be wrong. We must ensure that whatever answers we reach will stand rocklike against all efforts to prove that we are wrong. Clients, or the opposing side in litigation may always attack our opinions, but in the end, we must always prove our opinions to be right and opposing opinions to be wrong. A great expert witness must wear two hats — the hat of the plaintiff and the hat of the defendant.

Many documents filed with the court during litigation provide facts that suggest issues: documents filed with the court including a petition, complaint, cross-petition, counterclaim, answers to petitions, interrogatories, answers to interrogatories, requests for productions of records and resistance to production, answers or resistance to interrogatories, motions, orders, transcripts of trials and hearings, depositions and tax, accounting, specialized industry libraries and newspaper clippings in public libraries of news and profiles on individuals and business entities. Also included are the expert's discussions with the attorney and the attorney's memos and notes on the dispute.

4.5.5   How Do I Proceed?

If you still do not understand the facts and issues, read a magazine article, book or treatise on the industry or dispute. These may cite important sources of information and help you to understand the issues. Research the internal revenue code and tax decisions again to determine the nature of the dispute or the issues. One dilemma that confronts the forensic accountant is his limited privilege in the courts. An attorney may be reluctant to share his privileged communications or memos in case the privilege may be forfeited in the hands of the expert. In this event, the accountant must decide if he can reach a fully investigated and supported opinion without this information. If he cannot, then he must explain to the lawyer why he needs it. If the lawyer still will not give him the materials, then the expert cannot reach a valid opinion and must inform the lawyer.

State accountancy statutes and regulations and federal tax laws prohibit accountants from disclosing certain financial transactions and tax return information without permission of the client, or unless a court orders disclosure. The engaging attorney must be informed of what these items are so he can resolve these restrictions for the accountant and guide him through the myriad of laws.

Almost every accounting issue that is not resolved at the fact level is based on accounting and tax rules, regulations and statutes. Although a few accountants are also attorneys, most are not. Usually a dual licensee must practice either as an attorney or as a CPA.

Our intent is not to resolve the issue as to whether CPAs engage in unauthorized legal practice. Expert accountants must interpret the internal revenue code, regulations and tax decisions and apply them to facts — and have the right to do so. During protests and conferences in the IRS Office of Appeals, CPAs have had to interpret tax treaties, federal non-tax laws such as Title 19, The Elementary and Secondary Education Act, among other statutes. In some specialized industry litigation, CPAs have had to testify about the Interstate Commerce Act and related regulations, the Securities and Exchange Act and Securities and Exchange Commission rules and regulations and rules of State Boards of Public Accountancy. A liquidation of a partnership or a breach of contract are legal transactions that often require an accountant to interpret the financial and accounting meanings of some of the contract provisions.

Forensic accountants do not encroach upon the work of an attorney, but when working with one, can provide him with information on certain statutes governing income and taxation that they constantly work with. After receiving preliminary facts and issues from the attorney, the accountant must review the petition and other related documents filed with the court and list facts and issues that he believes to be relevant.

4.5.6   How Do I Know When I Am Finished?

Many forensic accounting expert witnesses or consultants find it difficult to recognize when their investigation is complete. If they have referenced and cross referenced all facts and issues to all relevant documents, investigated all testimony, looked up in a list of legal documents and citations pertaining to the case all court and other decisions they have relied on and briefed the cited cases that are in point, the work may be nearing completion. This work seems to be neverending. The investigation is complete when each issue has been accounted for and resolved and, when the many transactions and authoritative support studied are all beginning to lead to the same answer, then we are ready to reach valid conclusions.

4.5.7   How Should I Report My Findings?

All reports of an accounting expert witness should be addressed to a person or entity designated by the engaging lawyer. This will serve as a basis for deposing the witness or examining him in court. Generally, it should be organized in the order of conclusions, facts, issues, summary and a thorough discussion.

Discuss one issue completely and resolve it before discussing another one. If the report is arranged by issues, it is easier to read and understand. The end of the discussion of each issue provides a logical stopping point at which to state conclusions.

More than one conclusion often exists for each issue. A good expert witness report will discuss them all, but explain why one particular conclusion was chosen over all others.

An expert should write his report so the reader can understand it. He was hired to help the trier of fact understand issues that were not in his area of expertise. For example, an expert may report that the transaction is a 368(a)(1)(D) or merely a "D" reorganization without explaining what this means. A novice in taxation, whether a judge or an attorney, might not understand.

Correct grammar will make it easier for the reader to understand, but good grammar doesn't mean stuffy language. Reports are written for a reader to understand. It doesn't matter if he is the plaintiff or defendant, a trial attorney, the judge or a member of the jury. If the report bores the reader or confuses him, he may become indifferent and take a position contrary to the conclusion in the report.

4.6 The Expert's Work Begins

A review of any petition will provide us with many facts, issues and answers. What follows is an annotated example:

Case No: 77915

The Petition in the Iowa District Court for Otoe County City of Racine, Iowa, Plaintiff

vs. Seneca Sewer & Water Dept., Defendant

Petition for Declatory Judgment and Permanent Injunction

(The petition heading provides us with many facts and issues. The facts tell us that any trial, if there is one, will be held in the Iowa District Court for Otoe County. Facts in the petition also tell us which party is the plaintiff and which is the defendant. Finally, it tells us that the plaintiff wants the court to award it a declaratory judgment and permanent injunction.

What issues can we discover from this petition heading? One issue: Is the word "Judgement" misspelled? Although not common usage in the United States, it is listed as an alternative spelling. Because the spelling is part of the official document, the spelling is a fact and we have no authority to change it. If a fact is wrong, we can explain the erroneous facts in our opinion, but we must not change the records that we examine. Too often, examiners change facts because they are not willing to accept them. This is discussed in Chapter 6.

Obvious issues are: (1) Location of the court: Seneca, Iowa. Unless the expert answers this issue, he might miss the pending trial. (2) What is a petition for declaratory judgment and what is a permanent injunction? You can find basic definitions of these documents in a dictionary of legal terms, but an experienced expert witness who is not a lawyer will ask the engaging attorney to explain the terms in lay language with which the expert is familiar. Perhaps the meaning in the Iowa District Courts differs from the definitions in another state jurisdiction or in the federal court system.

After we understand terms, the next issues are: (1) Is the plaintiff entitled to both a declaratory judgment and a permanent injunction or just one or the other? (2) Does a basis exist for the defendant to defeat a declaratory judgment and a permanent injunction?)

COMES NOW the Plaintiff and for cause of action against the Defendant alleges and states that:

(This means that what follows is the facts that will give the plaintiff the right to the judicial relief that it has requested — a declaratory judgment and a permanent injunction.)

1. Plaintiff, City of Racine, is a municipal corporation duly organized and existing under the laws of the state of Iowa.

(The issue suggested by this allegation in paragraph 1 of this petition is: is plaintiff a municipal corporation organized and existing under Iowa Law? This seems to be a simple issue. The plaintiff has stated facts about itself. We need only pose those facts as a question. With this issue, the expert can delve into the history of the plaintiff, including its minutes during the negotiations and signing of the water contracts. Expert witnesses must report any discrepancies between statement 1 and the actual facts to their clients' attorneys.)

2. Defendant, Seneca Sewer & Water Dept., is a utility board organized by the City of Seneca, Iowa pursuant to provisions of Chapter 388, Code of Iowa and is responsible for the operation of the municipal water and sewer utilities for the City of Seneca, Iowa.

(These few facts require a review of the articles of organization, Chapter 388, Code of Iowa and a tour of the physical plant, offices and wells. This will help us to learn whether Seneca had the authority and physical capacity to carry out the contract. We should also have the attorney review our interpretation of Chapter 388 so we can begin with a correct premise.)

3. Plaintiff maintains a water distribution system but does not have its own water wells and therefore does not have the capacity to provide its own water for its residents.

(This will require us to visit plaintiff's physical plant and offices and review their articles of organization, board minutes and state audits to determine whether these facts are true.)

4. On or about May 10, 1972, Plaintiff and Defendant entered into a written agreement for the sale and delivery of water at a wholesale rate by the defendant to the Plaintiff for distribution by Plaintiff to its residents. A copy of this written contract is attached hereto as Exhibit "A" and by this express reference made a part hereof.

(The contract will provide more issues and reveal whether the statements regarding the duties of the plaintiff and the defendant as described in this petition agree with the provisions of the contract.)

5. The contract between the Plaintiff and Defendant at paragraph B (1) provided for a schedule of wholesale water rates to be paid by Plaintiff to Defendant for water sold and delivered to plaintiff.

(Paragraphs two through five give rise to the following issues: (1) What does the May 10, 1972 contract provide? (2) Was the contract carried out according to its terms? (3) Were the rates billed at wholesale? The answers to these issues are in the contract and in the billing and revenue records of defendant.)

6. On or about February 15, 1978, Defendant by resolution of the "Water Works Trustees" did increase the rate schedule to be paid by Plaintiff to Defendant. This increase was agreed to and acquiesced in by Plaintiff as follows:

0–300,000 gallons	$255.00
300,000–3,000,000 gallons	.76/1,000 gallons
3,000,000–	.83/1,000 gallons

A copy of the resolution of the "Water Works Trustees" of the City of Racine is attached hereto as Exhibit "B" and by this express reference made a part hereof.

(The petition should be reconciled to the actual contract and the actual resolution and not to mere copies, because this is a statement of fact and must be verified by reading city resolutions and contracts and amended contracts. These may be needed to resolve further allegations.)

7. There were no rate increases by Plaintiff between February 15, 1978 and May 9, 1990.

(This can be verified by a review of rate and billing records.)

8. On or about May 9, 1990 by resolution of the Racine Water Board Trustees, Defendant further attempted to modify and increase the rate schedule to be charged Plaintiff as follows:

0–2,000 gallons	$8.00
2,000–7000 gallons	1.92/1,000 gallons
7,000–	1.64/1,000 gallons

A copy of this resolution dated May 9, 1990 is attached hereto as Exhibit "C" and, by this express reference, made a part hereof.

9. The attempted rate increase of May 9, 1990 would constitute an effective rate increase to Plaintiff of over One Hundred Percent (100%).

(Paragraphs 8 and 9 allege that defendant increased the wholesale rates to plaintiff of over 100% on May 9, 1990. This allegation must be verified by examining the rating and billing records and resolutions of defendant. The issue in paragraphs 8 and 9 are: did defendant raise the rates and were the rates increased by over 100%?)

10. The rate schedule as set forth in the resolution of May 9, 1990 is an attempt by Defendant to materially alter the terms of the contract between the parties by altering the rate formula as set forth in the agreement of May 10, 1972 and the resolution of February 15, 1978 and as such constitutes a material breach by defendant of the terms of that contract and is, therefore, null and void.

Issues: (1) Is this an attempt by defendant to materially alter the terms of the contract? (2) What does "materially" mean and is there a formula to calculate "materially"? (3) What is a material breach of the contract terms and what amount of increase would not be material? (4) Does a rate increase make this contract null and void? While many of these questions can be answered by a review of the contract and rate and billing records, a comparison with the wholesale rate charged by nearby cities to smaller communities also will be helpful. Additionally, authoritative books on water rate making and billing for municipal water are published.)

11. Further, the rate increase as set forth in the resolution of May 9, 1990 is a material breach by Defendant of the terms and conditions of paragraph C(5) of the agreement dated May 10, 1972 in that this increase is not based upon a demonstrable commensurate increase during the period 1978 through 1990 in the cost of Defendant's performance under the terms of the agreement and further this rate increase includes and reflects increased capitalization costs of defendant and is an attempt by defendant to recover these increased capitalization costs, all in violation of their agreement with plaintiff and, therefore, null and void.

(Paragraph 11 adds two new and important allegations when it charges: (1) The increase is not based upon a demonstrable commensurate increase in the cost of the defendant's performance under the contract terms. What does this mean? If we can determine what this means, the dispute can be ended and resolved out of court. Four major issues in this paragraph are: (a) What is the cost of performance? (b) Is the increase based upon a demonstrable commensurate increase in the cost of performance? (c) Did consulting engineers prepare a rate making study? (d) Do the facts in the petition agree with the facts in the underlying agreements? (2) The increase includes and reflects increased capitalization costs and is an attempt by the defendant to recover these costs. The issues for this allegation are (a) Does the rate increase include capitalization costs increased, or not? (b)Are the rate increases an attempt to recover these costs? (c), are including capitalization costs and attempting to recover them a violation of the agreement?)

12. Plaintiff notified Defendant prior to the effective date of the resolution of May 9, 1990 that it considered the attempted rate increase of May 9, 1990 to be null and void under the terms of the agreement between the parties and has continued to pay the defendant under the previous rate schedule established February 15, 1978.

(This is easily confirmed by the defendant's cash receipts and billing records. However, it is merely a statement of fact and would mean that the plaintiff owes additional funds to the defendant if the defendant is successful in this dispute.)

13. Defendant has discussed disconnecting and discontinuing further delivery of water to plaintiff and has threatened to impose further penalties all

in violation of the contract between the parties unless Plaintiff makes payment in full to Defendant under the rate schedule adopted by Defendant on May 9.1990.

(*The foregoing paragraph is not an issue for the expert accountant and will be addressed by the attorneys for the parties. However, the attorney may ask the expert to determine the facts.*)

WHEREFORE Plaintiff prays for a declaratory judgment and an interpretation of the agreement between the parties dated May 10, 1972; that as a part of said decree and judgment that the Court find that the rate increase of Defendant of May 9, 1990 is a breach of the agreement between Defendant and Plaintiff and as such is null and void under the terms of that agreement; and further, that Defendant be permanently enjoined from enforcing the resolution dated May 9, 1990 increasing the rate charged Plaintiff for water sold and delivered to Plaintiff and for such other and further relief as the Court deems just and equitable.

4.7   Interrogatories

The defendant submitted 19 preliminary interrogatories to the court and the plaintiff. The only one relevant to the forensic accountant is discussed below:

4.7.1   Interrogatory No. 2

State whether you expect to call any person as an expert witness at the trial of this lawsuit and, if so, state the name and address of each such person and with reasonable particularity state the following:

a.The subject matter on which the expert is expected to testify. (*The expert usually must submit this to his engaging attorney to be filed with the court. It can be included in the expert's job engagement contract, but the engaging attorney often requests this in the form of a preliminary report to be submitted to the court.*)

b.The designated person's qualifications to testify as an expert on such subject.

c.The mental impressions and opinions held by the expert and the facts known to the expert, regardless of when the factual information was acquired, which relate to or form the basis of mental impressions and opinions held by the expert.

4.7.1.1   Answer to Interrogatory No 2:

b. James L. Wren, 18 Fluor Blvd., Des Moines, Iowa

b .Certified Public Accountant, Partner, Slovax and Associates

c .Generally, the above-named individual will testify as to the actual direct costs of water provided to Plaintiff by Defendant as reflected by the books and records of the Defendant.

(Even before Daubert *[see Chapter 2], this answer would have been considered by many courts, attorneys and expert witnesses to be inadequate.* Daubert *brought more attention to the credibility and professional qualifications of expert witnesses. Guidelines for expert opinions and testimony expectations are found in Chapter 3.*

Many examples of facts and issues, documents and depositions will be covered in following chapters. This water rate litigation required a study of many records including, among others, news clippings found in local libraries, interviews with other water boards, Federal Home Bank officials, study of water accounting manuals, reconciling contract costs with consumer price indexes, review of certified financial statements and related working papers issued by independent accountants or the state auditor's office, rate-making studies by consulting engineers, official opinions of the Attorney General of Iowa, Iowa Code and research in similar disputes in other jurisdictions.)

Upon review of the answers to interrogatories, the defendant filed the following answer, counterclaim and application for temporary hearing:

Case No. 77915

In The Iowa District Court For Doe County

City of Racine, Iowa, Plaintiff

Seneca Sewer & Water Department, Defendant.

Answer, Counterclaim and Application for Temporary Hearing

Division I

The defendant now comes forth and answers as follows:

1. Defendant admits the allegations of paragraph 1 of the Petition.

2. Defendant admits that it is a municipal utility board organized pursuant to Chapter 388, Code of Iowa and that it is responsible for the municipal water utilities of the City of Seneca, Iowa, but denies that it is responsible for the sewer utilities of the City of Seneca, Iowa and denies that it is the

Seneca Sewer and Water Department. Defendant affirmatively alleges that it is known as the Board of Waterworks Trustees of the City of Seneca, Iowa.

3-8. Defendant admits the allegations of paragraphs 3 through 8 of the Petition.

9. Defendant denies the allegation of paragraph 9 of the Petition.

10. Defendant denies each and every allegation of paragraph 10 of the Petition.

11. Defendant denies each and every allegation of paragraph 11 of the Petition.

12. Defendant denies each and every allegation of paragraph 12 of the Petition.

13. Defendant admits that it has discussed discontinuing delivery of water to Plaintiff, but denies each and every other allegation of paragraph 13 of the Petition.

(Almost all issues under Division I to this Answer to the Petition are factual accounting or factual recording issues. Paragraph 10 is a mixture of legal and accounting issues and requires guidance by the attorney before and after work on them.)

Division II

4.7.2   Counterclaim

The Counterclaim consisted of 13 paragraphs explaining why the petition of the plaintiff is not correct and alleging that defendant's interpretations are correct. Only paragraphs 1, 6, 7 and 13 are relevant to forensic accountants and are reproduced below:

Defendant, as its counterclaim, states:

1. Plaintiff was shown in public meetings of the Board of Waterworks Trustees of the City of Seneca, Iowa, held on April 9, 1990 and again on May 9, 1990, that Defendant's costs of performance under the May 10, 1972 contract had demonstrably increased to the extent that the rate increase declared and imposed in the May 9, 1990, resolution of Defendant was justifiable, within the contemplation of the parties and within the intent of the original contract.

This counterclaim paragraph blends partial truths with hyperbole and hopes to mesmerize the defendant into yielding. The minutes of the public meetings on April 9 and May 9, 1990 may show that the parties discussed and reviewed the costs of performance and the contract. Local news reports of the meeting might even confirm the minutes. The allegations that the contract had demonstrably increased and rate increases were justified must be proven and defended or rebutted. The parties view these issues subjectively. The accounting expert witness must distinguish between objectivity and subjectivity and convince both parties that his understanding of issues and answers is the sole objective understanding.

6. Plaintiff has thereby incurred a debt to Defendant of at least $120,000 as of April 12, 1991, as a result of Plaintiff's underpayment of bills for water sold by Defendant to plaintiff.

(Whether a debt was incurred and its amount requires accounting calculations and interpretations of the accounting legalese contained in the contract. This author was once engaged by a County Board of Supervisors to study the cost of indigent care by two local hospitals. The supervisors believed that the hospitals were overcharging for indigent care and wanted the costs to be determined before litigation began. My completed study determined that the hospitals were undercharging *for indigent patients. The Board called a public hearing over my report and threatened to withhold my fee. While any expert witness should sympathize with his client, his ultimate responsibility is to the trier of fact and to honesty and integrity.*

We all want to help our client to win, but an accounting expert witness must be aware that his conclusions require objectivity and his independence from the client.)

7. Said debt continues to grow with each passing month and is currently due and owing and Defendant now makes demand upon Plaintiff for payment in full of that debt.

(If a debt is found to exist, this is a reasonable statement. The plaintiff's expert will try to rebut it and the role of the defendant's expert is to defend this statement and rebut the conclusion of the opposing witness if possible.)

13. In the alternative, Plaintiff should post a bond that would satisfy Defendant's outstanding and accruing bill with Plaintiff. Such bond should be maintained during the pendency of this action and should be filed with the Doe County Clerk of Court.

Therefore, given the allegations of Divisions I and II above, defendant requests:

(*The defendant, among other requests, asked the court to: enter a declaratory judgment to interpret the original contract, find the rate increases to be justifiable, find that the plaintiff's demand for a permanent injunction is unnecessary, order plaintiff to pay defendant all amounts due and owing for water sold to the plaintiff including penalties, order plaintiff to pay defendant's attorney fees in full and to pay all court costs.*)

4.7.3 Application for Temporary Hearing

In the interim, defendant requests that the court set a date, time and place for a temporary hearing on the issue of establishing the escrow account or bond demanded in Division II above.

(*After the answer, counterclaim and application for temporary hearing are filed, the judge may grant a temporary hearing and order plaintiff to set up an escrow account. Not all litigation contains an answer, counterclaim and application for temporary hearing. The expert should determine his role in each instance with the engaging attorney.*

Paragraph 4 of the petition filed by Racine refers to an agreement (contract) to deliver water and attaches it as Exhibit A. The remainder of the petition alleges that rate increases by defendant have violated the terms of the contract. Plaintiff's expert witness will be engaged to testify that the defendant has violated the contract terms. Defendant's expert witness will be engaged to testify that the defendant has not violated the contract terms. Each expert must complete adequate research and investigation and apply acceptable methods, examples and authoritative support to prove that he is right and the other expert is wrong. The expert witnessing solution to right versus wrong is discussed thoroughly in Chapter 5 and is one of the more important concepts of forensic accounting, consulting and expert witnessing. It stands equally with substance versus form, real versus imagined facts and rational thinking.

Reading and understanding the contract and related resolutions (Exhibit A) will give the forensic accountant adequate information to make a preliminary determination of where to begin.)

4.8 Water Purchase Contract Seneca–Racine Exhibit A

This contract for the sale and purchase of water is entered on the 10th day of May, 1972, between the City of Seneca, Iowa by the Board of Trustees of its Municipal Waterworks Plant and System of said City, hereinafter referred to as the "Seller" and the town of Racine, Iowa, hereinafter referred to as the "Purchaser."

Witnesseth:

Whereas, the Purchaser is a municipal corporation authorized by law to establish and operate a water supply distribution system subject to approval of the voters residing within the town and Whereas, the Seller owns and operates a water supply distribution system with a capacity currently capable of serving the present customers of the Seller's system and the estimated number of water users to be served by the said Purchaser as shown in the plans of the system now on file in the offices of the Purchaser and

Whereas, by Resolution No. 1007 enacted on the 23rd day of May, 1972, by the Seller, the sale of water to the Purchaser in accordance with the provisions of the said Resolution was approved and the execution of this contract carrying out the said Resolution by the Chairman, Board of Trustees and attested by the Secretary, was duly authorized and

Whereas, by Resolution of the Town Council of the Purchaser, enacted on the 2nd day of March, 1972, the purchase of water from the Seller in accordance with the terms set forth in the said Resolution was approved and the execution of this contract by the Mayor and attested by the Town Clerk was duly authorized;

Therefore, in consideration of the foregoing and the mutual agreements hereinafter set forth,

A. The Seller Agrees:
   1. To furnish the Purchaser at the point of delivery hereinafter specified, during the term of this contract or any renewal or extension thereof, potable treated water meeting applicable purity standards of the United Sates Public Health Standards in such quantity as may be required by the Purchaser not to exceed 3,000,000 gallons per month and water furnished shall be of the same quality and purity as that sold by the seller to the customers of its own system.
   2. That water will be furnished at a reasonably constant pressure calculated at 75 lbs psi from an existing 18-inch main supply at a point located at the City of Seneca Platte River Water Treatment Plant. If a greater pressure than that normally available at the point of delivery is required by the Purchaser, the cost of providing such greater pressure shall be borne by the Purchaser. Emergency failures of pressure or supply due to main supply line breaks, power failure, flood, fire and use of water to fight fire, earth-

quake, or other catastrophe shall excuse the Seller from this provision for such reasonable period of time as may be necessary to restore service.

3. To furnish, install, operate and maintain at its own expense at point of delivery, the necessary watering equipment, including a meter house or pit and required devices of standard type for properly measuring the quantity of water delivered to the Purchaser and to calibrate such metering equipment whenever requested by the Purchaser but not more frequently than once every twelve (12) months. A meter registering not more than two percent (2%) above or below the test result shall be deemed to be accurate. The previous readings of any meter disclosed by test to be accurate shall be corrected for the three months previous to such test in accordance with the percentage of inaccuracy found by such tests. If any meter fails to register for any period, the amount of water furnished during such period shall be deemed to be the amount of water delivered in the corresponding period immediately prior to the failure, unless Seller and Purchaser shall agree upon a different amount.

   The metering equipment shall be read on the 15th day of the month. An appropriate official of the Purchaser at all reasonable times shall have access to the meter for the purpose of verifying its readings.

4. To furnish the Purchaser at the above address not later than the 30th day of each month, with an itemized statement of the amount of water furnished the Purchaser during the preceding month.

B. The Purchaser Agrees:

1. To pay the Seller, not later than the 10th day of each month, for water delivered in residences with the following schedule of rates:

   a. $150.00 for the first 300,000 gallons, which amount shall also be the maximum rate per month.

   b. $0.45 cents per 1000 gallons for water in excess of 300,000 gallons, but less than 3,000,000 gallons.

   c. $0.50 cents per 1000 gallons for water in excess of 3,000,000 gallons.

2. To pay as an agreed cost, a connection fee to connect the Seller's system with the system of the Purchaser the sum of $2,000 which shall cover any and all costs of the Seller for installation of the metering equipment, valves and meter pit.

C. It is further mutually agreed between the Seller and the Purchaser as follows:

1. That this contract shall extend for a term of 60 years from the date of the initial delivery of any water as shown by the first bill submitted by the Seller to the Purchaser and, thereafter may be renewed or extended for such term, or terms, as may be agreed upon by the Seller and Purchaser.

2. That 60 days prior to the estimated date of completion of construction of the Purchaser's water supply distribution system, the Purchaser will notify the Seller in writing the date for the initial delivery of water.

3. When requested by the Purchaser the Seller will make available to the contractor at the point of delivery, or other point reasonably close thereto, water sufficient for testing, flushing and trench filling the system of the

Purchaser during construction, irrespective of whether the metering equipment has been installed at that time, at a flat charge of $50.00 which will be paid by the contractor, or on his failure to pay, by the Purchaser.

4. That the Seller will, at all times, operate and maintain its system in an efficient manner and will take such action as may be necessary to furnish the Purchaser with quantities of water required by the Purchaser. Temporary or partial failure to deliver water shall be remedied with all possible dispatch. In the event of an extended shortage of water, or the supply of water available to the Seller is otherwise diminished over an extended period of time, the supply of water to Purchaser's consumers shall be reduced or diminished in the same ratio or proportion as the supply to Seller's consumers is reduced or diminished.

5. That the provisions of this contract pertaining to the schedule of rates to be paid by the Purchaser for water delivered are subject to modification at the end of every 1 year period. Any increase or decrease in rates shall be based on a demonstrable increase or decrease in the costs of performance hereunder, but such costs shall not include increased capitalization of the Seller's system. Other provisions of this contract may be modified or altered by mutual agreement.

6. That this contract is subject to such rules, regulations, or laws as may be applicable to similar agreements in this State and the Seller and Purchaser will collaborate in obtaining such permits, certificates, or the like, as may be required to comply therewith.

7. That the construction of the water supply distribution system by the Purchaser is being financed by a loan made or insured by and/or a grant from, the United States of America, acting through the Farmers Home Administration of the United States Department of Agriculture and the provisions hereof pertaining to the undertakings of the Purchaser are conditioned upon the approval, in writing, of the State Director of the Farmers Home Administration.

8. That in the event of any occurrence rendering the Purchaser incapable of performing under this contract, any successor of the Purchaser, whether the result of legal process, assignment, or otherwise, shall succeed to the rights of the Purchaser hereunder.

In witness whereof, the parties hereto, acting under authority of their respective governing bodies, have caused this contract to be duly executed in four counterparts, each of which shall constitute an original.

Seller: The City of Seneca, Iowa

By its Board of Trustees of the Municipal Waterworks Plant and System

By _____, Chairman

Attest: _____, Secretary

Approved by City Council, City of Seneca, Iowa this 23rd day of May, 1972.

By _____, Mayor

Purchaser: Town of Racine

By _____ , Mayor

Attest: _____ , Town Clerk

This contract is approved on behalf of the Farmers Home Administration this 22nd day of June, 1972.

By _____ , Acting State Director

Resolution: Whereas the Waterworks Trustees of the City of Seneca, Iowa, did enter into a Water Purchase Contract with the town of Racine, Iowa, now the city of Racine, Iowa, on or about May 10, 1972, for the purchase of water by said city of Racine, Iowa,

and

Whereas said contract provides that the provisions of the same pertaining to the schedule of rates is subject to modification at the end of each one year period and

Whereas the cost of performance on the part of the Board of Waterworks Trustees of the City of Seneca, Iowa, has increase (d) substantially since the making of said contract and it is now necessary to use a new schedule of rates for the sale of water by the Board of Waterworks Trustees of the City of Seneca, Iowa, to the city of Racine, Iowa.

Now, Therefore, Be It Resolved by the Board Of Waterworks Trustees of the City Of Seneca, Iowa, that the schedule of rates for the sale of water by the Board of Waterworks Trustees of the City of Seneca, Iowa, to the city of Racine, Iowa, shall be as follows on a per month basis:

First 300,000 gallons	$255.00
Next 2,700,000 gallons	.76/1000
Over 3,000,000 gallons	.83/1000

That the rate set out above shall be effective with the billings and statements sent in April of 1978 and shall apply to the statement to be sent to the city of Racine, Iowa, on or about April 15, 1978.

Duly passed this 2nd day of February 1978.

Resolution #144

Resolution Setting Bulk & Wholesale Water Rates

Whereas, the Seneca Water Board Trustees hereby states that the following scale shall be used for the purchase of wholesale and bulk water from the Seneca Water Department. A minimum charge will be billed each trip if purchase is less than 2,000 gallons.

2,000 gallons or less	$8.00 plus tax
For next 5,000 gallons	1.92 per 1,000 gallons
All over 7,000 gallons	1.64 per 1,000 gallons
(All above rates add sales tax)	

Said fee shall be billed the first of every month with all current Water Department penalty and collection procedures in effect.

Effective date of rate will be July 1, 1990.

Duly passed and approved this 9th day of May 1990.

Attest:

_____, City Clerk   _____, Chairman

4.9 Deposition of Plaintiff's Expert

The plaintiff's expert did not issue a written report but gave his opinions orally by deposition. Chapter 5 discusses and illustrates depositions and begins with an analysis of the deposition of Racine's expert. Chapter 9 discusses and illustrates expert witness reports, but the report of Seneca's expert witness appears in Chapter 5 for continuity. The deposition of the plaintiff's expert and the report of the defendant's expert show the relationship of each to this water-rate-dispute petition and contract. Opposing lawyers and their forensic accountant expert witnesses must determine facts and whether the opposing expert has irrefutable theories and knowledge. Can he be rebutted?

How to Continue

5

5.1 Discovery

The expert witness must review and understand all petitions, interrogatories, contracts, record production requests, counterclaims and all other court legal documents generated in response to the litigation before he reads depositions. This allows him to make preliminary notes, observations and a listing of information he will need from the depositions. All issues might be answered by these documents in themselves, without need to examine books, records, correspondence and other original records of the parties. Armed with this information, the expert witness can read the depositions objectively because he is armed with knowledge of several of the facts. If the opposing expert has prepared and filed an expert's report and has been or will be deposed, attend the deposition if you can. Whether you have attended or not, always read, cross-reference and make notes on his report. You must rebut it. All expert reports can be rebutted. Determine whether the opposing expert's deposition and report are supported by factual and substantive authority. The analyses and commentaries on depositions, transcripts, court-filed documents and accounting records will assist an expert to arrive at and to testify on an expert opinion. It shows how one discovery leads to another and the expert's report shows what accounting questions and answers the accounting expert witness should provide for his attorney to be used in direct- and cross-examination in depositions or in the court.

In *Racine v. Seneca*, the plaintiff's expert accounting witness did not issue a written report of his expert opinion. All of his opinions were part of his testimony when he was deposed. It is vital for an expert to analyze the deposition of the opposing expert to determine his opponent's scope of work, his conclusions and how to prepare his own report.

Attorneys often provide their summaries of depositions to the expert. These summaries are the attorney's concepts of what is informative in a deposition. Insist on an original deposition. An accounting expert witness's understanding of the accounting issues may be different from the attorney's.

5.2 Deposition of the Expert Witness for the City of Racine

In the following deposition, William Rayney, attorney-at-law, represents the plaintiff and Robert I. Max, attorney-at-law, represents the defendant. Also present was Zeph Telpner, CPA. Deposition was taken of James L. Wren. Each deposition begins with establishing the deponent's name, address, business, education, and other qualifying credentials. Except where designated otherwise, Q represents Max, and A represents Wren.

5.2.1 Direct Examination

Max: Before we begin, I guess we should stipulate, Bill, that any objections should be reserved. (*The deponent should stop speaking during objections or off-the-record requests during the deposition. Your engaging lawyer will inform you when to begin again. Also, for "yes or no" questions, give "yes or no" answers. One bad habit of many deponents is to answer such questions with "yes it is" or "no it isn't" instead of "yes or no." This lengthens the court record and can annoy judges and practicing attorneys.*)
Rayney: Right.
Max: Except as to form of the question.
Rayney: Okay.

Q. Could you give me a brief description of your education background?

A. I graduated in 1969 from the University of Iowa with a bachelor of science degree.

Q. And was that in accounting?

A. Yes.

Q. Any further degrees after that?

A. No.

Q. What has your employment history been?

A. I worked for Chester and Chester Company from 1969 to 1975 and with Slovax and Associates from 1975 to the present. (*Accounting firms have reputations as competent or not so competent. So have accountants. A successful expert will determine the skill and reputation of his opponent. This can provide a psychological edge in reviewing his depositions and reports. You will have read his* curriculum vitae *for advance preparation and will learn of the representative cases in which he has testified. An expert witness economist serving as an expert on over-the-road truck tractors claimed to be an expert because he had grown up in and worked in his father's International Harvester (now Navstar) dealership. Information obtained by his opposing expert determined that the dealership sold farm machinery and equipment and pickup trucks. He was not an expert on over-the-road trucks.*)

Q. Were you employed with any accounting firms during your college years?

A. No.

Q. And what's your specific job title now?

A. I'm an audit partner.

Q. What does that entail?

A. Planning and reviewing audits mostly.

Q. And have you had much experience with utility rate disputes?

A. Well, yes. The first one I worked on was way back in Dubuque when Iowa Power was — for the rate they ended up with, that was as a staff accountant. Most of my experience with utilities has been as an auditor since then. (*What does this mean? When we read our depositions, or the trial transcripts of our testimony, we often regret not thinking before we answer. Always listen carefully to the question and think about your answer before you give it.*)

Q. So you're referring to one possible dispute?

A. Right.

Q. When was that, if you recall?

A. Probably 1972 or '73.

Q. Okay. Did you have to testify in that dispute?

A. No.

Q. Have you ever testified in a rate dispute — utility rate dispute?

A. No, I don't think so.

Q. Have you ever participated in audits of municipal utility boards?

A. Yes.

Q. And if you can, which municipalities were involved?

A. Well, North Platte, Nebraska, Hastings, Nebraska. There's various small cities. I may not even be able to tell you the utilities anymore. And Missouri Valley Waterworks, Hancock Municipal Utilities. *From this testimony, we have learned that this expert witness has little or no water-ratemaking expert knowledge experience. His audit experience alone is not sufficient to make him a ratemaking expert. Unless he cites authoritative support for his opinions, his opinions probably will be easy to dispute.)*

Q. And how long have you been involved in this particular case with Racine?

A. A week and a half? *("A week and a half" could mean 60 hours of solid work hours, or sporadic hours during a week and a half of different days over more than several weeks. We must determine the number of hours he worked on this opinion. We can compare it with our estimate and discover that this job would entail between 150 and 200 hours for an opinion and testimony that will satisfy the client, the attorneys, the judge and the jury (if there is one). An expert witness has a responsibility to give an opinion based on substantive work and authoritative support. When an expert witness holds himself out to be an expert in a particular field, he owes the clients, attorneys, the courts and the jurors enough respect to provide them with honest and skillful representations.)*

Rayney: Or two.

A. Maybe two weeks.

Q. With whom have you consulted?

A. With Bill Rayney.

Q. Okay. And have you spoken with anyone from the Town of Racine?

A. No.

Q. Have you spoken with Rodney Dale?

A. No.

Q. Do you know what his involvement in the case was?

A. No.

Q. Is he an accountant for Racine, or do you know?

A. I don't know.

Q. And have you had an opportunity to prepare any memoranda regarding this dispute?

A. Yes, I have. (*This witness has spoken only with Racine's trial attorney. He has not spoken with employees or citizens of Racine, nor has he spoken with Racine's accountant. He did not visit the water plant or distribution facilities, nor did he consult any authoritative texts, laws, or persons. He did not examine any original accounting records of the parties. His answers show that he was not prepared, knew little of the topic, did little work for his fee and was not qualified to be the plaintiff's expert. He will be easy to rebut. The memoranda he prepared were minimal computations and he did not prepare an expert's report. If the opposing expert accounting witness is a knowledgeable and honest accountant and exercises what it takes professionally to give an expert witnessing opinion, he will easily rebut the plaintiff's expert.*)

Q. Okay. Have you brought those with you today?

A. Yes, I have.

Q. Would they be available to us?

Rayney: Those documents.

Q. Okay. And you're referring to what's lying on the desk in front of me, the three sheets labeled 3, 4 and 5?

A. (The witness nods head affirmatively).

Q. Is that right?

A. That's right.

Q. Okay. That's for the benefit of the court reporter.

A. I understand.

Q. Why don't you just take a minute and explain what these are, in any order you care to refer to them. Let's refer to them by number.

A. Okay. First of all, No. 5 is a computation of the percentage of rate increase from the '73 rates under the contract to the '78 rates to the 1990 rates. That's assuming a million and a half gallons, which is roughly what was being used. 4 is a summary of the operating expenses for 1973, 1978, 1979, 1984, 1986, 1989 and 1990 and the increases and decreases of that. And 3 is just a summary of the capital improvement fund.

Q. Referring to Sheet No. 4?

A. Yeah.

Q. You have many different columns. Where did you arrive at these figures?

A. These figures came from the audit reports and there is a reconciliation to the audit reports at the bottom.

Q. Okay. And you're referring to the audit reports, not to some financial statements?

A. (The witness nods head affirmatively).

Q. The actual audit reports?

A. The actual audit reports.

Q. Are you familiar with some figures that were provided by Shirley Krug of Gerard & Company?

A. Yes.

Q. Are these figures from those sheets?

A. The figures for 1979, '84, '86 and '89 are the same figures that she's got, yes, on her report. (*Accountants* — *let alone nonaccountants* — *without someone to explain them could not understand these schedules of computations.*)

Q. And what was your purpose in setting forth this Sheet No. 4? What was your ultimate goal?

A. My ultimate goal was to see what the operating cost increases were from the period of the contract to the rate — between the rate increases. I did include the years that she included just so that...

Q. And what was the percent of increase per year between 1972 and 1978, if you know, per year, not over the six years?

A. Per year?

Q. Yes.

A. I didn't divide it. It was 46.8% over that five-year period. (*Was the period five or six years? Was his opinion based on the correct period?*)

Q. And what you're referring to is what you've called the operating costs?

A. Yes, the net operating costs.

Q. And what was the percentage increase in revenues?

A. This doesn't have revenues on it.

Q. Okay. I see a penciled-in figure of 69 percent. What is that?

A. That's the rate charged to Racine. That was the rate increase charged to Racine.

Q. So would it be fair to say that each year the rate went up about 11 and a half percent between 1972 and 1978?

A. The rate charged Racine, yes.

Q. And what would the per year increase between '78 and '90 be?

A. '78 and '90 was — it's 45.7% on the rate increase?

Q. Rate increase.

A. It was — I can do that. 111.3.

Q. Is it fair to say about 9.2% or 9.3% per year?

A. Yes.

Q. I see you have some notes at the bottom of Sheet No. 4.

A. Yes.

Q. Could you explain No. 1 for me?

A. Note No. 1 is a quote from the contract. I removed the capital outlay, depreciation — which depending on the year was in here — and the interest costs because the contract said costs shall not include increased capitalization of the seller's system. Increased capitalization relates to either capital outlay or depreciation and related interest costs. There are several other problems with the interest costs too.

Q. So it's your understanding — First of all, let's understand what contract we're talking about. When you say contract, you're referring to the May 23, 1972 contract between Racine and Seneca Water Board?

A. Yes.

Q. And the specific language you've alluded to is found at Paragraph C-5, I believe. Is that correct?

A. Yes.

Q. So is it your contention that increased capitalization of the seller's system must mean any capital outlays?

A. Yes.

Q. In other words, if some of the capital outlays shown on Sheet No. 4 were for replacement of this current system of the seller, you maintain that those costs do not properly belong in a calculation of the cost of performance?

A. That was my interpretation, yes.

Q. And how did you arrive at that conclusion?

A. That's the only way — the only interpretation I could make of capitalization. I think that refers to the act of using the system. It's not a defined
term though. (*From the preceding testimony, can this conclusion be correct
or is it even comprehensible? What did this expert mean by this opinion.?*)

Q. Is cost of performance a term of art in the accounting world?

A. No.

Q. Does it have a particular meaning?

A. No. (*The deponent states that "cost of performance is not a term of art in
the accounting world. How does he know? What is his authority? If you sit
in on a deposition, advise your engaging attorney on accounting questions
to ask and on questionable answers. If you sit in on the trial, make notes
to advise your attorney on accounting aspects of the accounting testimony.*)

Q. And does increased capitalization have a particular meaning in the
accounting world, as far as you know?

A. No. It could either mean investment in production of assets or it can
mean — it could relate to the capitalization of the capital portions.

Q. So basically do you have some accounting authority for removing certain
items from the calculation of operating expenses? I see on Sheet 4 that
you've taken out capital outlay and you've taken out interest. Is that
correct?

A. Yes.

Q. Is there some accounting principle or accounting authority that causes
you to do that?

A. Well, neither buying equipment or paying interest is an operating
expense.

Q. According to your own theory, or ...

A. Well, accounting theory, the act of buying equipment is not an expense.
Understand that they are cash basis financial statements up through
1987, I think, Gerard's audit. (*Has he cited his accounting authority? Has
he even testified that there is any? Should you notify Robert Max so that*

he can probe deeper? If you do not notify him until later, Max and his
expert accounting witness will be able to rebut him easier in the report of
Max's expert and during testimony at trial.)

Q. And after that, what are they?

A. They are accrual basis.

Q. Can you explain the difference basically between the two types of accounting?

A. Cash basis is simply the cash receipts and cash disbursements that are either received or expended. An accrual basis takes into account the amounts people owe you and the amount you owe them.

Q. So have you — in comparing these two systems on Sheet No. 4, have you made any adjustments for the change in method?

A. No. I looked at the change in method. There was relatively insignificant differences, which are shown on that audit report in 1987. I think it was 1987, the year that it was switched to accrual. (*Is this answer true? Are the differences insignificant or are they material? The opposing expert must review every document used by his opponent and then some.*)

Q. What do you mean by insignificant differences? I'm not following you.

A. There wasn't much big difference between the amounts owed at the end of the year of transition and the amounts that were receivable from customers.

Q. Now what are you referring to?

A. I'm referring to the audit report of June 30, 1987, where we had 103,390 receivables at the beginning of the year, 25,091 inventory and 112,710 payables.

Q. Okay. You referred to no significant difference in the accounting principle?

A. Yes.

Q. And what does that tell you?

A. That the difference in the operating — operations here only came to 20-some thousand dollars, the difference between cash and accrual.

Q. In that year?

A. In that year. We don't know what they are every year. But assuming this is a fair representation of what the years looked like, what I'm saying is there's not a gigantic difference between the cash basis and accrual basis.

Q. In going back to the sheets you prepared, these are labeled Sheets 3, 4 and 5. What are Sheets 1 and 2?

A. Sheets 1 and 2 were a comparison of the four years that Gerard's people had prepared.

Q. And you just didn't happen to bring those with you today or what?

A. Well, I brought them.

Q. You didn't feel they were too useful?

A. They weren't — they showed a lot lower percentage of increase in costs, but I did these on the same years they did them. And so from '73 to '79, they showed 102% increase; however, that wasn't the year of the raises and that didn't make any sense to me. It also shows from '79 to '89 only 5.6% increase. I didn't think those were very apropos, however, because they're not covering the years between the years the raises took place.

Q. Here you're referring to calculations at the end of Sheet No. 1?

A. Right.

Q. What does Sheet No. 2 show?

A. Sheet No. 2 just shows the four years that Gerard's people showed. It shows that 5.6% increase.

Q. And that's after you've taken out the interest?

A. Yes. Their figures only show 11.8% increase.

Q. I see you've taken out sales tax. Why is that?

A. I didn't — She took that out too. Both of us have. Because they collect sales tax from the customer and remit it to the state, that's not an income or a cost to the system. These are exactly the figures that are shown on hers. Okay? And this is the reconciliation from the financial audit, financial statements, to her figures.

Q. What you're just referring to is Sheet No. 2?

A. Yes. In my opinion, it really didn't make sense though.

Q. Okay.

A. Because of the years involved. But if you want to go with 5.6 percent, it's okay with us. Those same years were carried over to here (Indicating).

Q. So basically you considered Nos. 1 and 2 to be worksheets that prepared you for No. 4?

A. Right.

Q. To get to No. 4?

A. Right — well, we thought we'd just look at the years that were used in this and see what the rate increase was. The problem is, it doesn't cover the years between the years the rate increases took place.

Q. What are the other problems with the interest costs that you alluded to?

A. Okay. First of all, I don't use them as operating expenses. Burns & Company paid part of those interest costs and so I don't think they should be included in the computation.

Q. Okay. Burns & Company paid interest costs on what basis? Through a contract?

A. Right. Burns & Company signed a contract to pay for $232,000 worth of capital improvements, plus interest on it. So the capital improvements and the interest are partially paid by the Burns contract. Part of the proceeds from the note or the bonds were never spent. They were just earning interest income, which if you use interest expenses, I think you've got to use that interest income too. As a matter of fact, the interest income becomes more than interest expense during this period.

Q. Which period are you talking about?

A. Between 1973 and 1989. I don't think they can take interest — It makes no sense to take interest expenses as expense, but we will leave it in if you want.

Q. How much of the interest expense is attributable to that contract in your estimation?

A. It's different in different years. There's not a set percentage, because of the difference in the length of the issues and the difference in the interest rates.

Q. So we could be talking 10% one year, 50% another year, or what?

A. In the audit report, there is a schedule that showed the amount of the interest from Burns ...

Q. That's all right, Jim. We'll go on. I'll just withdraw the question. I can see it would take a little research.

A. It's a schedule in the cash basis audit early on when the state auditor was doing it and you'll find it in there.

Q. What's your understanding of why you've been asked to participate in this lawsuit?

A. To determine the — help to determine what the increase in costs have been.

Q. So to look at the history of the costs?

A. Yes.

Q. Have you ever been hired by any municipality to help determine what its utility rate should be?

A. No, not specifically.

Q. Do you think it's valid to look only at historical costs in determining utility rate or water rate, based on your accounting experience?

A. Most of the time, it's based on the net income from utilities. In other words, the whole financial picture, not only cost. (*Is this true? Is rate-making based on the past transactions, or future needs?*)

Q. So looking at a projection of what revenues are desired is also a valid portion of the determination of a utility rate; correct?

A. Yes. (*It is doubtful that this expert would have supplied this information if the attorney hadn't thought to ask it.*)

Q. And have you done any of that in your work so far? Have you looked at any of the projections made by the Water Board?

A. No, I haven't, because I was asked to look at this in relation to the contract between the parties.

Q. Is there some reason in your mind that the cost of performance — which refers only to historical costs — cost of performance is a term used in the contract. What I'm asking you is whether you interpret that based on your accounting experience to mean only historical costs or whether we'd also include revenue projections in that definition.

A. Costs aren't revenues. I assume it doesn't have anything to do with revenue.

Q. Is there some authority for saying that? I mean, is there — Again, it's not a term of art, is it — or is it?

A. No. In accounting, costs are what it costs to do something. Revenue is a completely separate thing and that's the income you receive from the services you perform.

Q. Okay. Have you examined any of the water rate studies on file with the Seneca Water Board?

A. No.

Q. If you were to set out to set a new rate for the Water Board, would you set an audit study? Would you strictly look at the audits or the financial statements from prior years?

A. I'd start there.

Q. And then what else would you use?

A. Then I think you have to look at what your plans are, what you think is going to happen in the future.

Q. What it's going to cost to perform the contract, in other words, in the future?

A. Yes.

Q. Okay. And how would you as an accountant go about determining that?

A. Well, accountants can't always determine that. Other people usually do that.

Q. So is it your contention that capital recovery items don't belong in the charges to the City of Racine?

(*Max continued direct examination by rewording this question seven times. He received the same answer each time. The repetitions have be deleted here for brevity.*)

Q. If the parties intended otherwise, would that change your calculations of costs?

A. Sure.

Q. Of operating expenses?

A. Yes. However, it would never get me to this, because there are some things in there that aren't capital improvements even (Indicating).

Q. You're referring to ...

A. Gerard's ...

Q. Gerard & Company's memo?

A. Right.

Q. Do you know when that memo was first presented to the City of Racine?

A. No.

(*Whereupon an off-the-record discussion was held.*)
(*Whereupon, Deposition Exhibit No. 1 was marked for identification.*)
Max: Let the record show that we've asked that Sheets 3, 4 and 5 be introduced into the record as Exhibit 1.
Wren: Those are a whole bunch of different things I was just bringing back to Bill.
Rayney: Just copies of the contract.

Q. I'm showing you now an eight-page document. Have you seen that before?

A. Yes. This is the water rate by gallon that was prepared by Gerard.

Q. It states, Subject, Seneca Water Department Rate Increase …

A. Yes.

Q. And that's what's been given to you by Mr. Rayney for your review of what Gerard & Company prepared for the Water Board?

A. Yes, it is.

Q. Okay. Referring for a moment to the sheet entitled Schedule of Expenses Per 1,000 Gallons of Water Pumped for the Year Ending June 30, 1979, can you tell me what in there pertains to increased capitalization of the seller's system?

A. Yes. There's $56,037 that is listed in the capital outlay.

Q. What else is a capital outlay on that sheet other than that figure?

A. That's all.

Q. And do you know where that figure came from, 56,000?

A. It came from the capital outlay list on the audit report, plus the $43,134 in cash transfers capital outlay fund.

Q. Is there some other reason for your eliminating that, other than your belief that that isn't part of the definition under the contract?

A. $43,000 of it is a cash transfer.

Q. Okay. And in 1984's sheet, we have capital outlay of $77,434. Did you remove all that from your calculations of operating expenses?

A. I removed it, yes.

Q. What else was removed?

A. The interest expense.

Q. How much was that?

A. $32,350.

Q. And again, you don't know how much of that is allocable to the Burns plant …

A. No.

Q. ... without further research?

A. Yes. But we do know that out of the 77,000 capital outlay, 60,000 was simply a cash transfer to the capital outlay fund — capital improvement.

Q. And what is that capital improvement fund for? Do you know?

A. No. But it's simply cash transfers in and out of that fund and the cash — the vast majority of the cash.

Q. As an accountant, what would you think they were set aside for?

A. I would think the Board was setting it aside for future capital improvements.

Q. Or perhaps replacement of current plant equipment?

A. No. I wouldn't think that would be the case, because the bond reserve funds are for that.

Q. Okay. Going on to the Gerard sheet for the year ending June 30, 1989, what figures did you remove?

A. I removed the depreciation of $100,494 and the interest figure of $20,300.

Q. Anything else?

A. No.

Q. All right. Next is 1986. Could you tell me what you removed from those calculations?

A. The capital outlay figure of 105,497 — however, that's not on this sheet — and the interest of $29,188.

Q. Okay. In any of these calculations, did you include any depreciation?

A. I removed the depreciation. First of all, there is no depreciation until 1987. So if you're going to compare, you're going to find it very difficult, because there is no depreciation on the cash basis one. You're not going to get a comparison.

Q. All right. So then you removed it all after '87 also?

A. That's correct.

Q. And it's your feeling that that makes the comparison more valid somehow?

A. Yes.

Q. Isn't there anything else you should do to adjust between the two methods, other than removing depreciation, between the two accounting methods?

A. Cash and accrual?

Q. Yes.

A. Probably, but I obviously can't go back and recreate the accrual method.

Q. So what you've tried to do is change the accrual figures to cash figures?

A. No. I did not try to adjust. I did look at the restatement and it was a relatively minor restatement amount. So I assume each year, you know, is fairly consistent. But that is — there is no way to tell that.

Q. Okay. What other documents have you reviewed with Mr. Rayney other than those we've just been discussing?

A. The audit reports for those years.

Q. Okay. And has he shown you some calculations he's made on his computer?

A. I know he's made some calculations, but I haven't been over them, no.

Q. Okay. I want to get back to a more basic question though. What is a water rate? Is it a charge per gallon?

A. In some form.

Q. Or per thousand gallons?

A. Or per thousand.

Q. Cubic foot?

A. Whatever, yes.

Q. So when we speak of the cost under the contract, would that be normal for a water board to refer to a cost of producing each gallon of water in order to come up with the cost — or rather, the rate it's going to charge? Wouldn't it have to calculate the cost per gallon?

A. I've never seen anyone do it on a per gallon basis, but certainly a board can do anything they want.

Q. What I'm asking is, isn't it relevant how many gallons are being sold when you're figuring water rate?

A. I would think so, yes, especially if you're projecting.

Q. And it doesn't take an accountant to know that, surely?

A. No.

Q. You have to know how many gallons you have to sell in order to know what your cost per gallon is; correct?

A. Yes. We don't have those amounts going back because, again, Seneca Water Board did not keep track of the gallons they sold. So, obviously, they didn't have that in the early years when they signed the contract.

Q. Although there may have been some projections of usage in the rate studies, which you haven't seen?

A. Yes.

Q. Correct?

A. Yeah. But for the first five years or so of the contract, they didn't know how many gallons they were selling, so obviously they weren't computing something on a per gallon basis.

Q. What's your understanding of when they first were aware of how many gallons they were selling to Racine?

A. They know how many they were selling to Racine. They didn't know how many they were selling overall.

Q. Okay. What's your understanding of when they first became aware —
when the Water Board first became aware of that number of gallons?

A. 1979 — I have to see here. I think …

Max: While you're doing that, I'd like to have this document, the Gerard
memo, marked as Exhibit 2, with counsel's permission.
Rayney: That's okay. No objection.
(Whereupon, Deposition Exhibit No. 2 was marked for identification.)

Q. That's an eight-page document.

A. June 1978 is the first year they knew how many gallons of water they sold.

Q. How did you determine that?

A. Because that's what the state auditor's report said in the year before. It's
in the audit report.

Q. For which year?

A. For June 1978.

Q. Okay. What is it that you're referring to now?

A. I'd have to find it again. What the state auditor said is that they didn't
have a system in place to get the number of gallons sold.

Q. They surely had a way to bill though, didn't they?

A. They billed. They just didn't accumulate the gallons that were sold. And
they had — in some of those years, they had — yeah, they had the
gallons per customer, but they never had the total gallons sold.

Q. I see.

A. This is the state auditor's report here in — What year is this?

Q. Do you just want to read the line you're referring to?

A. 1975 audit report.

Q. '75?

A. The total number of gallons was not determined exactly because the present billing machine does not record the total gallons. So we obviously were not going to know the total gallons up until 1978, because that's the first one that shows gallons sold in the audit report.

Q. But you say they always knew how many gallons they were selling to Racine, right?

A. Right. And they would know how many they sold to specific customers. They just didn't know how many they sold to everybody.

Q. So it could be reconstructed through a lot of effort?

A. A lot of effort, yeah.

Q. Now, referring again to Exhibit 2 — what's been marked Exhibit 2, the Gerard memo, is it your understanding that the document was put forth as the Water Board's rate study or simply …

A. I don't know.

Q. Or was it possibly just a justification for the rates after the dispute arose?

A. I don't know.

Q. Do you have any dispute with the — strike that. Have you inquired what the gallons unaccounted for in that Gerard study refer to?

A. There's always gallons unaccounted for. There's leakage and there's — they use gallons to flush the system and evaporation and all kinds of things. For instance in 1979, 10.7% is pretty normal.

Q. Based on your experience looking at other audit reports?

A. Yeah. June of '84 gets very high, 17.1%.

Q. Okay. Do you know why it's high?

A. No. It appeared to be losing more as they went along for some reason.

Q. Do you know how water is supplied to the City of Seneca to the municipality itself?

A. No.

Q. So you have not reviewed that portion of this dispute with Counsel yet?

A. No.

Q. When you removed the depreciation, did you have some accounting principle that you came in with and said, these items are properly included in the operating expenses or the operating costs?

A. No. Except the biggest inconsistency between the cash basis and accrual basis of accounting is, of course, the capital outlay versus depreciation. We simply have no way of going back and reconstructing what depreciation would have been in 1972.

Q. Okay. What else have you prepared other than Exhibit 1?

A. That's it.

Q. No written memoranda?

A. No.

Q. Okay. Knowing what you know now, would you base a rate study on prior audits of a water board?

A. That's where you'd have to begin.

Q. What other financial documents would you use if you were doing — I realize you're not a ratemaker. That isn't your trade.

A. Well, some of the things that you would have to consider is whether your increase in capacity, interest rates, have an effect and so forth, if you were looking forward in the future.

Q. So you would want to know how many gallons were going to be pumped or sold?

A. That's one of the things that you would project if you were expanding a plant, certainly.

Q. Or if you were determining a rate for the sale of water, you would need to know how many gallons you were going to sell on the average in the next several years; correct?

A. To …

Q. To determine …

A. To one customer or all customers?

Q. To any customer.

A. Well, obviously you would look at your variable costs if you're looking at a specific customer. Fixed costs would not enter into it unless you were expanding your plant. In this case, there's very few variable costs.

Q. Based on your experience as an accountant and an auditor, is it valid for the Water Board to take into account the number of gallons it's going to sell overall when it determines the rate charged to Racine?

A. I … Yes, I think they … I would consider it if I were on the Board. If I were negotiating a contract with Racine, I would get completely different costs.

Q. Completely different from what?

A. I would look at only variable costs if I were negotiating with a large customer, as you see done all the time with companies, for instance.

Q. And can you expound on that a little bit?

A. Because it probably only costs us 25 cents a gallon, 20 cents a gallon something like that, to produce an additional gallon of water. So that's cost we would look at if we were negotiating. Anything we could get over that would reduce costs to the other customers or raise your net income.

Q. That cost per gallon would be affected by the total number of gallons sold, wouldn't it?

A. That's the additional cost of each gallon you pump would cost. In other words, completely variable cost is one that …

Q. Let's get back to the actual dispute here. Burns & Company went away. That's the point.

A. Right.

Q. There is a decreased demand for water overall from the Seneca system. Is it your contention that that should not affect the rate charged to Racine?

A. Well, I would think the increased costs would affect Racine on the contract …

Q. Just as it affects everyone else?

A. Right.

Q. Is there some … Have you formed an opinion yet as to whether the rate which was determined in 1990 by the Seneca Water Board to charge Racine is too large?

A. Yes. I think it should be the 45-point …

Q. Go ahead.

A. 45.7% on Exhibit 1. That's my opinion.

Q. And why do you think that?

A. Because that's the amount — the costs that went up.

Q. So you would link — that's your reading of the contract? Is that what you're saying? That's your interpretation of the contract?

A. That's my interpretation. That's all, yes. And that's what costs have gone up, you know, if you take the capital outlay and the interest out of there.

Q. And yet you can see that in 1978 the rate went up at a greater percentage than the costs, according to your calculations?

A. Yes, they did.

Q. So there wasn't a direct link between the two, the increase in costs and the increase in rate?

A. No, apparently not.

Q. Is there anything in the contract that says there must be a direct link?

A. Well, it … it says …

Q. Here is the contract.

A. The costs shall not — Well, yeah. It refers to the increase or decrease in the rates shall be based on a demonstrable increase or decrease in the costs of performance. And I think the costs of performance went up 45.7 percent. *Earlier in this deposition, he testified, in effect, that there is no "cost of performance in accounting."*

Q. So you're arguing that it should be exactly the same increase and percentage?

A. In theory, that makes perfect sense to me, yes.

Q. Have you gone back and calculated any of these figures for 1972 to see what the relationship between operating expenses and rate charged was?

A. Well, on Exhibit 1 there's 1973, which is the first year, I think, water was delivered under the contract. And from 1973 to 1978.

Q. But do you know what the relationship between the two was, between the actual operating expenses and the rate charged.

A. No.

Q. Okay.

A. Because we don't know the number of gallons, you're never going to be able to do that exactly. I'm sure somebody could estimate that.

Q. I thought we knew how many gallons were sold to Racine back then.

A. Well, we do to Racine, yes. We don't know — these are costs for everything, not just costs …

Rayney: Bob, if I might interrupt, Exhibit 1 on Page 4, what's marked Page 4, he has made a computation showing the increase in operating expenses of 76.4% and a net increase of 46.8% and that compares with what he's figured as a 69.1% increase in rate to Racine based on a million five a month.

Q. What do you mean by total and net?

A. Okay. I took the same method they used here and called that the total increase in cost.

Q. Okay. And then the net is your method?

A. Yes.

Max: I guess I'd just like to reserve the right to continue these depositions as we go on until the October 12th deadline.
Rayney: No objection.
Max: That will be it for today. Thank you very much.
(Whereupon, the deposition concluded at the hour of 10:30 a.m., September 8, 1992.)
(*This expert has given much testimony on what he didn't know or didn't do. Each answer he gave becomes a statement of fact and continues to be fact until it is rebutted. The defendant's expert must rebut almost every answer given by this witness and also address himself to questions not asked and answers not given.*)

5.3   The Issues

Issues are discussed briefly in Chapter 4. Illustrative cases are included in Chapter 6 that will show how to determine issues. The most important job in forensic accounting is to determine the issues from the facts. Of course, correct facts are needed to accomplish this

5.4   The Work Program

After an expert witness has reviewed the legal documents prepared and filed for the litigation, he may wish to prepare a work program so the expert and his staff will know what to do to arrive at a conclusion. A program depends on the complexity and needs of the case. Some experts use the petition, interrogatories, depositions and all related documents as the program. In the water board dispute, the petition, deposition and contract provide information on the work that lies ahead for the expert.

The deposition, for example, would provide us with the following representative sample of work to complete to arrive at a conclusion that will stand up at the trial and in our depositions:

1. Obtain and review Wren's *curriculum vitae* to determine his level of competence in expert witnessing.
2. Determine the actual number of hours that Wren has spent on his work on Seneca's behalf.
3. He has stated opposing opinions that cost of performance has no meaning in accounting and then he explains what cost of performance is in testimony on ratemaking. Determine by research whether cost of

performance has specific meaning in accounting. Obtain authoritative documentation.

4. Wren testified that he had not spoken with anyone from his client's administration. Determine from the evidence he provided during his deposition whether he needed to talk to the client to arrive at his conclusions. Also determine what personnel of both parties can provide information to prove or disprove Wren's calculations and testimony.

5. Wren testified about increases and decreases, accounting for income, expenses, from donated cash assistance from Burns & Company. Determine if his accounting explanations are correct and, if not, determine a correct explanation.

6. Wren testified that the change from cash to accrual accounting was insignificant. Review his calculations, if any, and recalculate based on facts from Seneca's accounting records.

7. Wren has testified about audit reports and engineers water rate study. Obtain the study and the audit reports. Do you reach conclusions different from Wren's? Explain.

8. Tour the physical plants of parties. Note your observations.

9. Cross reference the documents within themselves.

5.5 The Working Papers

Working papers to determine over- or understated accounts on a balance sheet, or income and expense misrepresentations, will require comprehensive trial balances of the general ledger and subsidiary ledgers.

In *Racine v. Seneca,* working papers would most likely consist of computations discussed by Wren for water, ratemaking, costs of providing water and essay explanations of facts. A report in Chapter 6 will demonstrate when detailed calculations are required for the judge and jury.

5.6 The Expert's Report

5.6.1 Coversheet to the Expert's Report

REPORT ON BEHALF OF DEFENDANT RE:

THE PROPRIETY OF WATER RATES AND WATER RATE INCREASES

PUT IN EFFECT ON MAY 9, 1990 FOR SALES OF WATER

TO THE PLAINTIFF

IN THE IOWA DISTRICT COURT FOR DOE COUNTY

CASE NO: 77915

CITY OF RACINE, IOWA, PLAINTIFF

VS.

SENECA SEWER & WATER DEPARTMENT

5.6.2   Report Issued by the Expert

I. Reason for Report:
   A. The Board of Waterworks Trustees of the City of Seneca, Iowa ("Board" or "Water Board" or "Defendant" and also known as "Seneca Sewer & Water Department") had asked me to investigate the water rates and water rate increases to the City of Racine ("Racine" or "Plaintiff") to be put into effect on May 9, 1990.

II. Scope of Work:
   A. The Board has engaged me for expert accounting assistance in the above-mentioned litigation (Litigation).
   B. I have performed such analyses, observations, physical inspections, interviews, research and professional judgments as I considered necessary in the circumstances. The Board had requested that I direct my investigation toward the following paragraphs (within my scope of expert knowledge) of Racine's Litigation Petition For Declaratory Judgment And Permanent Injunction (Petition) that was filed on April 11, 1992.
   C. My work is not designed to constitute an audit prepared in accordance with generally accepted accounting principles and auditing standards. It is designed to comply with certain requirements of the Iowa District Court for OTOE County and for related appellate courts as interpreted by the Board's legal counsel for the sole purpose of resolving equitably the allegations of the plaintiff and the rate accounting disagreements between the parties.
   D. The Board asked me to design my work to help sustain, if possible, the following positions of the Board toward these specified Paragraphs of the Petition:
   1. Paragraph 9. That the rate increase of May 9, 1990 does not constitute an effective rate increase to plaintiff of over one hundred percent.
   2. Paragraph 10. That the rate schedule of May 9, 1990 does not materially alter the terms of the contract; and does not alter the rate formulas of May 10, 1972 and February 15, 1978.

3. Paragraph 11. That the rate increase of May 9, 1990 based on the terms and conditions of paragraph C (5) of the May 10, 1972 agreement is based upon a demonstrable commensurate increase during the period 1978 through 1990 in the cost of performance under the agreement; that the rate increase does not include and reflect increased capitalization costs and is not an attempt to recover increased capitalization costs.

4. Paragraph 12. That plaintiff has not continued to pay the Board under the rate schedule of February 15, 1978.

E. The additional purpose of my work was to allow me to testify and issue a written report as an expert on the above-specified contended matters if approved by the attorney for the Board.

III. Conclusion:

A. In my opinion:

1. The rate increase of May 9, 1990 does not constitute an effective rate increase to Plaintiff of over one hundred percent. The effective rate increase is 30.75 percent. Accordingly, the allegations contained in Paragraph 9 of the Petition are not correct.

2. The rate schedule of May 9, 1990 does not materially alter the terms of the contract; and does not alter the rate formulas of May 10, 1972 and February 15, 1978. Accordingly, the allegations contained in Paragraph 10 of the Petition are not correct.

3. The rate increase of May 9, 1990 based on the terms and conditions of paragraph C (5) of the May 10, 1972 agreement is based upon a demonstrable increase during the period 1978 through 1990 in the cost of performance under the agreement; that the contract does not require the increase to be commensurate; that the rate increase does not include and reflect increased capitalization costs and is not an attempt to recover increased capitalization costs. Accordingly, the allegations contained in Paragraph 11 of the Petition are not correct.

4. Plaintiff had continued to pay the Board under the rate schedule of February 15, 1978 in all material respects, except for initial delays in some payments. Accordingly, the allegations contained in Paragraph 12 of the Petition are mostly correct.

IV. **General Comments:**
   A. To reach my conclusions, I studied and made analyses from the Board's financial statements, accounting records, audit reports, minutes, resolutions and correspondence; certain reports and studies of Racine; certain tax and accounting publications, and physically inspected the offices, plant, pools, equipment, machinery, buildings and land of the Seneca Water Department; and obtained, studied and analyzed, as I considered necessary, various other items.
   B. I also interviewed or was involved in office or phone conferences with the following persons:
      1. Water Board Trustees: Daniel Jerome, Peter Leo and Barry Randall
      2. Water Board management employees: Betty Marvins, City Clerk; and Dennis Hall, Water Department Superintendent
      3. Gerard & Company, P.C., auditors: Shirley Krug, CPA; and Sarah Plautz, CPA
      4. Legal Counsel: Robert Max, Esq. (Max) for the Board; William Rayney, Esq. (Rayney) for Racine; Richard Gellan, Esq., Chicago, IL and Millard Cook, Esq., Cleveland OH for certain research information.
      5. Farmers Home Administration (FmHA) officials: Trevor Previt, Appeals Officer; Rebecca McEldowney, loan specialist; Lynn Noel (Noel), District Loan Specialist
      6. Independent Water Departments:
         a. Gene Rollo (Rollo), Metropolitan Utilities District, Manager of Rates and Regulatory Affairs
         b. Lawrence Trask (Trask), Superintendent of the Council Bluffs Water Department
         c. Also, I was present for the deposition of James I. Wren, CPA (Wren) who serves Plaintiff as an expert witness.

V. **General Approach to this Report:**
   A. I have been asked to express my expert opinion on certain issues that revolve mainly around the contract of May 10, 1972. This contract is identified in the Petition as a contract of May 10,1972 between the Seneca Sewer & Water Department and the City of Racine, Iowa. The defendant's Answer, Counterclaim and Application for Temporary Hearing identifies the defendant as the Board of Waterworks Trustees of the City of Seneca, Iowa. The contract of May 10, 1972 identifies the seller as the City of Seneca by the

Board of Trustees of the municipal Waterworks Plant and System of Seneca, Iowa. It identifies the buyer as the Town of Racine.

B. This report will identify the defendant-seller and the plaintiff-buyer as explained in paragraph I.A, "Reason for Report." The contract of May 10, 1972 will be indentified as the Contract.

C. The issues in the Contract that I have been asked to resolve might appear to be mainly accounting issues to be resolved under generally accepted accounting principles. These issues frequently have been explained by Plaintiff (and by Wren in his depositon) as either acceptable or not acceptable accounting.

D. This report will look at accounting interpretations of the Contract with the practical approach of the laity to technical terms and jargon. The issues identified as those to be resolved in paragraph II.D "Scope of Work" require interpretation of the accounting language of the Contract.

VI. Is the Rate Increase of May 9, 1990 an Increase of More than 100% over the Rates in Plaintiff's Resolution of February 15, 1978?

A. The Petition at paragraph 9 identifies the increase as over 100%. In Answers To Interogatories Propounded By Defendant (Answers) at No. 5, the rate increase is specificially calculated as an increase of 111.8 percent. Plaintiff's expert Wren calculates an increase of 111.3 percent.

These calculations are made on incomparable bases. Growing inflation was rampant between 1978 and 1980 with interest rates of up to 20 percent. A new presidential administration on January 20, 1981 took steps to slow and reduce inflation significantly. A meaningful computation of the percent of rate increases must be calculated on Consumer Price Index (CPI)-adjusted bases. The U.S. Bureau of Labor Statistics CPI for the years 1961 through 1990 designate 1982–1984 with the index of 100. By applying the CPI to the rates in Answer No. 5 of $1,303.80 and $2,761.31, the CPI adjusted rates are $1,597.50 for 1979 and $2,088.74 for 1990. This is an increase of 30.75% when the years are compared on the same bases.

VII. Is the Rate Schedule of May 9, 1990 an Attempt to Materially Alter the Terms of the Contract by Altering the Rate Formula as Set Forth in the Agreement of May 10, 1972 and the Resolution of February 15, 1978?

A. This allegation in the Petition at paragraph 10 distorts the facts of the rate schedules. The method of calculating charges to Racine is

identical for 1972, 1978 and 1990. Each rate schedule merely mul-
tiplies the gallons purchased by a rate per gallon to arrive at a total
charge. The imagined differences among the rates are clerical differences of form only and not of substance.

B. This allegation makes no objection to the amount of the rate —
only to the arithmetic of the method of computation or the rate
formula. The 1990 rate formula can be stated in identical form to
the 1972 and 1978 forms by simple multiplication and addition.
Thus the reformatted 1990 rates become:

0–300,000	$498.12
300,000–3,000,000	$1.64/1000 gal.
3,000,000 and up	$1.64/1000 gal.

No price break is granted on over 3,000,000 gallons because this
price is part of the rate increase. The CPI would increase the 1979
rates for the first 300,000 gallons to $312 and the 1990 rate to $377.

VIII. **Is the Rate Increase of May 9, 1990 a Material Breach by Defendant
of the Terms and Conditions of Paragraph C(5) of the Contract?**

A. Is the increase based upon a demonstrable commensurate increase
during the period 1978 through 1990 in the cost of defendant's
performance under the terms of the agreement?

1. The Petition has added the word "commensurate" to the
language of Contract Paragraph C. (5). That word does
not exist in the Contract. Contract Paragraph. (5) states
that "any increase or decrease in rates shall be based on a
demonstrable increase or decrease in the costs of performance hereunder." The Petition uses commensurate to
mean rate increases or decreases in proportion to cost
increases and decreases. Because water utility ratemaking
is based significantly upon future projected costs to provide water, historical costs serve as a tool to project future
revenue needs. If rates were commensurate with historical
costs, it would be possible for water utility boards to un-
dercharge for water.

2. The Board's attorney has identified statuory authority
(Code of Iowa, 384.84) that the governing body of a city
utility may charge rates at least sufficient to pay the expenses
of operation and maintenance, principal and interest of
outstanding bonds and to maintain a reasonable reserve for
future bond payments.

Confiscatory rates of a utility are rates that do not provide a reasonable return on value of property used in public service. Confiscatory rates do not provide a net return that is sufficient to preserve the utility's property, nor do they provide a sufficient security to attract financing to allow the utility to discharge its public duties. (See *Black's Law Dictionary*).

Commensurate rates, then, appear to be in violation of rational municipal utility policy.

3. Petition paragraph 11 alleges that the increase is not based upon a demonstrable cost increase during the period 1978 to 1990. This is not a valid allegation. Wren's deposition exhibit 1 calculated an increase in costs for the period 1973 to 1978 of 46.8% and from 1978 to 1990 of 45.7 percent. Although I do not agree with his calculations of increase, I agree that costs increased. Such increases comply with the Contract term "demonstrable."

4. Petition paragraph 11 alleges that the disputed rate increase "includes and reflects increased capitalization costs of defendant and is an attempt by Defendant to recover these increased capitalization costs, all in violation of their agreement with Plaintiff."

   a. This allegation contains issues that according to plaintiff seemingly have either no meaning within the scope of generally accepted accounting principles, or are in violation of the Contract.

   b. Petition paragraph 11 creates difficulties because I have reached conclusions on the issues it raises that differ from Racine's expert, Wren. Wren has testified that the Contract does not allow Defendant to include capital outlay, depreciation or interest costs in its cost of performance.

   c. Wren has identified certain items that appear to be deficiencies in the contract as he interprets it. He defines increased capitalization as any capital increases that occur after the date of the contract. He also calls our attention to the fact that the phrase, "increased capitalization" does not have a particular meaning in the accounting world.

   d. Wren has testified that "cost of performance" is not a term of art nor does it have a prticular meaning in the accounting profession.

   e. Deposition Exhibit 1 of Wren's testimony compares accrual basis financial statements with cash basis financial

statements. Defendant reported its financial statements
on the cash basis until June 30, 1987 when it converted
to the accrual basis of accounting. Additionally, Defendant reported on a calendar year until June 30, 1976,
when it converted to a fiscal year. Wren testified that the
conversion from cash to accrual resulted only in "insignificant differences" although he had made no analyses.
He concluded that the conversion difference amounted
to only about $20,000. He admits that he did not know
what the annual differences are, but, based on 1967, he
assumed that there was not a "gigantic" difference between cash and accrual.

f.   Wren testified he also eliminated interest from cost of
performance because Burns & Company paid part of
the interest costs. He also pointed out that Burns &
Company paid for $232,000 of capital improvements
and that part of the proceeds from the bonds were never
spent. Because the proceeds earned interest, he thought
that interest income should offset interest expense.

g.   Wren eliminated depreciation from costs because the
statements showed no depreciation before 1987. He said
that, with current depreciation, the costs would not
have been comparable to past years and that "we simply
have no way of going back and reconstructing what
depreciation would have been in 1972."

h.   Wren testified that the contract means that rates should
have increased in the same amount that historical costs
increased after eliminating capital outlay and interest.

5.   Generally accepted accounting principles often do not apply
to certain industries. I had been a member of the American
Institute of Certified Public Accountants (AICPA) Interstate
Commerce Commission (ICC) Regulated Carrier Sub-com-
mittee. This committee was charged with preparing a trucking industry auditing manual for its more than 200,000 CPA
members. Two of the Big Six accounting firms did not agree
with the industry and the rest of the profession about certain
accounting policies of the trucking industry. Although the
accounting was generally accepted by the trucking industry,
the ICC and most of the accounting profession for the
trucking industry, these two firms would not accept it.
Therefore, an audit guide was not issued because it would
be required to endorse the industry practice as generally

acceptable. Additionally, accounting principles for similar issues may differ because the Security and Exchange Commission has rules that differ from other agencies who make rules such as the ICC, the Department of Defense and Federal and State Regulatory Commissions.

6. Frequently, accounting must be interpreted on the basis of general language usage and common sense. Over and over, the courts have held that words do not have exceptional meanings. Mr. Justice Holmes delivered the court's opionion that "we see nothing to be gained by the discussion of judicial definitions. The Defendant in error has realized within the year an accession to income, if we take words in their plain popular meaning. As they should be taken. (*Burnet v. Sanford & Brooks Co.*, 282 U.S. 359, 364.)

7. The U. S. Supreme Court explained how it resolved a difficult depreciation accounting issue. In *Welch v. Helvering,* 290 U.S. 111, 54 S. Ct. 8, Mr. Justice Cardozo delivered the opinion that, "Here, indeed, as so often in other branches of the law, the decisive distinctions are those of degree and not of kind. One struggles in vain for any verbal formula that will supply a ready touchstone. The standard set up by the statute is not a rule of law; it is rather a way of life. Life in all its fullness must supply the answer to the riddle."

8. All of Defendant's rate increases are based on demonstrable increases in costs. A review of Wren's deposition exhibits and the financial statements show a cost increase each year. The contract provides that the rates be based on demonstrable increases or decreases. The ordinary meaning of demonstrable is that it is capable of being demonstrated or proved. Does "demonstrable" also mean commensurate even though the contract does not state this?

   a. The American Water Works Association Water (AWWA) Rates Manual (AWWA Manual M1 4th ed) states that since 1972, inflation and resulting cost impacts, together with the need for conservation, have put pressure on water rates. The AWWA Manual provides that the development of water rates begins with revenue requirements. To set rates, the water utility must determine its total annual revenue requirements for the period for which the rates are to be effective.

      i. Accordingly, water rates are based upon future needs and not historical costs. Next, the utility should allocate these annual revenue requirements to the basic functional cost components and design rates to recover these projected costs from customers.

ii. Costs to be recovered through revenue include in addition to operating and maintenance expenses, debt service, debt service reserve, capital improvements, city support facilities, cash for future plant improvements, depreciation and interest.

iii. These generally accepted water utility ratemaking principles preclude the term commensurate from the contract.

9. Does Defendant attempt to recover increased capitalization costs and does this violate the Contract?

a. History of Seneca Water Rates to Racine: In June, 1967, Johnson, Jones & Associates Architects & Engineers (JJ) issued its Preliminary Engineering Report on the Proposed Municipal Water System (Report) to the mayor and Town Council of Racine. The Report was a "comprehensive engineering study of a new municipal water system for the Town of Racine to obtain a safe, reliable and efficient supply of water to satisfy fire, commercial and domestic requirements."

This JJ Report included historical information on Racine and its water needs with the technical issues of treated and raw water sources, production, distribution and cost and financing matters. The Report considered four alternatives to provide Racine with a complete water system. Three required extensive expenditures by Racine. One required modest expenditures and the purchase of treated water from Seneca. According to the Report, annual costs that must be met from the water revenues include debt service on loans. Because of lower costs, the Report recommended that Racine buy treated water from Seneca.

In June, 1971, JJ issued a Water Rate Study and Report (1971 Study) to Defendant. This study "recommended improvements to the municipal water system ..." that "represent major capital improvements which require detailed financial planning." The 1971 Study reported that its primary purpose was to develop a schedule of water rates that "will provide sufficient revenue to meet the operating expenses for the utility as well as amortize bonds needed to finance the recommended improvements."

The cost estimates in the 1971 Study included water procurement and supply construction at the Racine plant, as well as other feeder and pumping improvements. The calculations of estimated revenue needs include revenues to retire bonds and provide debt service and capital improvements. The 1971 Study recommended an immediate rate increase for adequate income to pay interest on Revenue Bonds and other construction period costs.

This 1971 Study concludes that, in 1970, Seneca City customers paid about $0.49 per 1000 gallons of water. To continue to provide treated water, a 35% rate increase is needed immediately to pay for water production in 1972. This translates to about $151 for the first 300,000 gallons and about $0.45 a gallon over that gallonage.

The JJ 1978 Water Rate Study for Defendant (1978 Study) disclosed that its purpose was to reach a water rate schedule to provide sufficient revenue for operation of the system and retire the related bonds. This Study recommended rates to Racine of $150 for the first 300,000 gallons and rates in Seneca of $168.15 for the first 300,000 gallons. It also disclosed that rates were raised in 1972 to offset the 1971 deficit.

After considering the contribution of Burns & Company to the water costs, the study recommends that Racine's rates be increased from $150 for the first 300,000 gallons to $255. For the next 2,700,000, the rate would increase from $0.45 a thousand gallons to $0.76. Over 3,000,000 gallons would increase to $0.83 a gallon from $0.50.

Revenue projection requirements included debt service, capital outlay, reserve fund transfers and reserve funds.

The 1971 Study treated gallons information for 1966, 1968, 1969 and 1970. The 1978 Study contains total gallons pumped for 1974, 1975 and 1976.

b.   The fact that Defendant's rates to Racine would include capital improvements have been a part of the public records of Racine since 1967, of Seneca at least since 1971 and probably much earlier.

10. If capital improvements in the rate basis have been a public record of both Racine and Seneca, then the signers of the contract may have considered a definition of increased capitalization of the seller's system. To define increased capitalization, we must first define the term "costs of performance."

   a. Cost of performance logically means the cost of service specified in paragraph A of the Contract. Seller agreed to furnish potable treated water to buyer. Therefore, cost of performance means the cost of furnishing potable treated water to the buyer in accordance with revenue requirements to recapture these costs and make a profit.

   The phrase "cost of performance" is not unique to this particular contract. The Treasury Department issued Treasury Decision (T.D.) in June, 1940 to regulate defense contracts between the U.S. Government and defense contractors. Section 26.9 of T.D. 5000 entitled "Cost of performing a contract or subcontract" specifies what can be charged against a U.S. Government defense contract and regulates cost-plus accounting.

   In 1972, JJ released specifications for bidders on construction of a Racine water distribution system. The specifications included many FHA forms and the terms: "faithful performance of the contract" and "performance of said contract."

11. The foregoing facts lead to the conclusion that the parties to the Contract realized that capital costs are recoverable in setting rates. What then does "increased capitalization" mean?

   a. Lawrence Trask, Superintendent of Council Bluffs Water Department, believes that it means plant and equipment acquired to increase a water department's capability to add other communities to the lines. For example, if Seneca contracted to supply Avoca, the additional costs to supply Avoca should not be charged to Racine. However, rates to Racine should recover increased costs that are necessary to continue to serve Racine. If the plant should blow up, then the increased replacement cost should be included in rates, whether to Racine or to others.

   b. Lynn Noel of FmHA and believed the same as Lawrence Trask of MUD. Additionally, Daniel Jerome, who signed the Contract as Chairman, is still Chairman and believes that was the intent of the provision.

   c.   If Defendant does not recover increased related costs of capitalization they would appear to be violating generally accepted water utility accounting and ratemaking principles.

12. Plaintiff has compared accrual basis financial statements with cash basis financial statements. (Wren deposition). Wren testified that he did nothing more than look at the June 30, 1987 and 1988 certified financial statements when the records were converted from the cash to accrual basis. He said that the difference was immaterial. Several years are involved. As a minimum, the audit working papers and the Defendant's records should be reviewed to determine whether the difference was material for each year.

Note J to the June 30, 1988 financial statements states that retroactive adjustments resulting from the change to the accounting method amounted to $828,690.

13. Wren eliminated interest from cost of performance because Burns & Company paid for part of the interest and capital improvements.

   a.   It is generally accepted utility accounting, especially for regulated utilities, to charge fixed asset accounts with interest costs incurred during the construction. This applies whether the utility performs its own construction or a contractor does it. Capitalization of interest is permitted because income is not earned during construction to offset the interest. Interest cannot be recovered before operations begin, so the utility is permitted to recover it by including it in the ratemaking base. (W. Meigs, et al, *Intermediate Accounting*, 3rd ed 412-13, 1974; H. Finney & H. Miller, *Principles of Accounting Intermediate*, 425-26, 1954).

   b.   Even if Burns & Company paid for capital improvements, the value of the Burns & Company contribution becomes part of the asset base. (W. Meigs, supra at 418-19; H. Finney, supra at 426-27; and C. Niswonger & P. Fess, *Accounting Principles*, 420-21, 1969).

14. Wren disallowed depreciation because the statements showed no depreciaton before 1987. He said that, without

it, the costs would not have been comparable and there is no way of going back to reconstruct it.

    a.   The Board accounted for assets and recorded them at the date of conversion to the acrual basis. It went through old records to determine acquisition dates. We calculated depreciation for the years ended December 31, 1973, June 30,1978, 1979, 1984, 1986, 1989 and 1990.

15. Wren testified that, under the Contract, rates should have increased proprotionately to the increase of historical costs. This is rebutted by the AWWA Accounting and Rate Manuals and in *Village of Niles v. City of Chicago*, 558 N.E. 2d 1324 (Ill. App. 1 Dist. 1990).

16. Dennis Hall, Water Superintendent, prepared the 1990 water rate study. The Board believed that he was capable of presenting the information to them for their use because of his water utility experience.

17. Had Racine been paying rates on the 1978 schedule as it maintained? I reviewed the schedules supplied to me by Betty Marvins. I also discussed it with Max. Apparently, they have paid on the 1978 schedule but had been delinquent with some earlier payments.

18. Overall Conclusion:

    Defendant has complied in substance with the Contract and generally accepted water utility accounting practices.

Substance versus Form
and the Nonfactual Fact

6

6.1 The Most Important Concepts of Forensic Accounting and Expert Witnessing

Neither expert reports nor expert testimony have substance within themselves. No matter how carefully we prepare our reports and testimony, no matter how knowledgeable and experienced we are in a subject, we cannot give substance to our work. Substance can be conferred upon our testimony only by our engaging attorneys, the trier of fact, juries, administrative law judges, IRS appeals officers and the opposing attorneys, clients and experts or anyone with the authority to make the decision. If, for example, the judge or jury believes that our expert report and testimony is substance, then that's what it is. If they believe it to be form, then that is what it is.

Until an expert masters the ability to make all readers who are able to reason accept that what he has given as opinion or testimony is substance and the only correct solution, that expert witness can never be truly great. An expert without this ability will not recognize the correct and relevant issues, will not understand when a fact is not a fact, will not be superior at cutting through extraneous facts and evidence to arrive at the one superior conclusion.

The lessons in this chapter will include more examples of right reason in these matters than any of the other chapters. Examples and commentary will come from actual litigation and from non-litigated matters.

Some of the best examples in my mind of substance versus form arose while I was teaching my CPE seminars to CPAs. In Oregon, I gathered the evaluations after I had taught a 2-day seminar, on Creative Tax Research. I was elated with the first evaluation. It read, "This is the best CPE course I have attended and without a doubt the best presentation. Mr. Telpner is a genius. (Years later, this same CPA sent me a letter to say, "Not only do I still believe that this is the best course, but four years later, I use it daily.")

I was elated with that first evaluation when I read it. The next evaluation deflated me. It read, "This was the worst CPE course I've ever taken. The discussion was an entirely self-serving lecture. If it were my money that I paid for this course, I would be demanding a refund."

This was an opportunity for me to learn. Was this the best CPE course, or the worst CPE course? Was this "without a doubt the best presentation," or was it a "self-serving lecture?"

It was both. It was the best to the CPA who liked my materials and my lecture and it was the worst to the CPA who apparently hated them. This is what happens to our expert reports and testimony in trials, in the IRS appeals office and when we give consulting advice to someone. What was it about my presentation and the materials that caused this participant to experience such adverse passion? I reread his sentence that said, "If it were my money that I paid for this course, I would be demanding a refund." I realized at that moment that it wasn't the materials or my skills that offended. If his opinion had been objective, he would have demanded a refund on behalf of his employer, who had paid his tuition and travel expenses.

I did wonder if my lectures were self-serving. In those early years, I wasn't aware of what a self-serving lecture was. Did the student believe that I had illustrated the topic with tax disputes and protests that I had personally resolved in order to bring acclaim for myself? I had told them that, in tax disputes that involved a protest, I would have none other but my own as a teaching example. Protests are not published and other CPAs would not give theirs to me. My lectures were not meant to be self-serving. They were meant to teach my students. I cared about them and wanted them to be winners. The first evaluation stated, in effect, that my materials and lectures were all valuable substance. The second evaluation indicated that my materials and lectures had no substance — they had only form. Later in this chapter, we will discuss what innocent causes create resistance to reports and testimony.

To determine the correct issues and ensure that we have actual facts instead of nonfactual facts, we must be able to recognize what is substance and what is form. These principles will be repeated over and over again by example in this chapter. Whether you believe them or not, the repetition is designed to embed them into your mind by osmosis. When you master this chapter, your expert report will always be the winning one and your testimony will always convince a judge, a jury, or an appeals officer, so long as they are rational people.

6.2   What Causes Testimony or Reports to Be Rejected?

- The expert has reached conclusions that have no basis in fact or in law.
- The expert has misinterpreted the facts.
- The expert has misinterpreted the law he is allowed to interpret such as the Internal Revenue Code (IRC).
- The expert has misinterpreted the accounting.
- The expert has chosen the wrong issues.
- The expert's investigation and research skills are weak and he did not find the correct answers.
- The expert's communication skills are weak and his report and his testimony did not convince the adjudicator.

The goal of this book is to discover how to overcome these common deficiencies in the work of a forensic accountant expert witness. Each expert witness engagement, each protest excerpted in it are from actual cases that were resolved before appropriate regulatory authorities when necessary. Each one used in this book was selected for theory and reasoning. They were not chosen to provide updates in the IRC or other statutes. Chapters that contain legal requirements for an expert witness, such as *Daubert*, are approved and annotated when necessary by my co-author, attorney Michael S. Mostek.

6.3   What Are Issues?

Issues are questions asked about facts to determine if they are real and actually exist and to determine if the facts and answers to the issues have substance or form. The correct issues provide the bases for the expert's scope of work, his conclusions, his report and his testimony.

Most accountants and attorneys are familiar with the IRC. When we read a Code section (sec.), we can formulate several questions (issues) to determine whether a transaction complies with the sec. Then we can advise a client whether to recast a planned transaction, or we can convince an appeals officer that his examining agent has erred with his adjustments. Sec. 162(a) provides a good example of law alone that provides many issues.

6.3.1   Section 162: Trade or Business Expenses

[Sec. 162(a)] In General — There shall be allowed as a deduction all the ordinary and necessary expenses paid or incurred during the taxable year in carrying on any trade or business, including:

1. A reasonable allowance for salaries or other compensation for personal services actually rendered
2. Traveling expenses (including amounts expended for meals and lodging other than amounts which are lavish or extravagant under the circumstances) while away from home in the pursuit of a trade or business
3. Rentals or other payments required to be made as a condition to the continued use or possession, for purposes of the trade or business, of property to which the taxpayer has not taken or is not taking title or in which he has no equity

For purposes of the preceding statement, the place of residence of a Member of Congress (including any Delegate and Resident Commissioner) within the state, congressional district, or possession that he represents in Congress shall be considered his home, but amounts expended by such members within each taxable year for living expenses shall not be deductible for income tax purposes in excess of $3,000. For purposes of paragraph (2), the taxpayer shall not be treated as being temporarily away from home during any period of employment if such period exceeds 1 year. The preceding sentence shall not apply to any Federal employee during any period for which such employee is certified by the Attorney General (or the designee thereof) as traveling on behalf of the United States in temporary duty status to investigate or prosecute, or provide support services for the investigation or prosecution of, a federal crime.

6.3.2 [Sec. 162(c)] Illegal Bribes, Kickbacks and Other Payments

1. Illegal Payments to Government Officials or Employees — No deduction shall be allowed under subsection (a) for any payment made, directly or indirectly, to an official or employee of any government, or of any agency or instrumentality of any government, if the payment constitutes an illegal bribe or kickback or, if the payment is to an official or employee of a foreign government, the payment is unlawful under the Foreign Corrupt Practices Act of 1977. The burden of proof in respect of the issue, for the purposes of this paragraph, as to whether a payment constitutes an illegal bribe or kickback (or is unlawful under the Foreign Corrupt Practices Act of 1977) shall be upon the Secretary to the same extent as he bears the burden of proof under sec. 7454 (concerning the burden of proof when the issue relates to fraud).

If an Internal Revenue Agent has disallowed an expenditure as a deduction from your client's income tax return because it does not qualify as a deduction under IRC sec. 162, what issues are involved?

To determine the issues, we must understand the language of 162.

The expenditure must be ordinary and necessary. It might be ordinary for a lawyer or CPA to drive a Rolls Royce, but is it necessary? At times it may be necessary, if, for example, he is a lawyer or CPA to movie stars who earn $20 million for each movie and drive expensive cars. It could also be necessary for a businessman to bribe a government official to stay in business, but is this ordinary?

The deduction must be paid or incurred during the taxable year. This provision is distinguished from "ordinary and necessary," by the use of the word "or" instead of "and." The "ordinary and necessary" test requires that both ordinary and necessary be complied with. However, "paid or incurred" means that it can be one or the other, but doesn't have to be both. "During the taxable year" specifies that, for the expense to be deductible, it must have been paid for the year if the taxpayer is on the cash basis. Why then, does it specify "incurred" instead of accrued for an accrual basis taxpayer? This limits an accrued Sec. 162 deduction to an actual determinable expense rather than to an estimated one.

The expenses must be for carrying on any trade or business. This limits Sec. 162 deductions to trade or business expenses only.

We can now determine the issues. A few are:

1. What kind of expense is it?
   a. Is it ordinary?
   b. Is it necessary?
2. Is the taxpayer on the cash or accrual basis?
   a. When was the expense paid?
   b. When was the expense incurred?
3. Is the taxpayer engaged in a trade or business?
   a. What is his trade or business?
4. If the expense isn't deductible under sec. 162 can it be deducted under a different section?

Section 162 illustrates how easy it is to develop issues. Issues often are merely restatements of the facts followed by a question mark. IRC sec. 162(c)(1), for example, addresses illegal bribes, kickbacks and other payments only to government officials or employees. We can begin our investigation by asking if the beneficiary of the payment was a government official, or a government employee. Next, we might ask if the payment was a bribe or a kickback or a payment that was neither a kickback or a bribe. What is a bribe? What is a kickback? If it was neither, was it another kind of payment?

Other issues are: does this section apply to officials or employees of non-federal governments? Does the law apply to state and city governments and their instrumentalities? Section 162(c)(1) applies to illegal transactions. Why does the code use the term "illegal?" Does this mean that legal bribes and kickbacks exist? Were the bribes and kickbacks in question legal or illegal? Many more issues must be resolved before other transactions can be solved. Once you have resolved all of these issues, your work is done and you can conclude that the expenditures were legal, or that they were illegal and not deductible.

Section 162 can teach us lessons on determining issues from statutes, legal documents such as a petition that states what they require or ask for. When people are charged with crimes or sued, the charges or the facts are not always as orderly as a statute or a petition. Facts are not always true and can mislead an expert witness from correct issues. The following actual cases were selected to help us understand and develop correct fact and issues.

6.4   What Is the Significant Issue?

An individual received a landscape architect degree in 1976 and a law degree in 1979. Upon graduation, he was employed by the U.S. Army Corps of Engineers as a landscape architect to design and supervise landscaping for bridges and highway overpasses. In 1990, he became interested in politics. He ran for the position of district attorney in his county even though he had no experience in law practice. His father was a popular politician and the former governor of the state. The candidate's political party won by a landslide and he was swept into office.

As district attorney, he was also allowed to maintain a private law practice in separate offices. He rented an office, furnished it and purchased a law library. When he filed his 1990 income tax return, he failed to depreciate any of his depreciable assets.

His private practice grew, but with no previous experience, he didn't know how to run a business. He also was a procrastinator who had been reprimanded twice by the Bar Association for missing deadlines. He did not file income tax returns for 1991 and 1992 and he failed to pay to the IRS withholding taxes on his employees.

The state's largest statewide-circulation newspaper discovered that the district attorney had not filed returns and printed larger than usual front page headlines: **"DISTRICT ATTORNEY FAILS TO FILE 1991 AND 1992 INCOME TAX RETURNS — SON OF FORMER GOVERNOR."** After the headline and news story appeared, an Internal Revenue agent reviewed the records of the district attorney's private law practice and called in a special agent to determine if fraud was involved.

There are so many issues in this situation that it is easy to discover most of them. Did he or did he not file? Why didn't he file? Can the 1990 return be amended to report depreciation? Is non-filing a commission of fraud? Should the taxpayer hire an attorney instead of a CPA? Will failure to pay withholding taxes trigger a 100% penalty on the taxpayer?

Each one of these issues is correct, but none is as crucial as the one major issue. Why didn't the attorney file? The fact that he was a procrastinator provides a clue that there was probably no intent to not file. Also, he had just begun to practice law for the first time after he graduated from law school 13 years earlier and had no business or tax know-how. He was represented by an attorney who claimed ignorance of tax matters and laws. The attorney preferred to have a CPA represent his client but, to protect him, agreed to review all information given to the IRS.

When events seem to be so cut and dried as in this case (he did not file the returns), we must look to unusual aspects of a transaction. Usually, the IRS will write to a taxpayer asking for nonfiled returns, or a field agent may ask the taxpayer to file, or exercise his authority to file a return for the taxpayer in lieu of the taxpayer's return. It is also unusual for a special agent to be called into a case upon initial discovery that returns were not filed. After working on the case, an agent might discover that his income was too small to require a return. In that event, a special agent would not have been needed. The agent might have determined that, even after returns were prepared, no fraud existed. Also, the newspaper headlines were unusual and suspicious. Failure to file, revenue agent's examinations and special agent investigations are not published and are not made public record until a petition on the matter is filed with the courts. Therefore, a newspaper should not have had access to the record.

Most CPAs have prepared delinquent returns or been asked to prepare returns for people who have not filed. These stories don't appear in newspapers.

Only two real issues now exist:

Why is a special agent investigating this case before any charges that require a special agent have been made?

Who told the newspaper that the district attorney had not filed his 1991 and 1992 returns?

The special agent admitted that he was investigating the source of the leak to the newspaper. If non-litigated confidential tax return information appeared in the newspapers, taxpayers would be upset and would be hesitant to file. Additionally, it is not legal to disclose tax return information without permission of the taxpayer, or by court order to a CPA or other preparers who are not lawyers. The agent wanted to settle with the district attorney as quietly as possible because the IRS did not want more information about the case to be printed in the newspaper.

The agent requested an amended 1990 return and completed 1991 and 1992 returns to be filed. The refund on the amended return, together with properly prepared delinquent returns with all expenses accounted for, resulted in a tax due that was lower than the minimum amount that should trigger fraud charges. The IRS district office waived some rules and told the special agent to accept the returns as filed returns, without change to the delinquent returns. After receiving the returns, he dropped fraud charges.

Payroll taxes are a different matter. However, the delinquent payments of payroll tax returns had not been reported in the newspaper, so the IRS agreed to installment payments and interest, but no 100% penalty.

In this instance, the genuine issues had nothing to do with nonfiling and everything to do with leaked information. When issues do not leap out, a forensic accounting expert witness must use his imagination to recognize unusual issues of substance.

6.5   The Nonfactual Fact

The nonfactual fact arises when people fail to recognize substance or to distinguish it from form. A forensic accounting expert witness must learn to recognize the effect his words and deeds will have on others. No matter what our words or actions are, our opposition is likely to misinterpret what we have said and what we have done. The following true example will illustrate the problems that confront us when we try to communicate to others.

6.5.1   The Nonfactual Fact in Action

A taxpayer's return was examined by the IRS. The IRS issued the agent's report and the taxpayer's CPA had filed a protest against the adjustments and additional tax, interest and penalties. Twelve months elapsed between the initial examination and the protest. The CPA had attended two conferences with the IRS appeals office. The IRS asked him to bring further documentation for what was expected to be a final conference, but the CPA died before he could attend with the additional documentation. Now another 2 months had passed and the taxpayer hired a new CPA to represent him.

The new CPA contacted the appeals office and assured them that after he familiarized himself with the examination facts and items in dispute he would resolve the case with the IRS. The taxpayer assured his new CPA that he had all the documents that the IRS had requested and would bring them to him at their next meeting. Unfortunately, the taxpayer cancelled several meetings with the CPA on the grounds of exceptional business circumstances.

On the morning of the day when the CPA was due to meet with the IRS appeals officer, the taxpayer confessed that he did not have the documents required. The CPA told the taxpayer that the IRS would probably overcome the original protest and assess the taxes, interest and penalties. The CPA left to meet with the appeals officer with a two-handled briefcase. It contained one slim manila folder with one only document from the client. The rest of the briefcase was stuffed until it bulged with magazines, research memos and correspondence that had no relation to the taxpayer. It was so full that it could not be fastened and papers stuck out of the top.

In the appeals office, the conferee and the CPA introduced themselves. The CPA waited for the conferee to ask for the documents. He would have extracted the manila folder with the one document furnished by the taxpayer. The conferee didn't ask. Instead, he stared at the briefcase. His face tightened. His expression was one of disappointment and disgust. He sighed and said to the CPA, " Look, this has taken so much time, I don't want to spend any more on it if we can agree. Will you settle for half?" The CPA said, "Sure."

What had happened? If the conferee had asked to see the documents, he would have assessed the tax in his report. Instead, his thoughts raced. What was he thinking? "Darn, this has gone on for 14 months. I don't want to look through everything in the briefcase. They're probably not in order and I'll have to sort them and add them and tie them to the return and the agent's report. It might take the rest of the day, or a week or a month. Then this new CPA will probably want to rebut my analyses of the documents. I hope he's willing to settle for half."

Why did this happen? The imagination of the conferee was on fire. He imagined facts that didn't exist. He assumed that the briefcase was jammed full with the taxpayer's documents and that they were not in order. He imagined himself working for hours more on the case, only to have his final decisions challenged by the CPA.

The conferee had seen the form of the briefcase and not the substance of the documents. He had imagined facts to exist that did not exist. He had discovered the nonfactual fact.

Usually, IRS agents and CPAs believe that the CPA deceived the conferee and was not honest with him. They have said that the CPA should have known what the response of the conferee would have been. This situation is easy to criticize and implies that this CPA could read minds, something even Harry Houdini could not do.

This case is not presented for admiration or reprimands. It is not an indication of IRS errors. All of us, public accountants, attorneys at law and forensic expert witnesses swear that facts exist when they do not. We frequently choose form over substance This case is merely a true occasion of failure to distinguish substance from form and facts from nonfacts. An expert who mistakes form for substance and imagines facts to exist when they do not will succeed only until he faces opposition that has mastered these concepts.

6.5.2   Substance versus Form and the Nonfactual Fact Recognized

Whether we attend the deposition and trial or read deposition and trial transcripts, we seek to understand the opposition viewpoint. We will try to determine if that viewpoint has substance and facts that we must overcome.

The following deposition occurred because a couple involved in divorce proceedings quarreled over the value of a drive-in owned and operated by the husband (Howard William Conseki). The deponent, Michael E. James, is the expert witness for the petitioner (Shirley Ann Conseki). The respondent's expert was not called until long after the litigation had been in process and the expert for the petitioner had been deposed. Attorney for the petitioner is Robert R. Lewis, and for the respondent, Donald J. Ritchard. Unless otherwise designated, **Q** is Lewis and **A** is James. We will dispense with the formal cover page, introductory questions to qualify the witness and other identifying questions not relevant at this stage for the expert witness.

6.6 Deposition of Michael James

6.6.1 Direct Examination

By Lewis (Q):

Q. What's your occupation?

A. I'm a Certified Public Accountant.

Q. What is the name of the firm that you're with?

A. Jones, James and Associates.

Q. How long have you been associated with that company?

A. Oh, it's an successor to many, but about 19 years.

Q. And would you tell me your education?

A. I have a degree from Columbia University.

Q. And what kind of degree is that, sir?

A. A BSBA.

Q. In what field?

A. Accounting, major in accounting.

Q. When did you obtain that degree?

A. 1966.

Q. Then after you obtained that degree, were you certified by anyone?

A. By the states of Iowa and Nebraska.

Q. And what's the certification that you have?

A. Certified Public Accountant.

Q. And how long have you been certified by the State of Iowa?

A. Since 1969.

Q. And how about the state of Nebraska?

A. Same.

Q. Okay. And is your firm that you're now associated with engaged in all kinds of accounting work?

A. Yes. *(We have learned that the deponent is a CPA and studied accounting at Columbia. He also has practiced public accounting for about 20 years. We will expect him to have a reasonably good knowledge of accounting, but we do not know what his specialty is.)*

Q. What fields did you operate in or what do you do in this business?

A. We do basically everything, auditing, accounting, tax work, management advice, tax planning, we do … we've done a lot of things, business valuations. *(The question to this answer seems to be addressed to his experiences as opposed to those of his firm. However, he has answered for the firm. We do not yet know if he is a general practitioner or a specialist in one of the fields he mentioned. We do not yet know if he is qualified to testify as an expert on the facts and issues on which he has been hired to testify.)*

Q. In connection with your firm, have you had occasion to come into contact with Mrs. Shirley Ann Conseki?

A. Yes.

Q. And about how long ago, sir?

A. About a month, month and a half ago, I believe.

Q. And did she request that you assist her in evaluating some assets and reviewing some financial documents?

A. Yes.

Q. And have some financial documents been submitted to you?

A. Yes.

Q. Will you tell us just generally the documents that you have?

A. I have the tax returns of Howard W. and Shirley A. Conseki for the last three years, '84, 3 and 2. I have some other papers concerning the … documents regarding the purchase of Con's Drive-In and numerous papers concerning that, papers regarding CDs, the apartment house on 5th Street.

Q. All right. One document you asked me for and I think we've obtained it for you just recently, is the depreciation schedules for the drive-in. Did you obtain those?

A. Right. This afternoon. *(Whatever he intends to do with the depreciation, he hasn't much time between receiving them and being deposed. If he uses calculations based on these schedules, for testimony at this deposition, we must review them carefully to determine if he has used them honestly.)*

Q. Now, with regard, first of all, to Con's Drive-In, did you receive some documents concerning the drive-in?

A. Yes.

Q. Okay. And were you asked to place a value upon Con's Drive-In?

A. Yes. *(Now we know what James is to do as the expert witness for the petitioner. When the attorney qualified this witness, none of the preceding testimony supports the expert knowledge of the witness to place a value on Con's Drive-In or any other drive-in. From his testimony, we may believe that his firm is qualified, but nowhere does the testimony support the deponent's expert ability, except that he is a CPA with a degree who has practiced public accounting for about 20 years. His present firm is an outgrowth of several other firms. We do not know the quality or reputation of the witness or of his firm. We will review his valuation in great detail* *to find weaknesses in his work. If his background is weak, his valuation may be weak.)*

Q. And would you tell us if you did that?

A. I did.

Q. And would you tell us how you go about doing such a thing?

A. How I did it or how I go about doing it?

Q. Both. How you go about it and then how you did it or how you applied your principles?

A. We try to get financial information for the last several years on a business. Normally try to get 5 years. In this case, we only have 3 years. *(If he normally wants 5 years, why does he have only 3 years for this valuation? Have they filed only three returns? Have they refused to provide more than three returns? If he normally needs 5 years, how can he compute a reasonable value with only 3?)* That, along with any financial statements, what I said before, whatever, put values of assets. That's basically it. Depends upon the type of business and how we value it. *(What did he say? What does this explanation mean? What is the substance of this statement? The substance is confusion. This confusion and incoherence can be used to discredit the valuation by this expert. To discredit his opinion is only half the work. The respondent's expert must calculate a value that is acceptable by the court. Without a value to replace the value computed by the petitioner's expert, the court has no alternative to decide upon.)*

Q. All right. And then what do you do?

A. Then we in this particular case … I guess that would be the easiest way to explain.

Q. Okay.

A. I took the information that was on the daily sales sheets and, to arrive at sales for the year, looked at the income and expenses that were reported on the Schedule C on the income tax returns for the last 3 years. Using that, I determined what the income was. *(It seems that the petitioner's attorney had not adequately prepared his expert for a deposition. Is there any substance to this explanation of how the witness determined what the income was? He said that he took the information from the daily sales sheets, but he doesn't say what use he made of that infor-*

mation. Next, he said that to arrive at the sales for the year, he looked at the income and expenses that were reported on Schedule C for the returns of the last 3 years. How can looking at income and expenses on a Schedule C help one to arrive at sales? How do income and expenses on any return help to arrive at sales? Did he add the "information" from the daily sales sheets to the tax return income and expenses? He looked at the daily sales sheets for only 1 year and the tax returns for 3 years. He said he had financial statements. Did he use them? Did Con's Drive-In have a general ledger? That would be an ideal location to find total sales for the year. He testified that "Using that, I determined what the income was." This indicates that he used the daily sales sheets and the income and expenses from the Schedule C to determine what income was. We cannot know whether he made correct computations until we review his calculations. Perhaps his work was right but his ability to explain himself was poor. Before an expert witness testifies, whether by deposition or at trial, our attorney must prepare us. We will not be able to testify adequately until our attorney understands what we tell him and we understand what he tells us. During this deposition, the petitioner's attorney indicates that he understands his expert. This is evidenced by his next statement. The witness did a poor job of preparing the attorney on accounting matters. Any opposition witness should become suspicious of the testimony and work of this deponent.)

Q. All right.

A. I believe the drive-in was purchased in 1981. I don't have the figures for that year, so I used, like I said, '82, '83 and '84. *(Earlier in his testimony, the deponent testified that he likes to have 5 years for a valuation. The Drive-In was purchased in 1981, so why didn't he obtain "figures" for that year? Did the previous owner have financial information that he would make available? After only 3-plus years in business did the value appreciate considerably or none at all from the purchase price?)*

Q. All right.

A. Next from that income there's a number of different methods that you can use, but the method that I used on this was I took the income and since there are people down there that run it, I assumed that there would not be any additional salaries involved in the operation of it, deducted from the income what could be considered to be a fair return on the capital that was invested based on risk and so forth and came down to an adjusted income figure which I termed excess income, totaled that, took the average of it for the last 3 years, deducted income taxes from it at an assumed rate to get the excess earnings, which I then capitalized at a rate of 15%. That all came down to capitalized earnings of $42,056.

Using the depreciation schedules which were furnished to me I looked at the original purchase price, after talking to Mrs. Conseki, made some assumptions as to the rate that the assets should be valued, came up with a total valuation of $38,488. Added that to the capitalized earnings and came up with a total value of $80,544. (*Once more, the issue starts with what did he say and what does it mean? Apparently, he capitalized earnings based on some method that is not clearly explained. Did he arrive at the correct basis to capitalize? Is capitalization of earnings the only method of valuation that would apply in this case? He used a capitalization rate of 15%. Is this a correct rate? How did he arrive at 15%?*)

Q. All right.

Ritchard: Total value of how much, please?
The witness: eighty thousand five forty-four.

Q. Mr. James, where do you ... a key figure in your equation is 15% capitalization. Will you explain that to me and how you arrive at that?

A. That's the same rate I used on the ... in the capital that was invested. Capitalization rate varies according to the business. If a service type business has a low capitalization rate, a business like this should have a higher rate and, since I had used the 15% for the invested capital, I thought the capitalization rate should be the same. (*All form and stated incoherently. The substance of his answer is that he guessed at the rate.*)

Q. I see. All Right. (*Does the attorney really understand? If a CPA doesn't understand what the witness has said about accounting methods and techniques, how would this particular attorney understand? A reasonably competent forensic accounting expert witness should be able to reason that this attorney understands little of accounting.*)

A. Right.

Q. And then as far as the ... financial statements that you have ... you've seen the financial statements filed by the parties and you've taken all of those figures that are shown except for Con's Drive-In figure that you've adjusted that you've told us?

A. Right. (*This question and answer means that the parties have agreed on the value of all other marriage assets except for the Drive-In, which the expert adjusted to what he believes is fair market value.*)

Lewis: That's all. I would offer into evidence Exhibit — Deposition Exhibit No. 1

Ritchard: I'd like to ask some foundational questions first, Robert, before I either make or withhold an objection.

6.6.2 Cross-Examination

By Ritchard (Q):

Q. When you prepared this document, this proposed exhibit, did you consider in connection with Con's Drive-In value the fact that this is a ground lease, he doesn't own the building, he ... he doesn't own the land, but he owns the building?

A. Yes.

Q. You said that there are several approaches, there are a number of different methods that could be used to determine the value of Con's Drive-In. Did you use what we would commonly call the capitalization of income approach?

A. Yes.

Q. And I suppose ... Does this rule apply? The higher the capitalization rate the lower the value, the lower the capitalization rate the higher the value?

A. Right.

Q. When you go out into the market to determine the cap rate, where do you pick up the 15% capitalization? (*We hope that we will learn precisely how the capitalization rate was determined. We will have a basis to prove or disprove. We will learn the substance of his conclusions.*)

A. Like I said, it's based somewhat on the market, the type of business that it is. (*This answer tells us nothing except that he seems reluctant to provide the method he used to determine the capitalization rate.*)

Q. Did you use your own judgment, too?

A. Yes.

Q. Have you had occasion to value other businesses in the past year?

A. Yes.

Q. What cap rate have you used?

A. One which was heavily service oriented. I believe I used a 20% five times.

Q. Have you in the past year used a cap rate as low as 15%?

A. I don't … I don't remember, to be honest.

Q. If you had used a 20% cap rate, then the value would have been lower, would it not?

A. That's right.

Q. Did you talk to any banks or lending institutions or financial institutions about what an acceptable cap rate would be at this time?

A. No.

Q. Did anyone suggest to you what the cap rate ought to be?

A. No.

Q. Might two persons such as yourself reach different conclusions as to what the cap rate ought to be?

A. That's possible. I ran this one past another person here in my office and he concurred with me. *(Finally, we have it in this testimony for the second time, that the witness guessed at a capitalization rate. His rate is form only, without substance. Running a rate past another person in your office does not constitute the research needed to arrive at a reasonable rate that is supported by substantive evidence. However, this deposition indicates that an attorney should have his expert accounting witness present at the deposition of an opposing expert accounting witness. Had another accountant been present, the capitalization rate of 15% might have been thrown out earlier as an unsupported capitalization rate.)*

Q. What are some of the other methods that could have been used to value the business?

A. Like I said, it depends a lot on the type of business that it is. If it was a, say a farm corporation, generally those are valued strictly on assets, not on earnings. The method that I used takes into consideration both the earnings — and they're adjusted; there's some deductions taken out of them; it's not a strict capitalization of earning — plus the asset values. That's generally the one that we've used on a lot of different businesses. *(This answer and several of his other answers were an opportunity for the respondent's attorney to discredit this witness both during direct examination and cross-examination. Did the witness answer the attorney's question: "What are some of the other methods that could have been used to value the business?" No. He described incoherently, how he did arrive at the value. Other accountants may have been able to guess what he meant — how he calculated the value, but they cannot have any certainty as to how he valued Con's Drive-In.)*

(We must also note that the attorney did not challenge his answer and continued his questions until he was able to understand the answer. It is imperative that lawyers bring their experts in to help them understand and question the opposing experts. Often, with small amounts like the amounts in this litigation, an expert may be willing to reduce his fee substantially merely to stamp out imbecilities found in the testimony of many expert witnesses.

The petitioner's attorney was remiss in not preparing his expert to enable him to testify with substance, and his expert was remiss when he allowed himself to testify without adequate preparation by his attorney. If the preparation was slight or didn't occur, then the expert was remiss in not preparing himself to testify with substance on the work he had performed.)

Q. Have you ever been familiar with a sale of this particular kind of drive-in, not a franchise drive-in, just a local drive-in of some kind?

A. I don't know of any.

Q. Do you know what the market would be realistically at this time for a drive-in like that?

A. Probably fairly high, based on all the other fast food restaurants in town. *(This would have been a great opportunity to have once more discredited the testimony of this witness. His answer alleges that he is familiar with the values of "all the other fast food restaurants in town." How does he know? Is he the accountant for them? [There were 23 fast food restaurants located on the main street of this city.] Also, none of the testimony alleges that this drive-in is a fast food restaurant. It may be a full service restaurant with full meals and table and car service.)*

Q. In other words, it would be a good market? Is that what your opinion would be?

A. I would think so.

Q. Would this be a ... Is this a partnership or was this a corporate business, according to your records? Was it a partnership?

A. Sole proprietorship.

Q. There was no partnership tax return?

A. No.

Q. Strictly sole proprietorship?

A. Right.

Q. If this had been a ... owned by a closely held corporation, would that have made any difference on the value?

A. No.

Q. Are you familiar with the Iowa case law that holds that in a dissolution case that the value of the ... of a closely held corporation is the value of the underlying assets?

A. No.

Q. Did you consider ... I know, as you've indicated, that you based your opinion as to value on income, but are aware of the actual value of the ... of the inventory and equipment other than what you saw in the tax returns?

A. Just what I saw in the tax returns and the depreciation schedules.

Q. Do you remember any figures? Could you tell us what ... what those values are of inventory and equipment and anything else that might be an asset of the business?

A. Just what I saw in the tax returns and the depreciation schedules.

Q. Do you remember any figures? Could you tell us what ... what those values are of inventory and equipment and anything else that might be an asset of the business?

A. Building cost was shown as $20,653, the equipment at $21,044. Inventory was approximately a thousand.

Q. And what are you looking at when you tell us those figures?

A. The tax returns, the depreciation schedules.

Q. For what year?

A. Depreciation was the 1984.

Q. Do you know anything about the terms of the lease of the ground lease?

A. I've read it, yes.

Q. Okay. Do you know when it expires?

A. Not … I don't recall without looking.

Q. Could that have an impact on the salability of that business?

A. Yes.

Q. The terms of that lease?

A. I would think so.

Q. Do you know whether that lease is assignable by Mr. Conseki to anybody else?

A. I, I don't remember.

Q. Do you have a copy of the lease with you?

A. I have a copy. *(Most experts prolong their answers. Remember to use "Yes" or "No" to a question that requires a "yes" or a "no." I had a habit of answering yes, it is, or no it isn't until a judge asked me to limit my answers to yes or no if appropriate. He reminded me that it would be less for the court reporter and less for the judges and lawyers and the expert witnesses to read. The transcripts would also use fewer pages and use less storage space.)*

Q. May I see it for just a minute, please?

A. (Witness complies.)

Q. Thank you.

Ritchard: Would you mark that as an exhibit, please, for identification.

(*WHEREUPON, Deposition Exhibit No. 2 was marked for identification.*)

By Ritchard (Q):

Q. Would you look at what has been marked Exhibit 2 and tell us what that is please?

A. That's the business property lease for Con's Drive-In, the land.

Q. And would you look at … Page 1 and tell us what the term is. I think it's shown on Page 1. Do you see what the term is?

A. For term of 5 years.

Q. Expiring when?

A. 31st day of December, 1986.

Q. And would you look at Item 3, Possession.

A. Okay.

Q. What does that say?

A. Tenant shall be entitled to possession on the first day of the term of this lease and shall yield possession to the landlord at the time and date of the close of the lease term, except as herein otherwise expressly provided.

Q. And the lease term expires when, did you say?

A. December 31, '86.

Q. What is Item 7? What's the caption?

A. Surrender of Premises at End of Term — Removal of Fixtures.

Q. Is there a sub-paragraph b under that?

A. Yes.

Q. What does that have to do with?

A. Holding over.

Q. What does that say?

A. Continued possession beyond the expiration date of this lease by the tenant, coupled with the receipt of the specified rental by the landlord shall constitute a month-to-month extension of this lease.

Q. Then would you look at Item C — sub-paragraph c, I should say, under 7? What does that say?

A. Termination of Lease. The lease shall terminate upon expiration of demised …

Q. Demised.

A. … term. If tenant wishes to extend or renew said lease, landlord or its representatives shall negotiate with tenant to that end.

Q. Look at Item 8, please.

A. Assignment and Subletting. There shall be no assignment of this lease or subletting of the premises or any part thereof without the landlord's written permission.

Q. Would the ability to sell a property, whether it's readily marketable, would have … whether or not it's readily marketable, would that have an impact upon its value?

A. Yes.

Q. And with those restrictions in the lease, would a sale that depended — in your opinion, based upon what you just read — would it depend at least in part on the ability of a buyer of some business to negotiate a satisfactory lease with a landlord?

A. Yes.

Ritchard: I'd like to offer Exhibit 2 into evidence.

Lewis: No objection.

Ritchard: That's all.

Lewis: That's all the questions I have. Anything further, Mr. Ritchard?

Ritchard: I don't have any other questions.

(*WHEREUPON, the deposition concluded at the hour of 4:50 P.M.*)

(*It is apparent that the expert witness did not attempt to perform all of the services necessary to determine the value of the Drive-In. If the respondent's attorney had brought a forensic accounting witness to the deposition, that expert may have been adequate to demonstrate that the valuation by the petitioner's witness was unacceptable and did not comply with existing rules of evidence and requirements of generally accepted valuation principles. Because of failure to hire an expert for the respondent at the time of this deposition, petitioner's erroneous and incorrect valuation would stand until proven wrong. Respondent now had to hire an expert who would now need to prove two premises: (1) that the petitioner's valuation was wrong and (2) that the valuation computed by the respondent's expert was right. The report of the respondent's witness is in Chapter 9.*)

6.7   Understanding Simple and Basic Accounting

To understand simple and basic accounting is never easy for forensic accountants, even if they are CPAs. After reading the facts, issues and resolution to this dispute over the dissolution of a partnership the best of forensic accountants and expert witnesses should have increased awareness as to how easy it is to misunderstand accounting.

6.7.1   Statement of Facts

The Smith Co. was a family partnership of James and Mary Smith and their son Robert. James and Mary operated as partners under an oral agreement until 1940, when they executed a written agreement. The main purpose of the agreement was to affirm only that the partnership assets were owned equally by James and Mary.

In 1958, their son Robert became a partner. A new agreement was prepared that provided that profit and losses would be shared one half by Robert and one fourth each by James and Mary except for certain modifications. The modifications provided that any rental income and expenses should be borne by and accrue only to James and Mary. They provided that Robert should pay for labor, supplies, depreciation on equipment, tractor and equipment repairs, all equipment, feed, inventories and his personal expenses. (*The Smiths' two daughters had no interest in the Smith Co. because they owned and operated farms and cattle ranches with their husbands in a different state. Robert's wife, Sarah, had no interest in the business.*)

The agreement also provided that James and Mary owned all farmland including fencing, buildings and improvements used by the partnership. Neither Robert nor the partnership should have any interest in it except for the right to use it for partnership business.

The contract provided that the partnership should keep its books on the cash basis and adopt a calendar year for accounting. Upon the death of James, the partnership should continue until the end of the calendar year in which James dies and then liquidate.

From the inception of the partnership, it had used the international CPA firm of AB & Co. (AB) Periodically, but at least annually, AB prepared cash receipts and disbursements journals to record partnership cash transactions. Additionally, they prepared a general journal to adjust accounts and to record non-cash transactions. The journals were posted to columnar working papers by AB & Co. to prepare financial statements and income tax returns. These working papers constituted the general ledger of the partnership.

The partnership had three bank accounts recorded on its balance sheet. The Robert or Sarah Smith bank account was used for partnership business and for personal transactions of their son. When Robert made a personal deposit to this account, it was debited to cash and credited to his drawing account. When he made a personal withdrawal from this account, it was credited to cash and debited to his drawing account. When partnership cash was deposited in the account, it was credited to the appropriate partnership revenue or note payable account. When partnership transactions were paid from this account, the debit was to the appropriate partnership account.

The James or Mary Smith bank account was recorded in the same manner as the Robert or Sarah Smith bank account.

The James or Robert Smith bank account was used only for partnership transactions and no personal transactions of any of the partners occurred in them.

In addition, James Smith had a personal bank account in another bank that was used solely for his personal nonpartnership transactions.

James died in October 1976 and the partnership was continued until December 31, 1976. Just before AB prepared a statement of liquidation, Mary became ill and unable to manage her affairs or herself. Her two daughters were named as her conservators.

AB prepared a statement of liquidation. All farmland and related structures were distributed to the Estate of James Smith and to the Mary Smith Conservatorship. In accordance with the partnership agreement, they distributed all equipment and inventories to Robert, because their working papers showed that he had paid for them. They distributed liabilities to the partners or assignees in the profit and loss ratio.

The liquidation distribution prepared by AB distributed $3,500,000 of assets to Robert and $1 million of liabilities. It distributed the unencumbered farmland and related structures to the estate and the conservatorship along with $1 million of liabilities.

Robert's sisters loved him dearly and they believed that he was entitled to his share of partnership assets after devoting most of his working life to the partnership. However, they didn't believe that the estate or conservatorshp should assume $1 million of liabilities that applied to Robert's assets. The farmland mortgages had been paid off in the 1930s. They sued their brother and the partnership's accountants for an accounting to determine what happened to the assets and liabilities and who they belonged to.

AB was located in Missouri so it hired Missouri attorneys to represent them. Robert also lived in Missouri so he hired a different Missouri law firm to represent his interests. His sisters lived in Kansas and hired a Kansas law firm to represent them.

The Kansas District Court Judge who was assigned to the case appointed a Kansas law firm as a special administrator to oversee and consolidate the work of the other three law firms. The special administrator hired a forensic accountant (expert) to resolve accounting problems and to serve as an expert witness on his behalf. He obtained an order from the District Court to authorize the forensic accountant to prepare an accounting of the partnership from 1958 to the date the assets were distributed; and beyond, to determine their final disposition.

During his work, among many other items, the forensic accountant uncovered the following additional facts, transactions and adjusting journal entries (AJE) recorded by AB:

In 1976, Robert Smith entered into a joint venture with Jane Jones to feed cattle. Robert purchased the cattle for this joint venture and the transaction was recorded in error on the partnership books in the following manner:

| Livestock Purchases | $9,500 | |
| Partnership cash account | | $9,500 |

Next, an entry was made to record the Jones Joint Venture cash on the books of the partnership in this manner:

| Partnership Cash Account | $15,000 | |
| Livestock sales | | $15,000 |

These entries were explained as being "to reimburse Robert for cattle and feed purchases." Both of the above entries should have been recorded as transactions in Robert's drawing and investment accounts and not as revenue and expenses of the partnership. To correct this, AB recorded an AJE as follows:

Notes payable	$15,000	
Feed		$5,500
Purchases		$9,500

At this point, notes payable were understated by $15,000, feed was understated by $5,500 and livestock sales were overstated by $15,000.

To correct this entry, AB prepared a compound AJE that included the following entries to attempt to correct the previous entries:

Robert Drawing	$15,000	
Notes payable		$15,000

Now, the uncorrected errors became an overstatement of livestock sales of $15,000 and an understatement of feed expense of $5,500.

Next, the following AJE was recorded by AB to attempt to correct the previous entries:

Livestock sales	$15,000	
Feed		$5,500
Livestock purchases		$9,500

At this point, feed expenses were understated by $11,000 and livestock purchases were understated by $9,500.

On December 14, 1976, Robert bought personal cattle that were recorded on the partnership records in error as follows:

Livestock purchases	$32,000	
Partnership cash account		$32,000

There was a corresponding note for this at the First City Bank recorded at the bank as Robert's personal note. Therefore, the following entry to record the cattle and note as personal were recorded by AB in a compound entry as follows:

Notes payable	$32,000	
Robert drawing		$32,000

However, this created an understatement in notes payable, so the following AJE was recorded by AB to correct the above entries:

| Hog sales | $32,000 | |
| Notes payable | | $32,000 |

Now, hog sales were understated by $32,000.

Next Robert paid $20,000 to the partnership for feed, which was recorded correctly as:

| Partnership cash account | $20,000 | |
| Feed | | $20,000 |

However, on December 31, 1976, AB adjusted this entry by recording the following AJE:

| Feed | $20,000 | |
| Robert drawing | | $20,000 |

This overstates feed expense and Robert's capital account by $20,000.

When the forensic accountant reviewed the partnership cash receipts and disbursements, he noted that when partnership labor, supplies, equipment repairs, equipment, feed and inventories were purchased, they were paid from the Robert or Sarah Smith bank account so that Robert would pay for them as provided by the partnership agreement. The transactions were recorded as a credit to the bank account cash and as a debit to the related expense or asset accounts.

In addition, he discovered the following transactions:

- On February 28, 1973, AJE 14 in AB's files (which are the accounting records of the partnership) records sales of $46,000. It is explained as "to record James' share of soybeans deposited in his personal bank account."
- On June 27, 1974, AJE 9 records $54,000 to "record cattle sales deposited in James' personal bank account." Again on June 27, 1974, AJE 10 records $57,000 to "record grain sales deposited in James' personal bank account."
- On January 16,1976, AJE 11 records $17,000 "to record checks from hog sales deposited in James' personal bank account."
- On February 23, 1976, AJE 13 records $15,000 "to properly record application of funds received from Jane Jones against note balance."

On February 24, 1976, AJE 15 records a reduction in notes payable of $152,000 "to [record] Robert's personal cattle transactions from the partnership."

On February 28, 1976, AJE 19 records $12,000 "to correct recording of personal note payment."

On February 28, 1976, AJE 25 records $32,000 "to record sales deposited to James' personal bank account."

6.8 Commentary

I had presented this partnership dispute to participants of a forensic accounting seminar a few years ago to determine its value as a teaching example. The feedback from the participants proved its value to teach us once more that professionals often assume facts that do not exist and fail to recognize the real issues in any dispute. The introduction to this book informs us that the cases cited as examples are actual cases resolved in federal or state courts, federal arbitration or an IRS appeals office. Therefore, the cases are not pages of fiction. The names have been changed to avoid identification of the parties and some of the cases have been abridged because the entire case was not needed. The preceding statement of facts informed readers that "a new agreement was prepared ..." It provided "that Robert shall pay for ... depreciation on equipment ... and his personal expenses." Three of the students in my forensic accounting seminar wrote almost identical comments. They wrote, "This case is stupid. How can anyone pay for depreciation on equipment?" The only stupid part of this case were the comments written by those three students. The case is real. It involved millions of dollars and was struggled over by the district court, four law firms, one international accounting firm (AB) and the special administrator and his expert for more than 1 year. The case is unfortunate, but real and therefore not stupid. The students' question, "How can anyone pay for depreciation of equipment?" is incompetent. Because the contract contained the words "Robert shall pay for depreciation on equipment," it took all involved professionals and a judge to determine what those words meant.

We have learned valuable and important concepts for expert witnessing, forensic accounting and accounting in general from these skeptical students. We must never assume something that does not exist. That is why the defendant, his CPAs and his attorneys lost this suit. They could not read and they also imagined facts that did not exist.

One important concept is that if the agreement states that Robert shall pay for depreciation on equipment, then that is what it states. None of us can help that. What you see is what you get. The real issue is how do we interpret the depreciation provisions of the contract?

Whether the provision is stupid or brilliant is not relevant. The relevancy of the provision is that it exists. We cannot wish it away — it exists. We cannot ignore it — it exists. We cannot even decide on our own what it means. This provision is subject to interpretation only by authorized parties — in this case, the district court.

Over and over, expert witnessing and forensic accounting work is destroyed by assumption of facts that do not exist; by misunderstanding of facts (we read broad meanings into facts that require narrow interpretations); and by failure to answer any facts that pose questions to us. In this case, the question is, what does "Robert shall pay for depreciation on equipment" mean? I know that it can mean many different things, but, in this case, the judge ruled that it meant that if Robert paid for the equipment, he still is not entitled to a 100% allocation of the depreciation on the equipment. The agreement provided for a special allocation for rental income and expenses. However, it does not provide for a special allocation to Robert of any other income and expenses other than in the profit and loss ratio.

The real issues in this case are not difficult to discover. The erroneous and confusing journal entries made by Robert's accountants indicate that they had not mastered accounting principles and theory of ordinary debits and credits. When we analyze the journal entries and the other records with the valuable and underused accounting tool called a "T" account, we will discover that if Robert had actually paid for the equipment and inventory as required by the contract, then the debits for those disbursements should have been charged to his drawing account and not to the partnership balance sheet. No technical accounting or tax issues were involved in this case. The most pervasive issue, the sole most important issue, was that AB did not understand the meaning of the basic accounting principle, assets equal liabilities plus capital. Accountants are taught that in their first textbook used in their first college accounting class.

Think of it. Accountants employed by an international accounting firm did not understand the meaning of assets equal liabilities plus capital — the accounting equation — our first lesson in accounting. How do you prove this? Proving this is unthinkable. A forensic accounting expert witness can never close his mind. The expert must think always of the unthinkable. What does the accounting equation mean? Does it mean that debits equal credits, or that the balance sheet balances? In a way, yes. When you think logically of the equation, you realize that its main function is to teach us accounting cause and effect. If we do *this*, then *that* must happen. If we charge equipment to an asset account of the partnership instead of to Robert's drawing account, then debits equaled credits, but the adjustment did not comply with the partnership agreement. We have discovered that the equipment had been recorded as if the partnership instead of Robert had paid for it and owned it. This does not comply with the contract. To show the equipment and inventory as Robert's would require a reduction in his capital account. Yet AB recorded it in the distribution as belonging to Robert.

In a 49-page report to the court, the expert witness wrote that AB was wrong and that that they did not understand that assets equal liabilities plus capital. He also calculated for the court that Robert's capital account, which had been recorded as $2,500,000 by AB for liquidation purposes, was really a deficit of $300,000.

His report made AB angry and they issued a scathing written rebuttal. The expert answered in 15 pages and AB conceded the issue, which was that AB had misconstrued the accounting equation. Robert was required to restore $2,800,000 to the partnership for proper distribution.

What helped to reverse the liquidation balances calculated by AB? They actually helped to reverse themselves. When they attacked the expert's report to the court, he was able to produce a letter written to him earlier by an AB partner. The AB partner wrote that "the inventory and equipment probably should have been charged to Robert's capital account to comply with the contract." However, the account charges to comply with the contract had never been made correctly since the inception of the partnership. Many court decisions had set a precedent that, when the partners of a partnership do not object to the accounting records even when they are wrong, then the accounting as recorded is considered to be correct. Therefore, the judge reasoned that Robert had not complied with the contract and that, for the past 40 years, the inventory and equipment had been recorded as assets of the partnership and therefore were assets of the partnership.

The expert had also reported that sales proceeds had been collected and applied to partnership loan accounts by the bank. The bank denied this. The expert was able to produce letters written earlier by the bank and by AB that admitted that sales proceeds had been collected and applied to partnership loan accounts by the bank.

In forensic accounting and expert witnessing, we must exercise caution about writing letters or making admissions. If AB or the bank had considered long before that the expert might be able to use their letters and working papers to show that their work or their later sworn statements were wrong, they might not have replied to him. Do not provide gratuitous comments. Information that we provide to the opposing parties must be approved first by the attorney for our side.

My comments about AB are not complaints about large public accounting firms. To the contrary, I have respect and admiration for them. They are so competent and so successful that I hold them in awe. Also, I have worked for Arthur Andersen & Co. and Peat, Marwick, Mitchell & Co. and am on good terms with their successors. Unfortunately, Andersen has seen its stature disappear in the Enron debacle. The entire firm has been declared guilty without a trial. When I worked for them in the late 1950s and early 1960s, such charges would have had no merit.

How is it possible for any small CPA firm (as an expert) to be on the opposite side to a large firm, or to help an international corporation? Even if the opposing CPA firm has 75,000 employees, they cannot all be in the same courtroom at the same time with you.

AB used one partner, two managers and three seniors to oppose the expert. The 3-year seniors were too inexperienced to challenge him. The 6-year managers were also too inexperienced and too far removed from the details of the transactions to challenge him. The partner had not seen any details for years. He knew the least about the issues.

Power does not matter. Size does not matter. Only your ability to reason, your recognition of trivia and your ability to cut through it, your determination of the right issues, your access to a research library and the communication skills needed to tell your story to the court matter.

6.9 Knowing and Understanding Facts Means Issues Will Resolve Themselves

An Illinois bank lent $30 million dollars to Corporation X (X). Twelve months after it had received the money, X filed for bankruptcy and was liquidated under Chapter 7 of the United States Bankruptcy Code. X had been a manufacturer whose financial statements had reported sufficient inventory, equity and net income to secure the loan.

The bank, as plaintiff, sued X and X's auditors, YZ & Co. (YZ). YZ in turn sued X as a third-party plaintiff.

The bank alleged malpractice against YZ. It alleged that inventory was the material income-producing asset, that it had been substantially overstated and that the auditors had not observed the taking of the physical inventory. It did not test count, price test, determine cutoffs, or ownership of inventory. Allegations were also made that YZ had erred by including incorrect income when it misapplied certain enumerated generally accepted auditing standards and standards of the Financial Accounting Standards Board. These errors resulted in a $3 million overstatement of income in 1992 and a similar amount in 1994. Further, the petition alleged that YZ violated independence standards because it participated in managerial responsibilities for X.

Before the bank made the loan to X on June 30, 1994, it had relied on the most recent certified financial statements, which were issued on March 30, 1993 for the year ended December 31, 1992. On April 22, 1995, YZ issued its audit report of X for the year ended December 31, 1994. Neither set of financial statements indicated that X was insolvent, nor did they indicate financial difficulties for X. On July 2, 1995, X filed for bankruptcy.

The bank had hired forensic accountants from two large accounting firms as experts. They proposed to testify that YZ had been negligent and incompetent. Further, they planned to testify that the misleading certified financial statements caused the bank to lose $30 million.

YZ's attorneys hired a different forensic accountant as an expert witness. They asked their expert, off the record, if YZ was incompetent. The expert answered in the affirmative, but declared that their incompetence did not cause the bank's loan or loss.

The bank's incompetence was the sole cause of the loss. The bank claimed to have relied upon the 1992 certified financial statements as the basis for its loan and loss. Further, it said that it also relied on the 1994 certified statements as a basis for the loan.

The bank relied on financial statements that were 18 months old at the time of the loan. These statements were worthless as support for a loan so much later. The business could have disappeared by then. The 1994 financial statements had not been issued until almost 10 months after the loan had been made and could not retroactively support the loan.

The bank should have insisted upon current financial statements and inspected the assets itself and checked with other creditors before making the loan.

Incompetence or negligence of the auditors were not the issues. The sole issue with substance was why the bank made the loan. The answer was the bank's negligence, incompetence and greed.

The suit against the CPAs was dismissed. An expert must begin at the beginning — in this event, the allegations made by the bank. On their surface, are they reliable? In this case, the date of the loan and the dates of the financial statements that the bank claimed to have relied upon should have triggered questions in the minds of the two other expert witnesses. They were so intent upon proving negligence and incompetence of the accused CPA that they missed the real issue, even though they were correct in their judgment of the work of the auditor.

6.10   Sometimes the Accounting Expert Witness Must Concentrate on Facts and Forget Accounting

A truck manufacturer with global sales sold trucks to its United States dealers for 70% of list price. If the list price was $100,000, the dealer's cost would be $70,000. Generally, the dealer would seek to add 10% to its cost for profit. Therefore, the dealer's minimum selling price would be $77,000 and its maximum selling price would be $100,000. This left a spread of $23,000 for negotiation with the customer.

The manufacturer also granted its dealers a holdback commission of 2% of the list price, or $2,000. This commission was paid to the dealer in the year following the year of sale by crediting the $2,000 to the dealer's parts bill from the manufacturer.

Dealer A was located in an extremely competitive trading area for over-the-road truck sales. To meet the prices of his competition, he had to offer his trucks for a price that was less than his minimum selling price of $77,000. To attract a large fleet buyer who wanted to buy 12 truck tractors, the dealer was forced to sell a truck below his cost, or, for example, $68,000. In the following year, the holdback commission of $2,000 would lower his cost to $68,000 so there would be no gain or loss. To make a profit, Dealer A — or any other dealer — could ask the manufacturer for sales assistance.

A sales assistance calculation can be tabulated in the following manner:

DEALER'S:	
LIST PRICE	$100,000
COST–70% OF LIST	70,000
ADD-ON FOR MINIMUM SELLING PRICE	7,000
MINIMUM SP	$ 77,000
NEGOTIATING RANGE	$ 23,000
DEALER'S HOLDBACK COMMISSION TO BE CREDITED TO PARTS:	
2% OF LIST OR	$ 2,000
DEALER COULD SELL 100 TRUCKS TO FLEET BUYER AT $68,000 EACH:	
DEALER'S COST AFTER SALES ASSISTANCE	$ 70,000
HOLDBACK – 2%	2,000
NET COST	68,000
GROSS PROFIT	-0-
MANUFACTURER'S SALES ASSISTANCE:	$ 4,000
DEALER'S COST	$66,000
2% HOLDBACK	2,000
NET COST	64,000
GAIN	$ 4,000

A large fleet buyer negotiated with Dealer A to order 100 trucks at a price of $68,000 each. Dealer A asked the manufacturer for sales assistance so he could still make a profit. Through its sales assistance program, the manufacturer offered to discount the cost another $4,000 based on Dealer A's assurance that he could sell them only for $68,000. This allowed Dealer A to earn a profit of $4,000 on each truck and helped him to acquire a customer that would become important. The manufacturer did not want its dealers to incur losses and was, therefore, willing to reduce its own profit.

The manufacturer would credit the amount of the sales assistance to Dealer A's parts bill after it had examined the transaction to determine that the selling price was $68,000 or less. If the dealer charged more — for example, $70,000, then the manufacturer would reduce its sales assistance by $2,000. At $70,000 with $2,000 of sales assistance, the dealer would still have realized a $4,000 profit.

Dealer A's sale of 100 trucks to the fleet buyer turned out to have been wishful thinking on his part. The buyer did not complete negotiations and bought a different make of truck. Dealer A did not notify the manufacturer of the change and was able to sell the trucks a few at a time priced in excess of $77,000. When the manufacturer discovered this, it refused to credit the $4,000 of truck sales assistance to Dealer A's parts bill.

Dealer A sued the manufacturer in Federal District Court. He alleged that the manufacturer was forcing him to sell trucks for $68,000 to receive a credit. The jury agreed with the plaintiff that the manufacturer was guilty of price fixing in violation of Section One of the Sherman Antitrust Act. They awarded the plaintiff $300,000. This amounted to $900,000 in treble damages plus attorney's fees and costs of $213,000 for a total of $1,113,000. Because the manufacturer had 531 domestic dealers, the potential liability was a minimum of about $591,000,000 to billions of dollars.

The manufacturer appealed to the 8th Circuit Court of Appeals. The manufacturer's law firm hired a forensic accountant to assist with the petition of appeal. They had provided him with a roomful of accounting records from both the original plaintiff and defendant. After reading the trial and deposition transcripts, the expert told the defendant's attorneys that he would not need to review the records that they had used in the District Court.

The expert explained that the concept of sales assistance was not to fix prices. It was only a plan by the manufacturer to hold its dealers free from losses on excessively discounted sales to meet competition. Once the dealer set the selling price, the manufacturer was willing to lower the dealer's cost to enable it to make an adequate profit. After receiving sales assistance, if the dealer then increased the selling price, it was obvious that it did not need as much sales assistance as it had originally requested. Therefore, although the manufacturer reduced the sales assistance, it had never fixed the selling price. The dealer was free to sell for any price.

The attorneys included this explanation in the appeal petition. Citing this language, the circuit court reversed the district court. The U.S. Supreme Court upheld the circuit court.

6.10.1   What Went Wrong in the District Court Trial?

The transcripts of the proceedings and of the depositions clearly revealed that no one at the trial was able to explain or understand sales assistance. The testimony of the defendant's officers made it sound as if they had engaged in price fixing. The petitioner's testimony upheld a charge of price fixing. The attorneys for both parties did not understand sales assistance, so they were unable to ask penetrating questions on direct- or cross-examination to help rebut the price fixing charge. The judge and the jury did not understand sales assistance, so a guilty verdict was rendered.

This entire case revolved around an explanation of sales assistance in language that would prevent the assumption that the manufacturer had engaged in price fixing. Sometimes, we must forget accounting and concentrate on the facts in existence before we examine accounting records. Always read the charges and answers before examining detailed accounting records and documents.

6.11   Can a Deposition Be Perfect?

The following deposition is the only case where we did not change names. The purpose is to allow readers to learn of the flaws of the authors. One mistatement can create unforseen problems. In this deposition, Zeph Telpner gave testimony using a case that involved a refrigerated motor carrier, Little Audreys. (It no longer exists.) Little Audrey's was a party in the litigation. The actual case was *Kizzier v. United States, 598 F.2d 1128 (8th Cir. 1979).* When the Department of Justice (DOJ) attorney asked me about it, I couldn't remember the case name so I called it the Little Audrey's case.

Although I had the right case but the wrong name, the U.S. DOJ attorney used this as a basis for a 49-page Motion In Limine to disqualify me as the expert for the plaintiff, Boles Trucking, Inc. Among other accusations, the government alleged that I was "fundamentally ignorant" and should not be allowed to testify. I am pleased to state that in the hearing on this motion before a federal district court judge, the judge ruled that I was not fundamentally ignorant. That ruling is my proudest legacy. I would have suffered untold embarrassment if a Federal Court had ruled that I had lost all my knowledge and was fundamentally ignorant. When you review this deposition, you will realize that my depositions are no better than the ones I have analyzed in this and other chapters. One name has been changed so the person will not be identified.

In this case, plaintiff was Boles Trucking, and the defendant was the USA. The deposition was taken at the request of the defendant. Zeph Telpner was deposed in the law offices of Michael Mostek, attorney for Boles, in Omaha, Nebraska.

Appearing for the plaintiff were Howard N. Kaplan and Michael S. Mostek, attorneys at law with McGILL et al., and, for the defendant, Robert D. Metcalfe, senior trial attorney with the United States Department of Justice Tax Division. Mr. David Boles was also present. Unless questions and answers are credited otherwise, **Q** refers to Metcalfe and **A** is the expert witness Zeph Telpner.

6.11.1   Direct Examination

By Metcalfe (Q):

Q. Sir, I would like to ask you to state your full name and spell the last name, please.

A. My name is Zeph, is the first name and Telpner, T-e-l-p-n-e-r.

Q. And while we're at it why don't we go ahead and have you spell your full legal first name? (*I had given my business card to the court reporter also.*)

A. Z-e-p-h.

Q. Do you have a middle initial?

A. No.

Q. Where do you live at the present time?

A. Council Bluffs, Iowa.

Q. Could you give me a street address?

A. 8 DeLong Avenue, Council Bluffs, Iowa.

Q. Is that D-e-l-o-n-g?

A. Yes.

Q. And how long have you resided there?

A. 8 DeLong, about 15 years.

Q. Are you presently employed?

A. Self-employed.

Q. What is your profession?

A. CPA.

Q. When you say "CPA," do you mean a certified public accountant?

A. Yes.

Q. And in what jurisdictions are you licensed as a certified public accountant?

A. Nebraska and Iowa.

Q. How long have you been self-employed as a CPA?

A. About 30 years.

Q. Have you always worked for yourself?

A. No.

Q. When I asked you how long have you been self-employed, I was confused when you said afterwards that you hadn't been self-employed all of those 30 years. Was there a time when you were employed by a firm?

A. Yes. Before I was self-employed, I was employed by Arthur Andersen, then I was a partner in a firm: Telpner, Bernstein, Friedman, & Tighe. Bernstein, Friedman & Tighe later merged with Elmer Fox and I merged with Peat, Marwick, Mitchell.

Q. Peat, Marwick, Mitchell?

A. Yes, at the time. Now I think it's KPMG or something like that.

Q. Are you on your own right now?

A. Yes, I am.

Q. How long have you essentially been operating as a solo practitioner or solo CPA?

A. About 30 years.

Q. Were you ever employed by the Internal Revenue?

A. Yes, I was, to teach a couple of seminars as an outside contractor.

Q. Have you ever been employed as either a revenue agent or a revenue officer examiner by the Internal Revenue Service?

A. No.

Q. When was the last time you were associated with an accounting firm?

A. Well, I, gosh, I think it was about ... see, I've had consulting agreements with ... it was about '87 or '88. I had one with McDermott & Miller for about 2 years, but I still had my own practice.

Q. I'm more familiar with the way law firms are operated than accounting firms. Do accounting firms have the same distinction between partners and associates the way a law firm might?

A. I don't know what distinction a law firm makes between ...

Q. Is there such a thing as an associate accountant in an accounting firm?

A. Well, yes. Sometimes, let's take Arthur Andersen, for example, and Peat, Marwick, Mitchell. I can compare those two. A brand-new accountant was called an assistant at Arthur Andersen and a junior at Peat, Marwick, Mitchell.

Q. I understand.

A. They had seniors at Arthur Andersen. It's changed now, at the time and supervisors at Peat, Marwick, Mitchell. They had seniors, but they had a higher level between senior and a manager called a supervisor. Arthur Andersen didn't have the term supervisor. They had manager, which would be M Class 1 through 5, with 1 being the lowest. One (1) and two (2) would be equivalent to Peat, Marwick's supervisor. And associates — well, I guess a principal would be a non-CPA, who is almost equivalent to a partner. He was the guy that just couldn't pass the exam, but they thought he was good enough to be a partner, so they called him a principal. Didn't share in the liabilities, but got a percentage of profits. And then I have what I call associates. I mean, it's different from other people.

Q. When did you obtain your license as a certified public accountant in Nebraska?

A. 1962, February. February is when I passed the CPA exam. I probably didn't get a permit to practice then because I was still with Arthur Andersen and you didn't, nobody at Arthur Andersen got a permit to practice except a partner at Arthur Andersen. So, it was probably 1963.

Q. When you became a certified public accountant in Nebraska?

A. No. I was a certified public accountant in Nebraska in 1962, but you have to have every year also a permit to practice under your own name. Otherwise, Arthur Andersen owned the permit to practice, so —

Q. Have you continuously held a permit to practice in Nebraska' as a CPA since 1963?

A. No, I think I registered as not in practice for one year. I was only — I didn't do any audits at the time of financial statements, so I didn't need to have a permit. But I've been continuously in Iowa.

(The deposition pages that followed were originally used to determine Telpner's work experience and qualifications over a 35-year period. They are omitted here for purposes of brevity.)

Q. Could you give me some type of idea as to exactly what you have done as a certified public accountant since, let's say, 1967, when you've pretty much been on your own?

A. Okay. I've audited, prepared tax returns, written protests before the appeals office of the IRS. The first case I ever worked on in litigation was in '66, as a master in chancery. Most of my work since about '74 has been tax and litigation and investigative accounting. Oh and continuing professional education. So, I prepared and taught continuing professional education for CPAs in approximately 26 state CPA associations and for the Internal Revenue Service.

Q. Are you familiar with the term "forensic accounting"?

A. Yes, I am.

Q. Does any part of your practice deal with what is called "forensic accounting"?

A. Yes, it does.

Q. How long have you been involved in that field?

A. Well, the first case I had was in 1966 and that was forensic accounting. As a master in chancery, I had to find facts for the court, so that the court could make a decision. I wasn't — I was a representative of the court and I've had cases in which there were so many law firms involved that the court appointed another law firm as a special administrator, who hired me to find the facts. I have been a special master and then I've been called in several times to help either a plaintiff or a defendant, the lawyers for them have asked me to come in.

Q. A master in chancery. I'm not familiar with that. Is that something in the Nebraska or Iowa courts?

A. No, that's — actually, it's interesting, because I said, what's a master in chancery? And a lawyer said, one of them told me, he said, well, we don't know. We studied it in law school. A master in chancery started out in England. I know about that because I had to find out. It's where we have, where the Court had an issue. This is an accounting issue, the first one. It was a, a painter and a paint supplier and a construction company got together. They were going to paint houses and split the profit. And the construction company, the contractor said the profit's $400 and the other people thought it was $30,000. So, it was technical accounting to determine what it was, so the Judge appointed me to find out.

Q. Okay, I see. Was this a state judge or a federal judge?

A. This was a state judge.

Q. Do you recall if it was in Iowa or Nebraska?

A. It was in Iowa.

Q. When you said before that you had done audits or that you audited, do I take that to mean that you audited financial statements?

A. Yeah, back in the '60s.

Q. Have you done that recently?

A. No, I haven't done that, a certified financial audit, since 1973.

Q. Do you hold any designations other than that as a CPA?

A. None. No, I — none that I can think of.

Q. Do you still prepare tax returns?

A. Oh, about 20.

Q. Are these what are called U.S. Individual Income Tax Returns or Forms 1040?

A. I have, all except one.

Q. What was that?

A. 1120S.

Q. Which would be an income tax return for an S corporation?

A. Yeah. And I have maybe two 1065s and a couple of 1041s.

Q. A 1065 would be a partnership return?

A. Partnership. And 1041 is a fiduciary income tax return.

Q. How long have you been preparing those tax returns?

A. You mean in general?

Q. Those types, yes.

A. Any tax returns or ...

Q. Yes.

A. Just those? Okay. The first tax return I ever prepared, I think it was in 1956. That was my first part-time accounting job. I'm not a kid.

Q. Well, I was born in 1956, so that goes back a ways.

A. Because back in those years when I was a student I worked for Bozell & Jacobs in the accounting department, and for John Begley, who was the head of the accounting department at Creighton.

Q. Would it be fair to say that within the last 10 years you have continued to prepare what are called U.S. Individual Income Tax Returns or Form 1040s for individuals in this area here in Omaha and Council Bluffs? Have you continued to do that?

A. Yes, I've prepared tax returns.

Q. But you don't seem to be preparing very many these days. Is that true?

A. Yeah, I don't choose to prepare very many. I like to research.

Q. I've heard the word or the term "controversy work." You've used the term "written protest." Would that be pretty much the same thing?

A. Well, when you write a protest and it appeared before the appeal's office …

Q. Right.

A. Would it be the same as … what?

Q. What is called by lawyers sometimes "controversy work"?

A. As a CPA?

Q. You're not familiar with that term?

A. No, I don't think of that. What happens is you have a taxpayer and your taxpayer is reviewed by an Internal Revenue agent and they adjust it so you have a right to file a protest against those adjustments and I've done a lot of that type of work.

Q. So, the protest would be in response to either a revenue agent's report or a 30-day letter?

A. Yeah.

Q. Have you done any of those type of things in the last, say, 10 years?

A. Yes, I'm sure I have, but I can't remember. I don't do a lot of those any more because I concentrate on forensic accounting.

Q. Could you tell me what your educational background has been?

A. Do you want me to start with college or with … ?

Q. Please.

A. Okay. B.S., Bachelor of Science in Business Administration from Creighton University.

Q. I understand they didn't have a B.S. in Accounting at that time.

A. Well, they called it Bachelor of Science in Commerce, when I started, BSC, but when I got out I started midyear, so I had to take one course, I think, in 1958 to get out and by then they had changed it to business administration. But it was the old school of commerce when I started.

Q. When did you get your bachelor's degree? What year?

A. That was 1958 when I received that.

Q. And have you received any degrees subsequent to that?

A. No.

Q. I take it since 1958 you have participated in what are called CLE courses or continuing legal education courses?

A. Continuing professional educational courses. That's what CPAs call it. I've taught them for 26 states. I've taught at the University of Nebraska in Omaha and Iowa Western Community College.

Q. Over the last, say, 10 to 15 years, can you tell me some of the subjects you've taught as part of your CPE?

A. Just how to research and write a protest, accounting for the trucking industry, how to borrow from the Internal Revenue Service, purchase, sale and liquidation of partnerships. The substance of examinations I wrote and provided to the IRS. I'm, I'm trying to think of some of them. The Bankruptcy Tax Act, I gave one on that a long time ago. That's, that's about all I can think of. There were 22 all together but, you know, some of them don't go over.

Q. Are you familiar with what is called a power of attorney form or a Form 2848?

A. Yes.

Q. Could you tell me when was the last time that you represented a client before the Internal Revenue Service under a power of attorney or a Form 2848?

A. Oh, a couple of years ago. Maybe a year ago.

Q. 1991 or 1992?

A. Yeah. But, see, I had surgery. I got sick in '91 and I had quadruple bypass so I was off work for a while. I didn't represent many people for a period of time. I've been misdiagnosed by five physicians. By the time I got to the doctor I was dying, actually, so I was off work for a while in those years.

Q. What kind of matter was that when you were representing someone before the IRS under a power of attorney in 1991 or 1992?

A. Well, the last one — well, let's see, '90 would have been a protest that I was asked to help with another accounting firm. In '91 it would have been, the first part before I had my surgery and then part of '90 would have been on a fiduciary return had a fiscal year and the IRS, inadvertently, couldn't find it.

Q. The Form 1041?

A. Well, they couldn't find the fiduciary return. I sent it to them three times and they finally got it. Some of the cases I handled as a delinquent application for tax exempt status., which I got a nice letter from the national office telling me I did a good job on it. I take my work very seriously.

Q. I'm sure you do, sir. None of my questions here are meant to question your competence or anything like that.

A. Oh, I understand that. I just said that because I really like this work.

Q. Did you ever write a protest either to a revenue agent report or to a 30-day letter with respect to any matter involving federal employment taxes?

A. I don't recall writing a protest on federal employment taxes.

Q. Okay. Let me make sure we understand what we're talking about here when we talk about federal employment taxes. I'm talking about what are called FICA taxes, social security taxes, federal withholdings. Do you understand when I'm talking about federal employment taxes that's what I'm referring to? Do you also consider those to be?

A. Yes, I certainly do.

Q. Would it be fair to say that your background as a CPA, insofar as it relates to federal tax matters, is mostly concerned with federal income taxes?

A. No, that wouldn't be fair to say that.

Q. Why not?

A. Because I have done a lot of research writing a protest on other taxes. In fact, in 1986, Arthur Andersen hired me to write a checklist for their auditors, 18 pages, on examination of taxes other than income taxes.

Q. What other types of taxes were these?

A. You have unemployment taxes, FICA and FUTA, SUTA, you have telephone Watts line taxes, you know, interstate carrier. You have sales taxes, use taxes, you had heavy highway use taxes and then in '82, with the Surface Transportation Act, we got the federal sales tax, the 12% sales tax. And then I taught about other taxes; operating taxes in my trucking course. In fact, I have a letter from Commercial Carriers telling me that I saved them money. They thought it was the first course they had ever been to that they made a profit on. And that was on taxes; property taxes, sales taxes, you know, payroll taxes.

Q. Excise taxes?

A. Yes, excise taxes.

Q. Such as highway and motor vehicle use taxes?

A. Yes, fuel taxes. I taught in there about reciprocity and prorate. You know, you discuss reciprocity and prorate in there. And state income taxes. You know, a lot of CPAs don't know much about state income taxes, but in the trucking industry you have some real problems with that.

Q. Mr. Telpner, as a CPA did you ever represent a client before the Internal Revenue Service in connection with an employment tax audit or examination by the IRS?

A. No, not that I can recall. State unemployment tax, yes, but not federal. (*Actually, I had, but I had forgotten them.*)

Q. Do you know what the acronym FICA stands for?

A. Federal Insurance Contributions Act, but I haven't heard it called that for years.

Q. Are you familiar with what are called Employer's Quarterly Federal Tax Returns?

A. 941s.

Q. I'll take that as a "Yes"?

A. Yes.

Q. Okay. Have you ever prepared an Employer's Quarterly Federal Tax Return for a client?

A. Yes.

Q. When was the last time you did that?

A. I don't know.

Q. Was it more than 10 years ago?

A. I don't know. I think it was less than 10 years ago.

Q. But you're not sure?

A. Not sure.

Q. Do you know what FUTA taxes are?

A. Federal Unemployment Tax Act.

Q. Have you ever prepared any Federal Unemployment Tax Returns for a client?

A. Yes.

Q. And when was the last time you did that?

A. I don't know. May I amplify here why I don't prepare a lot of those things?

Q. Certainly.

A. I've always thought it was ridiculous to hire me and pay my fees to prepare a tax return like that when any client can learn how to do it, so I taught them to do that. They're very simple returns.

Q. Mr. Telpner, do you claim to have any familiarity or knowledge of the procedures employed by the Internal Revenue Service in conducting employment tax examinations?

A. Just in information that I've read written up in journals of taxation and accounting magazines and so forth and the American Institute of CPAs they sent out some time ago, yes.

Q. Can you recall the names of any articles or publications that have given you any knowledge or familiarity with the procedures employed by the IRS in conducting employment tax examinations?

A. I can recall names of the periodicals, but I can't tell you the names of the articles. *Motor Freight Controller, Journal of Taxation, Journal of Accountancy, Transport Topics,* American Institute of CPAs, Tax Division releases or pronouncements, New York University Annual Institute on taxation. Commerce Clearing House loose-leaf reporting service, you know, stuff like that. And some court cases, court decisions. I can't think of the names of them though. And if there's any more, I just can't think of them right now.

Q. Are you familiar with the provisions of the Internal Revenue Manual as they relate to the conduct of employment tax examinations by the IRS?

A. Insofar as I receive them from the American Institute of CPA's Tax Division, yes. I didn't receive the entire manual.

Q. Have you been retained by Boles Trucking, Inc., to testify as an expert witness in a trial in a case called Boles Trucking, Inc. vs. United States?

A. Yes. Let me ask a question. May I ask you a question, Mike?

Mostek: Yes.
Telpner: You contacted me ...
Mostek: I think I can clarify it. He is retained by my firm. And we retained him on behalf of Boles Trucking.

Q. When was that?

A. Well, I don't know. It could have been — when they first contacted me it might have been last November or December. It may have been. I don't know for sure.

Q. Mr. Tepner, are you currently ...

A. Pardon me, it's "Telpner."

Q. "Telpner." Pardon me. Mr. Telpner, are you currently prepared to provide the court or a jury with an expert opinion relative to the liability of the plaintiff, Boles Trucking, Incorporated for certain federal employment taxes that were assessed against it for taxable quarters between January 1st of 1984 and December 31st of 1987?

A. Yes.

Q. Can you tell me what your field of expertise is with respect to this matter?

A. Well, I'm an acknowledged expert on the trucking industry and accounting and taxes in the trucking industry and tax research. And forensic accounting, investigative accounting, find out what happened.

Q. When you say you're an "acknowledged expert," can you tell me what you mean by that?

A. By other CPAs. In 1980, Arthur Andersen bought a lot of my ongoing trucking work. I was also appointed the examiner of Best Refrigerated Express bankruptcy. I testified in Greensboro, North Carolina for the Mason and Dixon Line. I have done work for the Central State's Pension

Fund on their multi-employer pension plan withdrawal lawsuits. I've testified in the federal courts on certain tax matters in North Carolina, Pennsylvania, Nebraska, Iowa. I can't remember where else.

Q. So, if I understand what you have told me correctly, you have been accepted as an expert by certain federal district courts in certain cases in the past; is that correct?

A. Yes, that's correct.

Q. Have you ever been accepted as an expert by any federal district court in any case involving federal employment taxes?

A. Not that I can recall. I would say no.

Q. These other cases where you testified as an expert, how many of them involved matters relating to, let's say, corporate income taxes?

A. Greensboro, North Carolina is one. That's probably the only one, Greensboro, North Carolina. Most of them had to do with withdrawal liabilities, things that took research. But there just haven't been too many adjustments in corporate employment taxes that I'm familiar with — or anybody's familiar with in my profession.

Q. So I understand this, could you tell me how, as a CPA …

A. Yes.

Q. … your professional training and background and experience qualifies you as an expert in any matters relating to federal employment taxes?

A. Yes, I can. Almost my entire professional accounting life has had to do with taxes. Income taxes, operating taxes. Many times I've had to research payroll taxes to give clients advice, then they end up in court. Many times I've had to research payroll taxes, unemployment taxes to teach my students about them. Because quite often when you act as a professor or teacher you do a lot of research, but you never happen to have it in court. So, I've given advice on this. I've dealt with state tax commissions because that's where I used to see most types of adjustments like that. But, never have I happened to have seen an adjustment or very many adjustments or very many cases on unemployment taxes. There just haven't been many in my career. And I'm sure that there's not near as many as there are in many other tax fields. But, I can research it, I can look it up and I can understand the Internal Revenue Code. I can understand the citations to the rulings, the cumulative bulletins, the treasury decisions, the district court, the circuit court, the Court of Claims and the Court of Appeals cases and New York University, Tulane Tax Institute. The reason I'm saying all this is because I do speak, myself, in tax matters. I really like tax, I can tell you, in this type of accounting.

Q. Would it be a fair statement to say that most of your familiarity with federal employment taxes comes from the research that you have done into statutes, the treasury regulations, the revenue rulings, revenue procedures, court cases and the like, as opposed to actually representing clients before the IRS?

A. I'd say I've been very lucky that nobody's had to adjust anything I've done in that matter, so, yes.

Q. Without telling us what your opinion is, can you tell us whether you have formed an opinion as to whether the truck drivers who performed services for Boles Trucking, Inc., during the period between January 1st of 1984 and December 31st of 1987 were independent contractors or employees, for federal employment tax purposes? I'm just asking if you've formed an opinion.

A. I have a problem with that question …

Q. Okay.

A. … and the way it's stated, though.

Mostek: Do you want to state it again?
Telpner: Well, could I …

Q. Could you just tell us what the problem is?

A. Could you read back the … could I ask him to read back the last three sentences or the last part of that sentence you gave?

Metcalfe: Why don't we have you read back the whole question.
(Whereupon, the requested portion of the testimony was read back by the court reporter.)
Telpner: I have formed an opinion.

Q. So your answer would be "yes"?

A. Yes.

Q. Are you aware that the Commissioner of Internal Revenue following an employment tax examination of the plaintiff, Boles Trucking, Incorporated, reclassified certain of its truck drivers who performed services for the corporation during the period between January 1st, 1984 and December 31st, 1987, as employees for federal employment tax purposes?

A. Yes, I'm aware of that.

Q. Okay. And how are you made aware of this, the reclassification?

A. I saw a copy of a claim for refund for taxes that disagreed with the reclassification.

Q. Was that a, to the best of your knowledge, was that a protest or a claim for refund that was authored by Mr. Truman Clare, to your knowledge?

A. I don't have any knowledge of that.

Q. Did you ever read any report or revenue agent report or revenue officer examiner report submitted by an employee of the IRS, in connection with Boles Trucking?

A. I did. That was over here. Yes, I did.

Q. And you're aware that certain federal employment taxes and unemployment taxes have been assessed against the plaintiff for the taxable quarters in periods between January 1st of 1984 and December 31st of 1987?

A. Yes, I am aware.

Q. Did you participate in any way in the employment tax examination that was conducted of Boles Trucking, Inc., by the Internal Revenue Service?

A. May I hear that question again?

Q. Certainly. Did you participate in any way or fashion in the employment tax examination that was conducted of Boles Trucking, Inc., by the Internal Revenue Service?

A. No.

Q. You didn't represent Boles Trucking in connection with the employment tax examination or audit?

A. No.

Q. Do you know when this employment tax examination of Boles Trucking, Inc., by the Internal Revenue Service was commenced or when it was finished?

A. No, I don't remember the dates in that report.

Q. Did you ever discuss the federal employment tax examination of Boles Trucking, Inc., with any officer or employee of the Internal Revenue Service?

A. No.

Q. Would it have been helpful to you in the formulation of your opinion as to whether the truck drivers of Boles Trucking were independent contractors or employees, for federal employment tax purposes, if you could have discussed this employment tax examination with the revenue office examiner who performed the employment tax examination?

A. No.

Q. Why not?

A. Because they had a thorough report and I was able to read that.

Q. When you say it was a thorough report, what do you mean by that?

A. Explained what they, as I recall, explained what they did and I think gave reasoning for why they did it. I can't remember now, but I got all the information I needed on that.

Q. During the period of time between January 1st of 1984 and December 31st of 1987, did you provide any accounting services or advice either to Boles Trucking, Inc., or to Bruce Boles?

A. No.

Q. You know who Bruce Boles is, don't you?

A. Yes, I do now. He's sitting there, yeah.

Q. When did you first meet Mr. Boles?

A. I don't recall. The last couple of months maybe. I'd have to look at my appointment calendar to see.

Q. Would it be fair to say that the first contact you had with Boles Trucking, Inc., came when you were retained as an expert sometime in, let's say, November, December of last year?

A. The first contact I had with …

Q. With Boles Trucking, Inc.

A. Yes. Yes.

Q. Mr. Telpner, do you have any personal knowledge of the terms and conditions under which certain truck drivers provided services to Boles Trucking, Inc., between January 1st of 1984 and December 31st of 1987?

A. What does "personal knowledge" mean? Talking with drivers or, or reading the documents?

Q. Talking to them, direct observation of how they performed their functions and duties.

A. No, I — just from what I've read in the depositions and the, the contract.

Q. Have you ever talked to any of the truck drivers who provided services to Boles Trucking, Inc., during …

A. No, I haven't. No, I haven't.

Q. … during the period of time between January 1st of 1984 and December 31st of 1987? Any of the truck drivers, have you talked to any of the truck drivers who were working during that period of time for Boles Trucking?

A. Not that I know of. I, I didn't know anything. I had never heard the name before even.

Q. So, you never met, for example, with William Morganthaler or Joyce Morganthaler?

A. No.

Q. Have you ever met Carl Ewart, E-w-a-r-t?

A. No.

Q. Or Ryan Clifford?

A. No.

Q. Okay. You've never met any of those people?

A. No.

Q. Okay. Would that have been helpful to you in arriving at any expert opinion concerning the status of those truck drivers for federal employment tax purposes?

A. No.

Q. Why not?

A. Because I read the depositions that were asked by — the questions of them that were asked by expert attorneys and they were under oath, so I, I accepted that.

Q. Would it be fair to say you have formed more than one expert opinion in this case?

A. I, I, I've got to think about that, if it's all part of one opinion or if it's — my, my — I'd say yes.

Q. Okay. Why don't I just ask you to give us whatever opinions you have actually formed as an expert in this case. Can you do that?

A. Yes. I'll be glad to give you my opinions. One, I'm talking about the truck drivers. Boles Trucking, Inc., is not the employer of the truck drivers that are involved here.

Q. Okay.

A. Cornhusker Motor Freight is the employer or was the employer of the truck drivers. Therefore, Boles Trucking, Inc., would owe none of the taxes that would accrue on the drivers' payroll, nor for any of the related penalties.

Q. Okay. Is that like one opinion?

A. Well, I divided it into three like that.

Q. Okay.

A. I was having problems with that expert opinion, whether that was one or whether it was three. But those were three. If you want it in one opinion, it could be. I don't care. But they are three different things, though.

Q. Isn't it three different things in what you've just told me?

A. No, no, no.

Mostek: You're asking him is that one opinion or three. It doesn't really matter, it's just …

Telpner: I gave you three different sentences, in effect.

Q. Oh, I see, I see, I see. I'm a little slow. Do you have any other opinions that you have formed as an expert in this case?

A. Yes.

Q. Could you tell me what those are?

A. That Boles Trucking, Inc. and Bruce Boles had reasonable basis to treat the drivers the way that both of them did.

Q. Okay. When you say it had a reasonable basis for treating the drivers, do you mean had a reasonable basis for treating the drivers as independent contractors for federal employment tax purposes?

A. As treating them as not being their employees at all, for federal tax purposes.

Q. Would that be with reference to Section 530 of the Revenue Act of 1978?

A. Yes.

Q. Do you have any other opinions?'

A. You know, when you're asking me that, really this is difficult. I haven't thought of some of the things I've done as being separate opinions, so could you help me with that a little bit?

Q. Sure.

A. Because I've done a lot of work and and I've been involved in trucking for a good number of years.

Q. Obviously, Mr. Telpner, I get from your testimony thus far that you looked at a good deal of documents, employment tax examination reports, protests, maybe some of the pleadings in this case. Certainly, the depositions of some of the drivers and perhaps some of the people who testified in this case; is that right?

A. That's correct.

Q. And based upon that you formulated certain opinions as to what, if any, federal employment tax consequences there were to Boles Trucking or to some other entity?

A. That's correct.

Q. Other than what you have given me thus far, did you reach any other conclusions or form any other opinions with respect to the federal employment tax liabilities of Boles Trucking for the period we've been talking about here between 1984 and 1987?

A. Yes, I did. But maybe it would be helpful to you if I gave you my trucking background. I don't think you ever asked me about my trucking background.

Q. We're going to get to that. I promise we'll get to that. But I'm just interested right now in other opinions that you may have, other conclusions you may have reached. And we've talked about whether or not Boles Trucking is the employer and we've talked about reasonable basis for treating the drivers under Section 530 of the Revenue Act of 1978. Were there any other conclusions or impressions or opinions?

A. Yes. I also based it on a prior decision by the Nebraska Department of Labor or Unemployment Commission. I can't remember which it is.

Q. Nebraska Department of Revenue perhaps?

A. No, it wasn't. The Nebraska — I think it was — was it the unemployment compensation department …

Mostek: (Counsel indicating by moving head up and down.)
Telpner: — down in –
Mostek: Labor.
Telpner: Department of Labor?
Metcalfe: I stand corrected.
Telpner: Whatever it was, you know what it is.
Mostek: Could we take a brief recess?
Metcalfe: Sure.
Telpner: I can't think of the name, either.
Metcalfe: We're off the record.
(Whereupon, a short recess was had.)
Metcalfe: Back on the record.

Q. Mr. Telpner, I'm trying to understand the substance of your opinion as an expert in this case here. Would it be your testimony as an expert in this case that the truck drivers, themselves, without regard to whether they were employees of Cornhusker Motor Lines or Boles Trucking, but just looking at them, themselves, the truck drivers who were performing these services during this period between 1984 and 1987, would it be your testimony that these individuals were employees, for federal employment tax purposes, under the, what are called the usual common law rules?

A. Go on.

Q. Would that be your conclusion?

A. That they were employees of whom?

Q. I'm not asking whether they were employees of any particular individual, but just looking at what they did by themselves, applying the 20 common law factors. You're familiar with that, are you not?

A. Yes. Yes, very familiar.

Q. Under that analysis, which is also known as the usual common law rules, applying that analysis to what these people actually did, these truck drivers actually did between 1984 and 1987, would it be your testimony that those individuals were employees, for federal employment tax purposes?

A. It's my opinion they were employees, for federal income tax purposes, of Cornhusker Motor Carriers, or whatever the name is.

Q. Cornhusker Motor Lines?

A. Cornhusker — what's the exact name of it? I can't — suddenly I got tongue tied. I couldn't think of it.

Q. I think it's Cornhusker Motor Lines. But we all know it's Cornhusker, right?

A. Yeah. Yeah, that's — yes.

Q. And you're pretty sure of that opinion?

A. Yes.

Q. Now, I brought up the issue of 20 common law factors or rules. Do you know what those are?

A. Yes, I do.

Q. Can you give me your understanding of what those are?

A. The Internal Revenue Service has ruled and it wasn't based just on a ruling, but based on some prior Court decision that there has to be a method to determine whether someone is an employee of yours, or whether he's an independent contractor. They list 20 rules as a rule of thumb. Not necessarily an exception to it, but 20 things to determine whether or not a person is an employee or independent contractor.

Q. Could you tell me out of those 20 factors which is the most important?

A: It would be helpful if you stuck it in front of me so I'd know what the other 20 factors are, but I'd say the most important are the — what the industry does. If there's a reasonable basis for relying on a decision to treat them as an independent contractor versus as an employee. What some of the other court decisions have been. You know, legal interpretations, industry interpretations and tradition. I think those are important. What's really been happening.

Q. But just focusing on the 20 common law factors, you indicated that you were familiar with those; is that correct?

A. Yes, but I would need them in front of me. It would be very helpful. My memory is not …

Q. Is it your testimony then that the most important of those 20 common law factors would be industry practice or custom?

A. No, I didn't say, mean that. I meant those are some I could think of right now. But without those 20 questions in front of me I'm going to have a heck of a time. There may be two or three others that I felt were very important, but they don't register right now.

Q. Believe me, Mr. Telpner, I'm glad no one is asking me these questions.

A. Well, you could give them to me and I could tell you.

Q. When I use the term "employee by statute," does that have any meaning to you?

A. You mean like a statutory employee?

Q. Well, there's statutory employees. There's certain people who are statutory employees that are specifically mentioned as employees for federal employment tax purposes.

A. All right.

Q. … in the Internal Revenue Code and you're familiar with that?

A. Yes.

Q. But when I use the term "employee by statute," I'm talking about a person who bears such a relationship to a corporation or business. In other words, they're a corporate officer, such as a president, vice president, secretary, who performs such services for the corporation of such a magnitude and duration that they must be regarded, for federal tax purposes, as employees. Are you familiar with that concept at all?

A. Yes, I am.

Q. Okay. Did you ever form any opinion as to whether David B. Boles, also known as Bruce Boles, was an employee by statute with respect to Boles Trucking, Inc.?

A. I haven't finished my review of that issue yet.

Q. Do you have any tentative conclusions or opinions?

A. No. No, I don't.

Q. Do you know of any fact or document or anything of that nature which would tend to indicate to you that Bruce Boles was not an employee by statute of Boles Trucking, Inc.?

A. Do I know of any?

Q. Right.

A. No, I don't. I haven't finished my review.

Q. Were there any particular documents that led you to conclude that the truck drivers that we've been talking about here were employees of Cornhusker Motor Lines during the period between 1984 and 1987?

A. The depositions I read, the contract between Cornhusker and Boles Trucking, what it said was different from what actually happened, according to the depositions from the drivers and also the document, the report by the State of Nebraska. Certain Supreme Court decisions and I can't name them right now and appeals court, district court, federal and some state decision, certain treatises written by experts in the field and what was happening in the industry and the ICC, the motor carrier statutes, et cetera. What was happening in the industry from about 1965 through about 1986 or '87?

Q. I'd like to go back and visit with you on the opinions that you have given us and make sure that I've gotten all of them. With respect to the first opinion that you mentioned that Boles Trucking, Inc. was not the employer of certain truck drivers between 1984 and 1987, for federal employment tax purposes; have I stated that correctly, that Boles Trucking was not the employer of those truck drivers?

A. Yes, you stated that, but I didn't mean just federal employment tax purposes, I meant FICA and FUTA, you know, all that.

Q. Federal employment and unemployment taxes?

A. Yeah and payroll taxes, you know, the total payroll tax package, withholding and so forth.

Q. Okay. And I believe it was also your opinion that Cornhusker Motor Lines or Cornhusker Motor Freight was an employer of those truck

drivers between 1984 and 1987, for federal employment and unemployment tax purposes; is that right?

A. Yes and the other payroll taxes that were …

Q. The whole package?

A. … yeah.

Q. All right. When I use "the whole package," I'm saying federal employment and unemployment taxes to mean withholding, FICA, FUTA,
everything that's at issue in this case.

A. Oh, okay, I'll go along with that.

Q. How did you arrive at that opinion? What's the basis for that opinion?

A. My experience in the industry, the documents I read. My knowledge of
the Motor Carrier Acts. My knowledge of ICC requirements. My knowledge of the Internal Revenue Code and experience with it. The research
I conducted. And there may have been other things, but I can't think of
them right now.

Q. In conducting your research with respect to whether these truck drivers
were employees, for federal employment tax purposes, did you happen
to run across or read what is called Revenue Ruling 71-524?

A. I recall that ruling. I saw several rulings, but I can't — tell me what it's
about and maybe that will …

Q. Well, I'll read the first sentence of that to you. And that's "Advice has
been requested whether a truck driver who performs services under the
circumstances described below is an employee of the leasing company
for which he performs services for purpose of the Federal Insurance
Contribution Act, the Federal Unemployment Tax Act and the collection
of income tax, its source, on wage."

A. I remember reading that. I mean, some ruling about that information.
I can't cite the number right now, I don't have my notes here.

Q. Didn't that revenue ruling tend to indicate that Boles Trucking was the
employer of those truck drivers?

A. Yes.

Q. Okay. And I take it then you disagreed with the findings or the conduction of that revenue ruling; is that correct?

A. Yes, I disagreed, along with several courts. Judges disagreed, also.

Q. How does your experience in the industry lead you to conclude that Cornhusker Motor Lines and not Boles Trucking was the employer of those truck drivers between 1984 and 1987?

A. Well, Cornhusker Motor Company advertised for the drivers, employed the drivers, trained the drivers, provided the rules for the drivers, told the drivers where to go, what to do, what they could be reimbursed for, what they couldn't, what they would be docked for. They exercised, I'd say, as complete a control as any motor carrier I've ever seen that had company drivers.

Q. Were you aware of the fact that Boles Trucking, Inc. leased certain trucks or power units or tractors …

A. Uh-huh.

Q. … to Cornhusker Motor Lines?

A. Yes, I was.

Q. When I use the term "power unit," does that have a meaning to you?

A. Yes, usually we would call them over-the-road tractors or trucks or heavy-duty trucks.

Q. Okay. Do you know who the owner of those trucks were during this period?

A. I didn't examine the titles, but from the documents I saw, you know, that I did read the depositions and stuff, Boles Trucking, Inc. was. But I wouldn't know positively without looking at the titles.

Q. Okay. Assuming for a minute that Boles Trucking in fact owned those trucks, wouldn't the ownership of the trucks give Boles Trucking a measure of control over what was done with those trucks and the activities of the drivers who drove those trucks?

A. No.

Q. Why not?

A. Because many equipment-leasing companies, Rollins, TER, or Ford, or Capitol Leasing don't have anything to do with the drivers. Even General Electric Leasing. I remember Cargo Contract Carriers used to lease revenue equipment — that's the tractors and even the trailers — from General Electric and furnish the drivers. They had nothing — General Electric had no say over the drivers. The person that owns the equipment doesn't necessarily control the people who drive the equipment.

Q. You mentioned control being exercised by Cornhusker Motor Lines over the truck drivers during the period in question here. Were there any of the other 20 common law factors that, in your opinion, preponderated in a finding that Cornhusker Motor Lines was the employer of those drivers?

A. This is difficult for me to answer, unless I have the 20 questions in front of me or some notes.

Q. Just from your memory.

A. Well, could you give me a clue to what some of the other questions were, the 20 points?

Q. Requirement to file written reports?

A. The drivers made trip reports out to Cornhusker. That's a requirement of Cornhusker. Usually they make the trip report out to the person that is responsible for approving the trip report and this happened to be Cornhusker. What was another of those?

Q. Provision of tools?

A. All right. They, they provided the tools and I've seen documents or I may have asked Bruce, I'm not sure, where they even provided their own CBs. Their tools for minor repairs, adjusting brakes, probably some tools that they didn't even mention like cans of ether to start in the winter. They're not supposed to use that, but drivers do use that, blow it over the carburetor.

Q. What was the most important tool of all?

A. The driver being able to operate the tractor. I — Clarence Werner gave me lessons in driving those and those babies are difficult. The ability to

drive a tractor, that's a tool. That, that driver, him or herself that can
drive a tractor, not have accidents, get the freight from point A to point
B and get back again ...

Q. Okay. Are you talking about special skills and knowledge?

A. Oh, yeah. The drivers have special skills. They're a very technical thing.
You know, you've got 32 gears. Even an automatic transmission, I think,
has 16 gears. I'd have to ask Bruce, but — but they certainly have skills.
Not everybody can drive a tractor.

Q. So, in your opinion, driving a tractor-trailer requires special skills?

A. Oh, yes, it does.

Q. Isn't it true that it requires more experience than special skill?

A. I would say it requires special skills and experience.

Q. In any respect, whatever tools and equipment were furnished by the
drivers, wasn't that very small, in terms of actual, you know, money
outlay, as opposed to the trucks, themselves?

A. Well, that truck equipment is irrelevant really, because you can buy a
truck anywhere, but you can't get a person who can drive one safely. I
mean, they drop a trailer and not ruin the king pin.

Q. Did you find that the truck drivers in this case had an opportunity to
profit by their management skills?

A. Oh, definitely.

Q. How?

A. In the first place, they had a good safety record. I saw one who said he
never had an accident in 29 years. You know, Cornhusker and most
carriers will, if you have an accident, if it's your fault they'll take it out
of your pay, your settlement. Also, fines for speeding, you know, if you're
not a safe driver you get those. And the regulated carrier takes that out
of the driver's pay, too, on the settlement. So, yes and it depends on how
many miles they drive. You know, you like to get a driver to drive so
many miles a day, but some of them don't like to drive that. They don't
like to be away from home. So, these drivers did participate. They were

responsible for their own percent of earnings when they got the stuff there safely.

Q. But, isn't it true that the earnings of the drivers were determined more by the number of miles that they drove than their management skills?

A. Well, let's say they drove, like a driver in Omaha, he left the terminal and drove under an overpass and took the whole top of the trailer and tractor off because he shouldn't have been under that overpass. He didn't drive many and he was fired. You see, they had to have these skills. Somebody furnishes miles. Cornhusker furnishes miles. But, if they didn't have the management ability, they couldn't drive those miles. You know, drivers have to be able to work computers even today in the cabs.

Q. You indicated before that you were familiar with a written agreement between Cornhusker Motor Lines and Boles Trucking, Inc., were you not?

A. Yes, I did read it once.

Q. You read it once?

A. Yeah.

Q. Did you read any provision in there which would tend to indicate that Boles Trucking was to be responsible for withholding and paying over federal employment taxes and federal unemployment taxes?

A. I read something in there that said that Cornhusker would consider them to be employees of Boles. Yes, I did.

Q. But you discounted that. Is that correct?

A. I had to. They didn't comply with it. Cornhusker said you're responsible for hiring, training, all of that stuff and depositions I saw from the drivers said Cornhusker trained them. Cornhusker hired them. So, Cornhusker never paid any attention to that. It doesn't matter what Cornhusker said if there, it's what they did. And that disappointed me, too, you know, not being a lawyer, I look at a contract a little differently if you've got to comply with it, but they didn't.

Q. Well, isn't it true that most of the truck drivers were reimbursed for their expenses, such as oil, gas, fuel, things like that?

A. I think they were, but that's common if they were employees of, of Cornhusker. They go out on the road and some companies had them charge and so forth, but they reimburse their company drivers.

Q. Do you know in this case who actually made those reimbursements?

A. Cornhusker, as I understand it from what I've read, you know, Cornhusker reimbursed Boles on the settlement sheet and so Cornhusker, in effect, told Boles how much went to the driver and how much should be withheld from the driver.

Q. But who was ultimately responsible for the payment of the gasoline, the oil, the tires and diesel fuel, things like that? Who is ultimately responsible for those things, if you know?

A. According to the contract, I think it said Boles Trucking.

Q. Doesn't that tend to indicate that these truck drivers were employees of Boles Trucking?

A. That has nothing to do with it. It tends to indicate that those tractors were owned by Boles Trucking, but the control over the drivers indicates that Cornhusker actually supervised, trained and were the ones who approved or disapproved of a driver. That's all the incidents of being an employer. It was Cornhusker who decided if a driver wasn't going to drive.

Q. Do you know if Bruce Boles ever fired a truck driver?

A. No, I don't know whether he did or not.

Q. Would you be surprised to learn that he did?

A. Whether he did or not? No, I wouldn't be surprised to learn it because if I had a contact with Cornhusker and they told me to get rid of a driver, I'd get rid of a driver.

Q. Did you review the deposition of Bruce Boles?

A. I think I did... how long ago was that ... well, I did. I'm sure I did.

Q. Do you recall any testimony in there by Mr. Boles that he fired a truck driver independently of anything requested by Cornhusker Motor Lines?

A. I don't recall. I'd have to read it again. It's been some time.

Q. Assuming that were the case, wouldn't that tend to indicate that Mr. Boles had a measure of control over the truck drivers?

A. It would depend on whether he had to report it to Cornhusker. And if that's the case and he said, Cornhusker, this guy's really rotten, can I get rid of him? Then that would be no control over him. He'd still have to go through Cornhusker.

Q. Suppose he fired him on his own?

A. I don't think he could because that means …

Q. That's not responsive to my question. Suppose he did fire him.

A. Suppose he did. It still would not be control because it would be an isolated incident. You know, when a truck runs into somebody that's nasty business. They're very safety conscious.

Q. Telpner, were you ever employed by any trucking firm or any firm that leased trucks and/or drivers to a common carrier?

A. Are you asking me if I was employed as a CPA, engaged as a CPA?

Q. Yes; as a CPA.

A. Yes, I have done some work for some companies like that. Or, for a company like that. Most of my work was with a company that was on the other side.

Q. What company are we talking about here?

A. Shada Truck Leasing. It would have been years ago.

Q. Ed Shada?

A. Yeah, "Big Ed." I haven't seen Ed in 10, 15 years.

Q. What did you do for Shada Trucking?

A. I can't even remember now. It's in the '70s, I think.

Q. Did you happen to read the depositions of a number of individuals who were associated with firms that leased drivers and trucks or power units to a common carrier in this case?

A. No, I didn't see those depositions yet.

Q. So you never read the deposition, for example, of a Betty Petty ...

A. No.

Q. ... or anybody like that? Do you have any personal knowledge of any trucking firm that leased trucks or drivers to a common carrier and treated its drivers as independent contractors for federal employment tax purposes?

A. Well, from the other side.

Q. Yes.

A. I did some, not for the carrier, but the carriers that leased to — are you familiar with Little Audrey's, Fremont? They're gone now. They were part of Midwest Emery. It was the ten largest carriers in the United States at the time, but Little Audrey's is a refrigerated meat hauler out of Fremont. About 25 million in revenue, which was huge a few years ago. They used almost exclusively independent contractors that had, you know, had truck drivers like that. And these contractors didn't withhold on their drivers. Now, occasionally ...

Q. When was this, by the way? If you can just tie it down a little bit better?

A. In the '70s.

Q. In the '70s?

A. Let me tell you, occasionally, the IRS, you know, they weren't doing a lot of audits of this. Occasionally, the IRS would examine the contractor and say, hey, you owe these taxes. And, in fact, there was a case with Little Audrey's. So, Little Audrey's, if you reviewed the contractor and he wasn't withholding and you put a lien on their tractors and their trailers, Little Audrey's revenue would be affected because it would be out of service. Why, they'd have freight. So, Little Audrey's did this: they set up a separate corporation that it didn't own and the sole purpose of it was to make settlements. And anybody that was an independent contractor for them at the time had to go through this corporation because independent contractors were not withholding and Little Audrey's said, hey, if you want to do it for us we're going to withhold. Whether it's right or wrong doesn't make any difference. We don't want them to tie up a truck.

Q. Were you aware of any trucking firm that treated its truck drivers as independent contractors for federal employment tax purposes between 1984 and 1987?

A. A trucking firm that treated them …

Q. Right, any firm. And whether it's a common carrier or someone who leases trucks or drivers to a common carrier.

A. Let me distinguish. When you say "trucking firm," to me that means a carrier with operating authority.

Q. Okay.

A. If you mean a leasing company that's a different situation.

Q. Are you aware of any leasing company that treated its truck drivers as independent contractors for federal employment tax purposes between 1984 and 1987?

A. That treated them as employees?

Q. Independent contractors?

A. Well, just as I said, only from the other side, because the ones that dealt with Little Audrey's and later Regal Trucking, but only from … they're in Georgia and they're bankrupt.

Q. That's Regal Trucking?

A. Regal Trucking. And Midwest Emery is gone, too, but they did the same thing. I mean, the people who leased to them. You want to check some more, I can think of some more. I can't right now, but …

Q. Let's go back to the second opinion you gave me here. And correct me if I'm wrong …

A. Okay.

Q. ... or if I've misstated you, okay? But, as I understand it, your opinion was Boles Trucking, Incorporated and Bruce Boles had a reasonable basis under one or more provisions of Section 530 of the Revenue Act of 1978 for treating its drivers as independent contractors for federal employment tax purposes?

A. That's right. There's three bases for that.

Q. All right. Could you kind of elaborate on those for me?

A. Yeah, but I can only think of two of them right now, because I can't remember the third. Okay. One, this report or the review by the, was it the Department of Labor in Nebraska we talked about earlier?

Q. How did that provide either Boles Trucking or Mr. Boles with a reasonable basis for treating the drivers as independent contractors?

A. Because their issue was: Are these drivers employees of Boles or are they independent contractors. And the way I read the report they determined that Boles was not liable for their taxes as an employer. Second, there were other court cases at the time.

Q. Such as?

A. Well, when you — some of them, I've got them in my notes. I don't have my notes with me. But you'll see some in that article he's making a copy of for you, in Wisconsin and so forth, but some of them actually said that the regulated carrier was the employer, the one with the operating authority, the one they were being leased to. So, there were cases like that around.

Q. Were those cases that dealt with who the employer is or whether the truck drivers were independent contractors or employees for federal employment tax purposes?

A. As I recall, you didn't determine one without the other. I mean, you have to look at both issues. I don't mean to hedge, but I just couldn't separate them in my mind. They're either somebody's employee or they're not, so you have to look at both. Now, we had ... the industry ...

Q. Industry practice or custom?

A. Yeah, the … you can go back to the '70s on up to the '80s and there's hardly any, any discussion about it. Clear back then, starting when Jimmy Carter came in, they were worried about deregulation. The truck drivers were worried about it. Then the truck drivers were worried about the embargo. Remember when fuel went up, that Arab embargo in 1973 in the Middle East? And so that's what they were concerned with. The truck drivers actually had a recession in '74. The biggest truck auction you ever saw, 86 tractors on the block at the Marina Inn in Sioux City. So, you had the drivers and the employers weren't concerned about payroll taxes, nor was the Internal Revenue Service. I was on the board of the National Accounting and Financial Council of the American Trucking Association 15 years and they hardly ever discussed this, I mean, once in a while an article would come through in *Motor Freight Controller*, but it wasn't until, oh, about '82, well, '78, but '82 we had some more talk about it. Dole wanted to make a different test for it, you know, just like we had in '78 and that never went through. But nobody talked about — I mean, really the IRS didn't say, hey, we're going to get these people until about '86. So, in all those years nobody was paying any attention to this industry and nobody at the governmental level was paying any attention to this until '86. You can look at cases, you can look in the writings, you can even look at the Internal Revenue agent audit manual and it wasn't until about '86 when they really cracked down on this. And then when they went to court they lost some of them and won some of them. So, this was not an issue. It was a nonissue. And there were a lot of … most of the cases originally came on the lumpers, you know, the loaders and unloaders. And that's when the congress kept putting moratoriums on because nobody knew what they were.

That's why all those moratoriums, you look at the history of this and I was around when that history was being written. No one paid any attention to this and when the agents would review, congress would say, stop making those adjustments, we don't know what they are yet.

Q. Mr. Telpner, I think your understanding of industry practice is somewhat different from mine as it goes with respect to Section 530 of the Revenue Act of 1978. My understanding is, as far as industry practice or custom is concerned and the treatment of the drivers for federal employment tax purposes, is that, in order to claim the benefits of Section 530, the taxpayer must show that it is the prevailing custom to treat the truck drivers as independent contractors for federal employment tax purposes within a certain geographical area where the taxpayer is located.

Mostek: I probably misheard it, but I thought you were paraphrasing what the statute said. This is just your understanding and not what the statute says. We'll proceed with that understanding.

By Metcalfe:

Q. Let's go back and answer the question again.

A. I've got the question — but it's really two questions that you've asked. One, you said treat as independent contractor and then you said within a geographic location. I'll answer the first one. I think you've misinterpreted what I said. I said leasing companies that owned the tractors were not withholding on the drivers. They were treating them as independent contractors. You and I have said the same thing. As far as geographic location went, I don't recall that in Section 530 or even in the history of it. But I recall the trucking industry because I was very involved in it in all those years from '64 on. — I served on its board for many years. This is an issue that doesn't have geographical boundaries.

Q. I'm going to read Section 530(a)(2)(C) and it says that, "A taxpayer in any case be treated as having a reasonable basis not treating an individual as an employee for a period if the taxpayer's treatment of such individual for such period was in reasonable reliance on any of the following:" And then it goes on to say "Long-standing, recognized practice of a significant segment of the industry in which such individual was engaged."

A. Okay. I agree with that.

Q. The way I interpret that, I'm talking about Bob Metcalfe's interpretation here, is that during this period between 1984 to 1987, in order for Boles Trucking to claim the benefits of that safe harbor provision of Section 530 of the Revenue Act of 1978, Boles Trucking would be required to show that a significant segment of the trucking industry within the Greater Omaha Metropolitan Area treated truck drivers as independent contractors for federal employment tax purposes. Is your understanding different from mine?

A. I didn't understand it as a limited geographical area, but I can respond to that with an explanation. I don't know how you got that interpretation, but the Internal Revenue Service, itself, in those years, especially in '86, said that a significant portion of the industry is not withholding and treating these people as employees and that's why we've decided to have a big drive on to examine them to make sure they start doing it. So, I know from the Internal Revenue Service, itself, that it considered a significant portion all over the United States as not having complied with it.

Q. What is the source of your information on that point?

A. Articles from the American Institute of CPAs, from *Transport Topics,* from *Motor Freight Controller,* interviews, statements by congressmen in there, et cetera, plus my knowledge of the cases that came out and the IRS audit manual in '86.

Q. So, under your view then, what was actually happening in Omaha, with respect to how truck drivers were treated for federal employment tax purposes during these years in question would have been really irrelevant then, right?

A. No, I don't see how you interpreted that from my statement.

Q. Well, let's say, for example, during the years between 1984 and 1987 all of the trucking firms and by that I mean both leasing firms and common carriers in the Greater Metropolitan Area from Omaha treated its truck drivers as employees for federal employment tax purposes, with the exception of Boles Trucking?

A. I don't think I said that.

Q. No, I didn't say you did, sir, but I'm giving you what is called a hypothetical here, okay?

A. Okay.

Q. Let us assume that, during these years between 1984 and 1987, all of the trucking firms, that is leasing companies and common carriers, with the exception of Boles Trucking, treated its truck drivers as employees for federal employment tax purposes. All right? Under this safe harbor provision that we've been discussing here, would it be your opinion that Boles would, nevertheless, be able to claim reasonable reliance on alongstanding, recognized practice of a significant segment of the industry in which it was engaged?

Mostek: Okay. I'm sorry, that was a very long question. I hate to interrupt everybody's train of thought, but the question as posed is ambiguous, because in the first part of your question you limit it to the years of examination '84 through '87. But the statute itself says a "long-standing practice." Now, I don't know how long is "long-standing," but I think that the question as posed is ambiguous because it's asking him in the first breath, limit your opinion or your response to '84 to '87, but then when you refer back to the statute, rather, your interpretation of the statute, when you refer back to the statute, which says "long-standing," creates an ambiguity and makes it difficult to answer the question.

A. Yes, it's a long question. It depends on who was right and who was wrong. Without looking at that, I wouldn't know who the employer was or who wasn't. You haven't really specified whether it was motor carriers which I'm talking about the one with the operating authority, or whether it was a leasing company, or what. And I couldn't understand the question, as such. But, I would also have to say that, hypothetically, no such thing would happen because I know just in Fremont, 30 miles away or however far it is, that Little Audrey's in those years, in the years '74 on were having the problems. And that anybody who would start in '84 would not have any experience in '84, except to look at history.

Q. Okay. Let's change the hypothetical a little bit. Let's say from 1970 up until 1987. There's only one firm in the Greater Omaha Metropolitan Area that's treating its truck drivers as independent contractors; that firm is Boles Trucking. Every other firm, leasing firm, trucking firm, common carrier, every other firm is treating its drivers as employees for federal employment tax purposes. Under your opinion would it be, would Boles be able to claim the benefits of the Section 530 (a)(2)(C)?

A. I would have to have more facts on what their transportation area was. Were they going to the East Coast, to the West Coast? Were they limited, just going from Omaha to Council Bluffs?

Q. Well, let's assume they were intercontinental.

A. Intercontinental? I would be of the opinion that they'd have to take the experience of the whole U.S. in order to determine whether they should withhold or not. Or, the experience of the trucking industry per se, and not narrow it down to a little bit. But, I do know that in this area there were many companies that were not withholding on their drivers and, therefore, I would say that Boles would still be handling it correctly.

Q. What firms were those?

A. I went over the cases with Little Audrey's, but you'll have to look up the cases or I suppose you would …

Mostek: We can supply you with additional information if you find more.

Q. Okay. With respect to your interpretation of the law, is there any relevant geographical area for implementing Section 530 (a)(2)(C) of the Revenue Code of 1978?

A. Well, there's a tax law and then there's other laws that lawyers interpret, but I didn't read anything about geographical limitations in there. And and, but I … are they in there?

Q. No, I'm just trying to get your best understanding, sir.

A. I could have overlooked them, but I don't recall any geographical limitations.

Q. So, would your testimony be that it's nationwide standard?

A. It's an industry standard.

Q. Yes, but is that nationwide or is it limited to something that happens locally where the taxpayer is located?

A. I suppose it could be somewhat of both, couldn't it?

Mostek: Bob, do you want to break for lunch or …

Metcalfe: I'd like to go straight through. Off the record. (Whereupon, an off-the-record discussion was held.) (Whereupon, this deposition was adjourned at the hour of 12:25 p.m.)

The Deposition of Zeph Telpner, CPA, was continued on the 10th day of June, 1993, commencing at the hour of 9:15 a.m., in the presence of Mr. Robert D. Metcalfe, Mr. Michael S. Mostek and Mr. Gary A. Barnes, as follows:

6.11.1.1 *Direct Examination (continued)*

Q. Back on the record here. Mr. Telpner, when we broke yesterday, according to my notes, we were discussing whether in your opinion Boles Trucking, Inc., could be relieved from liability for some federal employment and unemployment taxes under Section 530 of the Revenue Act of 1978. And as far as I can tell, what I was asking you was questions concerning other companies that may have been operating during that time. And when I talk about other companies, I'm talking about companies that either leased trucks and drivers to a common carrier or to a common carrier, itself. That's what I mean when I say companies using trucking firms and things like that. And I believe you identified for me a firm called Little Audrey's; is that right?

A. Yes. Yes, I did.

Q. Where was Little Audrey's located? I believe it was somewhere in Nebraska, I just didn't grasp where.

A. Fremont, Nebraska. I think Freemont's about 30 miles from Omaha.

Q. And if I also recall correctly, you're saying that Little Audrey's was operating during the 1970s; is that right?

A. Yes and into the '80s. I don't know how long ago they closed, but …

Q. Are you fairly sure that it's no longer in business?

A. Yes.

Q. Now, would I be correct in believing that your testimony is that Little Audrey's treated its truck drivers as independent contractors for federal income tax purposes?

A. I don't think that's what we were discussing yesterday. I mentioned that Little Audrey's had several companies similar to Boles Trucking that were leasing tractors to it and drivers. They had drivers, too. And these trucking companies were not withholding on those drivers, these lessors. And the Internal Revenue Service actually in 1973 or '74 had some cases against them. And because they weren't withholding and the IRS claimed they had to, one of them was a similar case to this. I think it was Titan Trucking, T-i-t-a-n. I can look up and I'll be glad to look up the reference for you when I go back to my office. But, anyway, they were not withholding and several others, which the IRS from time to time would seize a tractor and trailer and hold up Little Audrey's freight. So, Little Audrey's finally said we don't care what you are, if you want to go with us you're going to have to run your settlements through a separate corporation we're setting up so we don't get our tractors seized anymore.

Q. Throughout the term that it was in business, you're saying Little Audrey's had trucks leased and drivers leased to it?

A. Yeah.

Q. Do you know any of the firms that leased trucks or drivers to Little Audrey's?

A. Not that I can think of now. It's been so … except for Titan. It had about maybe 25, 30 tractors. I think Shada Leasing leased to Armour in those years. They lease to somebody else now, but in those years, I don't think they leased to Little Audrey's. I don't think Lowry … I think Lowry had leased to American Beef Packers. These are similar companies. Lowry's was huge, only they were just like Boles Trucking. And I know that they didn't because when Lowry's trucking filed bankruptcy I remember the IRS came in and claimed that Lowry's owed $900,000 in payroll taxes. And this was before the interest was very high. And I don't even know if they had the 100% penalty yet. I can't remember when it came due.

Q. In the case of Little Audrey's, who was actually paying the drivers for their miles?

A. Originally, it was Little Audrey's, I mean, you know, but after all these tractors were being seized, well, when I say originally with Little Audrey's, to the best of my memory. But, after the tractors were seized and they had problems with the independent contractors not being able to supply them tractors, if they had liens on them, were tied up, Little Audrey's formed a separate corporation to handle all the payments to the drivers and the settlements. They would actually withhold and pay over to the drivers through this separate corporation and I'm not sure whether, but then they decided because of the cases against the contractors that they might start withholding it. And I think they may have withheld. But, it was a, the corporation wasn't owned by Little Audrey's, the contractors, it was just a separate entity that had Little Audrey's lawyer and insurance agent and someone else as the stockholders incorporators and then the paperwork would go to them. They would bill Little Audrey's, who would give them a big check and then they would pay the individual contractors.

Q. Do you know what the name of this corporation was?

A. No, but I, I can't think of the name of it. I know the … Steve Johnson was the last president of it. Neil Larson would have been the one that set that up. He was the financial vice president. It was his idea to set that corporation up. And he later set one up for Regal Trucking and I think Midwest Emery had the same thing in Chicago where they went to.

After the Motor Carrier Act of 1980, we lost about 2,000 or so trucking companies. I think Midwest Emery was in the top ten largest trucking companies in the United States and then whammo. You know, operating authority was the largest asset. It used to be you have operating authority worth 8, 10 million and then came 1980 and they were worth nothing.

Q. How was it that you acquired this information that you just testified to as to Little Audrey's?

A. I was in the National Accounting and Finance Council with Neil Larson and I used to go out there and help them on some technical problems. And I was actually at Little Audrey's when he showed me how the whole thing worked. He went over the corporation with me. He showed me the settlement sheets and how the checks went out and how they settled everything up. I, I … he also did a fuel tax study out there.

Q. Did you ever become involved with respect to any federal employment tax liabilities of Little Audrey's?

A. No, no.

Q. Did you ever work, either as a CPA or as a consultant for any of the firms such as Titan Trucking that leased drivers and trucks to Little Audrey's?

A. Not, not for the ones that leased drivers and trucks to Little Audrey's. I have for other firms that leased drivers and trucks.

Q. I believe you said at one point that the corporation that had been formed by Little Audrey's may have begun to withhold federal employment taxes from the wages, or amounts, rather, that were paid to truck drivers. Can you tell me when that might have been?

A. It probably was about '75. That was after the Titan case. Probably about 1975. And they made the decision only for one purpose, because the Internal Revenue Service was seizing their tractors. And when you've got a trailer full of refrigerated meat sitting out on the interstate for 2 or 3 days, it's not too good — or sitting at a scale, because that's usually where they tie it up, is at the scale. The meatpackers get unhappy with you.

Q. Mr. Telpner, did you ever hear of a firm called Werner or Werner Enterprises?

A. Yes, I certainly have heard of a firm called Werner Enterprises.

Q. Do you know how long Werner Enterprises has been in business?

A. Clarence Werner started business in 1956 as a truck driver. He worked for Midwest Transportation for Frank Chulino. In about '59, I think it was, when he really opened Werner Enterprises. By 1963 or '4, they only had about $300,000 worth of revenue and they didn't have operating authority. They hauled lumber and grain and took title to it and then would resell it. About '71 is when they got their first authority. I think it was contract.

Q. And after that do you know what happened to the company?

A. Werners?

Q. Yes.

A. Yeah, I think it's the number — I've read now that it's the third largest truckload carry in the United States today. They're huge. About 1980 they really grew as soon as the Regulation Reform Act came in, July 1, '80. They jumped by 12 million dollars that year. All his stuff used to be reported publicly.

Q. Would Werner have been bigger, smaller or about the same size as Little Audrey's?

A. Oh, it would have been much smaller in 1974. It didn't get its growth … see, it was so restrictive. When the Motor Carrier Reform Act came out, if this will, maybe it will help you. Before it came out to get an operating authority you had to be fit, willing and able and then you had to be for the public good, a necessity, you know, convenience and necessity. In 1980, they got rid of the public convenience and necessity test, just be willing and able and serve a useful public purpose. So, it was much easier to get authority and took the monopolies away. So, that's when Werner really grew. The only reason that they didn't grow larger earlier was because of the monopolistic authority in regulation.

Q. Did you ever acquire any knowledge as to how big Werner was, let's say, during the late '70s and early '80s?

A. Yeah, I did.

Q. How big would Werner have been at that point?

A. May I ask a question of … could we go off the record a minute?

Metcalfe: Certainly. Off the record. (Whereupon, an off-the-record discussion was held.)

Mostek: For the record, Mr. Telpner has just advised us that he was formerly the CPA for Werner Trucking Company and through that relationship did obtain certain information which would, which would come to him by virtue of that relationship. However, most of the information which he obtained was public by virtue of the Interstate Commerce Commission filings. Nonetheless, we would like to proceed on the basis that Mr. Telpner's testimony regarding Werner Trucking or Werner Enterprises will be given on the understanding that any information given is to be used solely for purposes of this lawsuit and will not be disclosed or disseminated to anyone not involved with this lawsuit. Is that agreeable, Bob?

Metcalfe: Agreeable to the government.

Telpner: Thank you. Okay. Sorry for the interrupting.

Q. We were talking about how big Werner was in, I believe, the late '70s and early '80s and you indicated that you did have some knowledge as to the size of their operations. But before we go into that, would it be fair to characterize Werner Enterprises as an interstate hauler or carrier?

A. Interstate truckload carrier.

Q. Okay. And do you have any idea as to how big the size of their operations was during the late '70s and early '80s?

A. Okay, let me tell you in 1980 that the Motor Carrier Act came in July 1, 1980. If you put them on a calendar year at July 1, 1980 they would have had revenues, would have had annual revenues of 9 million dollars. Within a year, they had revenues of 21 million, which is a phenomenal jump in this industry because they used to, you know, just go up in little increments. I think by '71 or '72, you know, it's just, you know, it's a long time ago, but I think they only had a couple of million in revenues. Maybe only a million. I don't think we had to file Class I Reports. Let me see, in '73 you were Class I if you had a million dollars in revenues. We didn't file Class I reports in '73. In '74, it changed to three million. I think it wasn't until '76 or '7 they hit three million.

Q. Were you ever familiar with a firm called Driver Management, Inc.?

A. They hadn't formed that yet when I was there.

Q. Okay.

A. But I know of it.

Q. And what is your knowledge of Driver Management, Inc.?

A. Just the other day, I think when I was here, somebody told me and I don't remember who it was that I had heard Werner had a leasing subsidiary that they leased drivers to themselves and somebody told me it was Driver Management, Inc. But, I left Werner in '80, the last time I would have done any work for them. I had sold my trucking practice to a Big-Eight accounting firm. Clarence called me back ... this is still about Clarence. It's confidential.

Mostek: Yes.
Metcalfe: Oh, yes. The whole thing.
Telpner: He called me back. When he got the first divorce, I had been away from him for about three or four years, but he wanted me to do some work. But I hadn't heard of Drivers Management, Inc. then, so it wasn't formed probably till after '82. I don't know for sure, though.

Q. Okay. Did you ever acquire any knowledge as to how Werner Enterprises and later the Driver Management, Inc., treated its truck drivers for federal employment tax purposes?

A. Not Driver's Management, Inc. I can tell you how Werner's did in any earlier years. Clarence Werner was convinced that he should have all his own revenue equipment in the early years.

Q. Company drivers?

A. And company drivers. He didn't have the number of owner-operators he might have had. In later years he got a few owner-operators. When I left I don't think he had more than seven or eight. And he didn't have any contractors, he just had one individual and one truck. I don't recall that he had anything like Boles. So, in that case, if he had something, nobody was reviewing it at that time and he probably just settled with them. I wouldn't have handled the settlement sheets, but I know I saw the settlement sheets. I remember I set up a, I can't believe this, how big they are now, a peg board accounting system. Now they've got the main frames and ...

Q. Mr. Telpner, with respect to, though, how the drivers were treated for federal employment tax purposes by Werner during the period you were there prior to, let's say, 1982, would it have been fair to say that Werner was withholding federal income taxes and FICA taxes from the amounts that it paid its truck drivers?

A. Oh, yeah. when I prepared his return I always looked at the payroll tax returns when I prepared his ICC. I wanted to make sure that we didn't deduct both halves. Werner was a little different. For ICC purposes, when it became regulated in '71, it was still a proprietorship. They had to report on the accrual basis for the ICC, but it was still cash basis for income tax purposes. And in 1981, I think that was the last return I might have done was '81, or worked on. It was still cash basis and it was really big then compared to the trucking industry. It wasn't like it was today, but if you were 40 million dollars you were in the top 100 largest carriers back then.

Q. Where was Werner's located when you were associated or working as a consultant there?

A. When I first started with him, he was working out of his house in Council Bluffs in his driveway. That's how long. And then he moved to 32nd Avenue in Council Bluffs and from there he moved out to their present location. God, I can't remember, it was about '75, '77, he moved to Omaha. Maybe it was earlier. It might have been earlier.

Q. Do you have any knowledge of the operations of either Werner Enterprises or Driver Management, Inc., let's say, after 1982?

A. No, no.

Q. And just for my own clarification, I believe it was your testimony concerning a firm named Regal Trucking?

A. Yeah, they were in Georgia.

Q. I was going to ask you some questions now about an examination or inquiry that may have been performed of Boles Trucking, Inc., by the Nebraska Department of Labor. And before I do so, I'd like to ask you if you had the opportunity to review a deposition of an individual who was formerly with the Nebraska Department of Labor and who is now retired, whose deposition was taken in this case?

A. What was his name? I did review a deposition by somebody who was with the Department of Labor and now retired. Was there only one deposition?

Q. Right.

A. Okay, then I did. Yes.

Q. And this formed the basis for your conclusion that, or at least in part for your conclusion, that Boles Trucking was entitled to relief under Section 530 of the Revenue Act of 1978?

A. Yes, it did.

Q. And could you tell me what was it, what was the basis for your opinion that as a result of this audit or examination by the, or whatever it was, inquiry by the Nebraska Department of Labor, that Boles Trucking was entitled to Section 530 relief?

A. There were exhibits attached to the deposition. Forms from the Nebraska Department of Labor and so forth, investigation. There's a letter saying that they reduced the rate, you know, from, gee, I can't remember what, down to point five tenths of a percent or something like that. And in those exhibits, there was no adjustment that I saw to assess the taxes, state unemployment taxes against the drivers.

Q. Correct me if I'm wrong, Mr. Telpner, but as a result of that inquiry or examination by the Nebraska Department of Labor, isn't it correct that Boles Trucking agreed with the State of Nebraska that the … its president, David B. Boles, otherwise known as Bruce Boles, was an employee for the purposes of paying the state unemployment tax?

A. I don't know if that's why they agreed. But, as I understand, later on they did agree that David Boles was a statutory employee, but I don't know why. I don't know why his advisors agreed to that. I wasn't privy to that.

Q. Okay. With your accounting background perhaps you can tell me the answer to this: If Mr. Boles was a statutory employee for the purposes of requiring Boles to pay state unemployment taxes, why wouldn't he also be a statutory employee for the purposes of paying over federal unemployment taxes and employment taxes?

A. You know, I gave that considerable thought because we're talking about times in the past and so I had to think. I told him I prepared my first return in 1956 and so I had to try to figure out what was going on. Do you remember in 1982 we had the Subchapter S Reform Act? Accountants and tax return preparers always advised clients who had a Subchapter S that they didn't have to pay salary; that if they had a Subchapter

S corporation they wouldn't be subject to self-employment tax. Subchapter S income is not self-employment tax. The Subchapter S income goes right onto the 1040. So, people who have Subchapter S corporations never paid a salary. It was very rare. They withdrew cash and they didn't have to pay self-employment tax. I thought they were always a little strange because you couldn't retire. I mean, if you didn't have self-employment tax how were you going to draw social security? But, anyway, they always advised them not to pay it. So, there was usually no payroll for the officers coming out of there. So, if there's no payroll, even if they were a statutory employee and there was no payroll and I said "even if" because I hadn't considered it in those years, you wouldn't have any withholding anyway. And if they did take a distribution it was a dividend. Now, between 1986, '86 and current, some cases were decided. One was a lawyer, I recall, had a Subchapter S corporation. And the Court said you're not taking a salary, but you're the sole person in there, so obviously these dividends are really salary. This was just the opposite of unreasonable compensation. They made him pay. So, that was the first time when anybody really started this stuff. Nobody cared. If you got CPAs that are my age that were doing — I had one Subchapter S and they pay salaries, two brothers. But they always paid salaries from the time they started before the Subchapter S laws. But, if you're a CPA my age, you would probably still be advising clients not to take salary out of a Subchapter S.

Q. Do you know if Mr. Boles was taking any money out of the corporation known as Boles Trucking between 1984 and 1987?

A.   I can't remember which ones I saw. Mike, do you remember when their fiscal year ended?

Mostek: I can't. I'm sorry.

Telpner: Well, if I saw an '84 return, it would have been ended in something like February or March of '85, because it wasn't until '87, you know, when the Tax Reform Act of '86, that they had to go on a calendar year. So, I saw maybe the '84 return and I don't think there was anything taken out, the '85, '86. I may have seen '87, but I'm not sure. But, I don't think there was anything taken out, except on '86 or '87, I saw on the Schedule M of a balance sheet a distribution called a, I wish I had an 1120S in front of me. It said it was a nondividend distribution. There's a line on there. And that's what I saw, a nondividend distribution going on. I didn't know what that was. It might have been a previously taxed income going out, I'm not sure.

Q. Mr. Telpner, based on everything you've seen and your expertise and everything like that, did Boles Trucking, Inc., in your opinion, have any reasonable cause or basis for not filing the Forms 941 or Forms 940 with respect to the status of Bruce Boles, David B. Boles, as a statutory employee of Boles Trucking, Inc. during the period between 1984 and 1987?

A. All I saw were the records of the income tax returns, but I would say, he had a reasonable basis.

Q. And what was that?

A. No salaries were paid to him on there. I mean, I should say it this way: The returns didn't report any salaries paid to him. I didn't, you know, look at the books or anything.

Q. But, let us assume for a minute, hypothetically, that Mr. Boles was taking money out of the corporation and having the corporation pay for some of his personal expenses and was furnishing him with a car and was making him loans that turned out to be not loans, but simply payments, the way we would think of dividend payments. If those payments would be made by the corporation to David Boles wouldn't those be income on which the corporation would be required to withhold federal income taxes and FICA taxes?

A. You've asked me about different types of tax transactions here. Dividends, no. If it's a dividend it's not. If it's a loan, no. Under the law and I can't remember when it changed, the Internal Revenue Code I'm talking about, I think it was '86 or '87, I think you had to figure the value of an automobile, there was a table that IRS had and withhold on that. But I don't know what years that started. Before that, nobody enforced it from the days of George M. Cohan on up to 1962.

Q. The — but going back to my question here, if Boles Trucking had made payments to David Boles and let's say they're not loans, they're not dividends, they're simply out and out payments, either directly to him or payments of his living expenses, personal expenses, wouldn't that constitute income to Mr. Boles on which the corporation, Boles Trucking, would have been required to withhold income taxes and FICA taxes?

A. Well, I looked at the returns and I didn't see any payments like that going out, so it's a hypothetical question.

Q. All right, yes.

A. Let's say that if any corporation, if they paid something out to the stockholders and it wasn't recorded as an account receivable and it wasn't recorded as a dividend, then we have to find out how it should have been recorded first. Should it be a receivable? Did he pay it back? Did he intend to pay it back? This is just anyone. Or, is it a dividend? If it was a dividend, did the board of directors declare it a dividend? You know, you've got to do that. So, let's say it wasn't a dividend. Now what is it? Is it a loan? Did they record it as a loan on the books and did he pay it back? So, if it wasn't a loan, if he didn't pay it back, then you have to look at the minutes. Because a lot of times the minutes used to say in the event that a deduction is disallowed by the Internal Revenue Service, the stockholder agrees to pay it back. You're familiar with that?

Q. Of course.

A. So, then, if it wasn't that, is it salary? I don't know. I really don't know. That's a legal question on what the heck that is. I'm not trying to beg your ...

Q. No, no, I mean, if you don't know.

A. ... but, I will tell you one thing that, remember, when I prepare a return I look at a lot more things than a lot of preparers do. I would have, if I had seen payments going out and they weren't paid back I would tell the stockholder we had to record these as an account receivable or you have to pay them back. I would never, I would never have thought on a Subchapter S of the term "salary." I guarantee you that.

Q. Are you aware that the Internal Revenue Service reclassified certain payments made by, or monies received by Mr. Boles or payments of personal expenses or payments for a car as income to Mr. Boles, subject to federal employment taxes?

A. No, I didn't see those adjustments and I didn't hear about those adjustments, except I have one alluded to about the automobile, but I never was informed that the IRS had reclassified everything. I was told that — was it you that asked questions about the automobile or somebody did?

Q. We may have touched on it yesterday.

A. I mean, before. Somebody told me that somebody from the Internal Revenue Service had proposed withholding on the automobile. But that's the only adjustment I knew about. I would be glad to look at the adjustments if you've got a copy.

Q. Are you aware of any individual by the name of Etaoin Shrdlu?

A. Yes, I am aware of him.

Q. Who is Mr. Shrdlu, to your knowledge?

A. He's a tax return preparer. Was in Council Bluffs, Iowa and he did have an office also in Omaha and associated with somebody.

Q. And how is it that you happen to know him or know of him? ,

A. I've heard of him. I've talked to Internal Revenue agents who have talked to me about him. I've seen his work.

Q. Have you formed an opinion as to his work as a return preparer?

A. As a return preparer, I've formed an opinion of his work.

Q. And could you tell us what that is?

A. May I go off the record a minute?

Metcalfe: All right. Why don't we go off the record.
(Whereupon, an off-the-record discussion was held.)

Q. Did you understand the question?

A. Would you repeat it, please?

Q. Certainly. I would ask you, sir, if you have an opinion of Etaoin Shrdlu as a tax return preparer, based upon your prior knowledge of his preparation of tax returns, your ability to consult with him, to talk to him and any other information you may have acquired about his performance?

Mostek: Bob, may we have the same stipulation we did with regard to Werner Trucking and Werner Enterprises, that it will be used solely for purposes ...
Metcalfe: Oh, certainly.
Mostek: All right.
Telpner: First, I want to qualify something here, is that sometimes I get annoyed with the Internal Revenue Service, too, because the director of practice is benign. I think Mr. Shrdlu does work that does not comply with the Internal Revenue Code, does not comply with the regulations, does not

comply with accounting of any kind and I've seen enough of his work to know that the advice is bad. His clients are trapped by it because they don't know any better. He has a big practice and his work's terrible. And years ago, Roger Metzger, who is dead now, (he was an Internal Revenue Service agent) told me that they were going to get him disbarred. But the Internal Revenue Service has never done that, to my knowledge.

I've seen him — I had two people that were sent to me, two guys that laid carpet for a carpet store. And he advised them to form a Subchapter S corporation. He was deducting their house, their car and everything. These were just two guys that didn't know any difference. The average taxpayer knows nothing about this. And so these two men came to me and they had Subchapter S corporations, they were deducting their household goods, everything, you know. Etaoin Shrdlu was doing it. And they got reviewed by the Internal Revenue Service. They were two blue collar workers making about 10,000 a year or less. The IRS set them up with 8,000 bucks in taxes each. And they wanted me to help them. I said, pay the tax and thank God that they haven't brought criminal charges against you, because I would have had I been an agent.

Now, I think he's a menace to society and to his clients. However, he's got a lot of clients and he's got some big clients in Council Bluffs and in Omaha and he's giving them advice.

And I might explain to you, let's go back to Werner's. When I used to prepare Werner's return, if I said this is depreciation, this is an investment credit, we've got to do it this way, he said okay and signed it. I made those decisions, no matter how big they were. But, he was a very honest man.

I know I'm digressing, but I want to tell you how I happened to — Clarence would call me up if somebody wanted to buy something from him and he'd say, I want to tell you about this, so you'll tell me the right way to record and report it. He always thought to call me. Shrdlu gives terrible advice but, nonetheless, a lot of people use him because they think he's good. They don't know the difference. People will say, oh, my tax man, Etaoin Shrdlu. And I really get mad because I had a heck of a library and I am a tax man and if I gave advice like that, it's because I would research it and accidentally misinterpret, but not because I didn't bother to look it up. It's a long answer; he's terrible, but lay people rely on him.

Metcalfe: Let's stop right here. Off the record.

(Whereupon, an off-the-record discussion was held.)

(Whereupon, a short recess was had.)

Q. Back on the record here. I believe I was asking you and you were giving your opinion concerning Mr. Shrdlu. Proceeding on from that point, I would ask you now, Mr. Telpner, if you could tell me whether or not you have formed an opinion as to whether or not Boles Trucking, Inc., the plaintiff in this case, was entitled to rely on any advice given to the corporation by Etaoin Shrdlu as a tax-return preparer that would qualify the corporation for relief under Section 530 of the Revenue Act of 1978?

A. I'm going to expound a little on my answer. As a very experienced certified public accountant, I know that average taxpayers hire accountants and they always think we're right until they find out different. But, I reviewed the tax returns of Boles Trucking and they were prepared by certified public accountants, the ones I saw after Mr. Shrdlu was no longer there for the period '84 through '87. And the CPAs continued on with the same advice. So, I would say, yes, he's entitled to rely upon the advice of Mr. Shrdlu and the CPA firms that followed. I think there were two other ones. The IRS director or practice allows him to give tax advice.

Q. In arriving at your opinion did you ever have the opportunity to read or review a deposition that was taken in this case of Etaoin Shrdlu?

A. No, I did not see his or read his deposition.

Q. Do you have any personal knowledge of any advice that was given by Etaoin Shrdlu to Boles Trucking, Inc.?

A. You mean, like I heard it from Etaoin Shrdlu?

Q. Right. Or, heard it from anyone associated with Boles Trucking?

A. Yes, I heard it from Bruce Boles when I was over here and …

Q. And what did he tell you?

A. He told me that Etaoin Shrdlu said he didn't have to withhold on the drivers; that they were independent contractors.

Q. And would it be your opinion that Boles Trucking, Inc., was entitled to rely on that advice and not file Forms 940 and Forms 941 for that period between 1984 and 1987?

A. I would say that not only was he entitled to rely on it, because he could rely on his accountant, as a layperson. He got the same advice from the successor CPAs who prepared the return in '84 through '87. Those were signed by certified public accountants and they didn't change any procedures. When I say he got the same advice, they carried on the same way, so I make the assumption that the advice is the same.

Q. What do the corporate tax returns for Boles Trucking, the 1120S returns have to do with the liability of Boles Trucking, if any, for federal employment taxes?

A. Well, the corporation, if there were employment taxes due, would be the entity that would pay the employment taxes.

Q. Would it be entitled to a deduction on its Form 1120 for any employer share of FICA that was paid?

A. Yes, it would.

Q. Okay. And none of the 1120S returns filed by Boles Trucking, Inc., for the period between 1984 and 1987, according to your review, reflected any deductions for employer FICA or matters of that nature?

A. I don't recall seeing any. Did they ever ... you said that they made a change in, in the ... didn't you tell me that they agreed to pay it on ...

Q. I didn't say they agreed to it. I'm saying the IRS reclassified at one point some ...

A. Okay. Well, that would be after '87 though, wouldn't it?

Q. Well, no. Actually, it was for a period between '84 and '87.

A. No. But, I mean, the reclassification wasn't made till after those returns were all filed.

Q. Correct.

A. Okay. I was just trying to think, you know, remember the tax on there. No, I didn't see any payroll tax on anything.

Q. Okay. Based on your review of the 1120S returns filed by Boles Trucking, Inc., for its corporate years between 1984 and 1987 and I should have said fiscal years, not corporate years ...

A. Yeah, but '87 had two returns, you know, the one ended in the fiscal year and then a calendar year. But I don't think that I found that calendar year.

Q. Okay. Did you see on any of those returns any deductions taken by Boles Trucking for either the purchase or rental of any automobile that was used by any officer of the corporation?

A. No, I did not. That's another reason I thought that Boles was entitled to rely upon the advice of the accountants.

Q. Why is that?

A. Well, you said, unless I misunderstood and I don't know whether it's been agreed that he had the use of the car and if he did and if any expenses went through the corporation, the accountants were supposed to put an automobile, if any of it was used, on listed property on the back of the depreciation schedule. The only thing I saw as listed property was a computer. So, if there was any automobile expenses and they weren't put there it would be the fault of the preparers of the return or the advisors to Boles Trucking.

Q. Okay. Did you ever learn or were you ever made aware of any change made by Boles Trucking, Inc., with respect to the treatment of its drivers as employees for federal employment tax purposes after 1987?

A. I don't recall that. I may have been, but I just can't recall anything about it. Could you tell me a little more?

Q. Well, were you ever told that after December 31st of 1987 that Boles Trucking, Inc., began to treat its truck drivers as employees for federal employment tax purposes?

A. I just don't remember whether I was or wasn't. I, I …

Q. Would you be surprised to learn that?

A. No, I wouldn't be surprised.

Q. Why?

A. Because you've been reviewing them and probably told them they — not you, I mean, the Internal Revenue Service probably told them to withhold.

Q. Well, if I understand your position correctly, your opinion was that the truck drivers who were being paid by Boles Trucking between 1984 and 1987 were employees, for federal employment tax purposes, of Cornhusker Motor Lines?

A. That's right.

Q. And based upon that, I would expect you to be at least a little surprised to learn that after 1987, Boles Trucking was in fact withholding federal income taxes and FICA taxes from the amounts paid to its truck drivers?

A. I wouldn't be surprised if, even a little surprised. Oftentimes, we do expedient things in here. If the IRS is breathing down your neck and you're from the IRS, we want to end it. So we said, all right, do it. And we pass it on to somebody else's, you know, income. You're not surprised at the — let me give you an example. The Internal Revenue Service does it, too. One time I had a client that got a refund, said I made a mistake on a return. The client brought it to me and I looked at it and I don't want the client to have that refund if they weren't entitled to it. I checked the return, I couldn't find the mistake. I took it down to the Internal Revenue Service in Council Bluffs, they checked and couldn't find it. I said, should I have the client pay it back? He said, no. It would cost us more to process it than what we overpaid you. It was expedient. A lot of times we settled things at the appeals office level. Paul Ross once, did you know him, the appeals officer?

Q. Yes.

A. He said on a case I had, he said what would the tax court judge do if he were hearing this case? He said, I tell you, I'll try to be like a tax court judge. You want to split it down the middle? I said, that's fine. So we got it half and half. We do those things just to get rid of it.

Q. Mr. Telpner, in arriving at your opinions concerning whether or not Boles Trucking was entitled to any relief from the federal employment taxes assessed against it under Section 530 of the Revenue Act of 1978, were there any documents or writings which you relied upon to form your ... whether or not the corporation was entitled to that kind of relief?

A. Section 530, I read that. I did some research on some cases and I don't have my notes here, but they wouldn't be hidden cases of the court of claims, appeals and so forth. Some of them before 1974, even. I went clear back. And so treatises in New York University, articles in the *Journal of Taxation* with the research in the footnotes. The *Journal of Accountancy* and *Transport Topics* and *Motor Freight Controller*, my personal experience, the Internal Revenue Code Regulations and my many years in practice.

Q. But what I was really asking you are there any documents, in, you know, returns or letters or any documents that you might have observed that you relied upon to form your opinions?

A. Oh, yeah. The tax returns for one thing.

Q. Tax returns? Okay. Which returns are these?

A. Okay, the ones in — you said from '74 — '84 through '87 …

Q. Yeah. The 1120 …

A. — S's, yes, for one thing.

Q. Okay. What else?

A. The depositions of the State of Nebraska guy, of Bruce Boles, of the drivers and the contract that nobody paid attention to. The contract, itself, said you're the employer. But then they went ahead, Cornhusker did and treated themselves as the employer. They completely controlled everything. They — I thought that there was no way that anybody could haul for Cornhusker, without Cornhusker completely controlling it the way the depositions related everything. Then I reviewed some trip sheets and I saw advances going out. You know how they do it, by fax to drivers. Mike Fouts, you know, he was from Cornhusker, giving a driver $1,000 here, $1200 there, just sending it. They needed an advance so they call Mike Fouts from Cornhusker. That's control.

Q. Do you know if Mr. Bruce Boles ever gave his drivers any advances?

A. No, I don't, but …

Q. Would you be surprised to learn that he did?

A. No, I wouldn't.

Q. Wouldn't all those things you've just said about control apply equally to Boles Trucking if an officer of Boles Trucking was making advances to truck drivers?

A. It might have, if I wouldn't have met Bruce Boles and reviewed the returns and read the deposition. As far as this goes he didn't exercise control. He doesn't even have a terminal or a place for the trucks. If he did any advances, like an agent of Cornhusker … I was startled by the amount of control that Cornhusker actually exercised. But, I also thought, man, this wouldn't be a bad business to lease tractors and have somebody take care of everything. He leases tractors. There's no doubt in my mind.

Q. Mr. Telpner, from what you've said here and what you said yesterday, it's my understanding you've done quite a bit of research into a number of court cases where either the court or a jury was called upon to make certain determinations as to whether an individual was an independent contractor or an employee for purposes of federal employment taxes; is that right?

A. That's right.

Q. Were any of those cases that you reviewed cases where a jury was asked to make the determination?

A. As I recall, there were some.

Q. Okay. Do you know any reason why a jury of ordinary average citizens could not apply the 20 common law factors to determine whether or not Boles Trucking, Inc., should have been withholding federal income taxes and social security taxes from the amounts paid to its drivers?

Mostek: What was the question? Any reason why the jury couldn't do it?
Metcalfe: Right.
Mostek: I don't understand that. What does that mean?
Metcalfe: Well, it's a question to …
Mostek: That's vague to me. I guess that would be my objection …
Metcalfe: Okay.
Mostek: … it's just vague.

Q. Mr. Telpner, you've read some cases in which the jury determined whether or not certain workers were independent contractors or employees, for federal employment tax purposes?

A. Yes.

Q. Okay. Do you know of any reason why in this case a jury could not determine, after applying the 20 common law factors to the facts of this case, to determine whether or not those truck drivers were independent contractors or employees for federal employment tax purposes?

Mostek: Okay. I still think it's vague and ambiguous, because I don't know what cases you're referring to. They may have been cases …
Metcalfe: I'm not asking for cases, I'm asking with respect to this case.
Mostek: I know, but there's an important element that you're leaving out. Were there expert witnesses involved in those cases? Because you know that

this matter is very complex and you know that an expert witness is going to have the power to draw inferences that a layman would not have. And so if you ask his opinion as to whether a jury is capable of making that decision, that's a very important factor. Did they have help from somebody to explain this complicated subject matter?

Metcalfe: Your objection's noted. You may answer the question.

Telpner: Before ...

Q. I'm not asking you in any other cases. I'm asking you about this case.

A. I wanted to tell you my answer before you two had the discussion.

Q. Okay.

A. My answer was that I don't know enough about juries to answer that question. I mean, you know, I would think that a lawyer — you know, I've never even served on a jury, but doesn't a lawyer question people to see if they're qualified to be on a jury?

Q. Sure.

A. And I've never done anything like that. I don't see how I could answer that. And that's the answer I had in mind before, because you're asking me to make an opinion about what the jury can do or can't do. It would be almost impossible for me to do anything but guess.

Q. Okay.

A. And if I guessed, I'd say maybe or yes or no or perhaps, because I ...

Q. Well, why don't we have your best belief here or opinion? Is there anything — what is there about this case that is so complex that an average person could not, after receiving instructions from the court on the 20 common law factors and apply them to the facts of this case to determine whether or not those truck drivers of Boles Trucking, Inc., are independent contractors or employees for federal employment tax purposes?

Mostek: Before you go on, I just want to lodge an objection as to foundation. He's already said he doesn't understand juries.

Metcalfe: Go ahead.

Mostek: You may proceed.

Telpner: Accounting is very complex. Most people don't even understand what we do. But, if we say it, they say it must be right. For example, if they say, because it's my opinion that the certified public accountants are the ones who — plus Etaoin Shrdlu, were the ones who made these decisions. What happens, the jury is going to believe that that's right. I know from experience in here that they think that we have an unusual perception in the minds of lay people. They think we know everything about tax and accounting and if we say it, that it's gospel. So, it's very difficult for a jury to find anything other than the fact that he is not the employer.

Q. Okay. But, I'm asking you what is it about this case that is so complex or so difficult that an average person could not understand it?

A. Well, the real problem is that ... are you familiar with a huge line of cases of who is the taxpayer? No, I have to tell you this is a story, because I'm going to tell you what's so complex.

Q. Why don't you just go ahead and tell me why you think it's so complex?

Telpner: There are a line of cases in tax, in the Internal Revenue Code in cases that are very difficult for lay people to resolve. For example, who is the taxpayer for one. It's very technical to decide who is the taxpayer. For example, Subchapter S corporation doesn't pay taxes. They're still a taxpayer in many of these cases. Now we get to this. This is very complicated. I have testified that Cornhusker Motor Carriers is the employer. Now, when I said that, even the learned counsel in this room were startled at the conclusion of a certified public accountant who is an expert in trucking and taxes and accounting. Startled at that. Now, I imagine the lay people would look at that and they said Mr. Telpner said that Cornhusker Motor Freight is the employer. And the Internal Revenue Service says that Boles Trucking is the employer. Now, do we know from experience on who the employer is? How are we going to figure this out? So, if we believe Mr. Telpner, then we're going to say without looking at the technicalities, Mr. Telpner must be right. And if we said we believe that the examiner, the collection examiner that did it, then we'll say that she's right. But I, personally, believe that the jury, instead of basing this on knowledge of technical know-how in the trucking industry, from my experience in accounting, they're going to base it on belief in me, or belief in you. And they are going to be baffled by all the technical problems that arose. That's very complicated tax knowledge, it's very complicated transportation industry knowledge, it's very complicated who is the employer knowledge.

Q. Anything other than who is the employer?

A. On whether he's able to rely on accountants or not. On advice of the CPA preparer, on advice of the non-CPA preparer. The years in question were all prepared by certified public accountants. That's going to have a lot of weight that their advice could be relied upon. But, are they experts? The jury is going to have to be an expert on whether a CPA can be relied upon or not. Whether the Internal Revenue Code interpretations of one CPA as opposed to another, as opposed to an accountant for the Internal Revenue Service, which one's right. Very complex and confusing. Then they have to understand the court cases that said sometimes their employer's this person, sometimes they're that person, sometimes they're independent. You've got court cases going in every direction and the years involved. And then they're going to have to decide, when we come to the question of trucking companies who do the same thing and the question comes up, why did the Internal Revenue Service start examining so many in '86, unless they had already determined that many trucking companies don't withhold on their drivers? So, the only reason for this big push is because everything I've read tells me that the IRS suddenly said, oh, my God, there's a lot of people not withholding on their independent contractors. They're truck drivers. Well, let's go out and examine them. And there was never any push until 1986 and shortly after when it really grew big. So, that tells me alone that the Internal Revenue Service had considered that there are enough trucking companies that don't withhold on their drivers, leasing companies, that it pays to examine them. And so a jury is going to have to hear a lot of complicated stuff.

Q. Mr. Telpner, have you ever published any articles or papers on any subject concerning or relating to federal employment taxes?

A. I did some research on lumpers, a lot of research on lumpers and I came to a conclusion on that. I presented the paper before the Nebraska Accounting and Finance Council. I came to the conclusion that if you went to Tax Court the taxpayer usually lost and if you went to a jury the taxpayer usually won. And I tried to figure out why. I found in most cases in the jury trials the jury wasn't paying any attention to technical problems. The tax court did, of course. The driver would testify, "Do you think I was going to ask that loader for a Social Security Number? He lifts freight all day long. He's got arms this big. If he doesn't want me to withhold on him, I'm not going to withhold." And the jury says, we don't blame him. Now, it goes to the jury, the jury looks to people like me to make their decisions for them.

Q. Mr. Telpner, have you ever written or published any articles or papers on the determination of the employer-employee relationship under the usual common law rules with regard to federal employment taxes? In other words, have you ever written any articles or papers concerning whether or not an individual is an employee or an independent contractor for federal employment taxes?

A. Under the common law rules?

Q. Correct.

A. No, not that I recall.

Q. Okay. Do you belong to any professional accounting societies or groups?

A. Right now the American Institute of CPAs, The Iowa and Nebraska Society of CPAs.

Q. Any other societies?

A. No, not anymore. I was on the board of directors of the National Accounting and Finance Council of the American Trucking Association for 15 years and of the Nebraska Motor Carriers and the Accounting Council. But, after deregulation, you know, they started to not have very much information. Most of the information came in trucking over the years. I mean, for accountants came from me. I was the only non Big-Eight CPA at the time that was on the ICC Regulated Carriers Subcommittee of the American Institute of Certified Public Accountants. CPAs call me up from all over the country to ask my advice on trucking.

Q. With respect to those professional societies that you belong to, were you ever a member of a section or group within those societies that had anything to do with federal employment taxes?

A. I was a member of the tax division of the American Institute of CPAs for a while. That would have covered all taxes, but I thought that they didn't do as much good as the *Journal of Taxation* or *The Journal of Accountancy* or some of the others where you could learn more. I thought it was too basic.

Q. Mr. Telpner, over the years you probably met many, many CPAs and accountants who were living in this area here of Council Bluffs/Omaha and like that; is that right?

A. Yes.

Q. You probably know quite a few of those individuals, right?

A. Yes.

Q. Okay. Do you know of any other accountant and by that I mean a certified public accountant, who has testified in a federal district court concerning either Section 530 of the Revenue Act of 1978, or to the determination of whether an individual is an employee for federal employment tax purposes under the usual common law rules?

A. No, I do not.

Q. Are you aware of any particular cases where an individual was, an individual accountant or CPA, was allowed to give testimony in a federal district court on matters that we've just described here for you?

A. I don't know of any.

Metcalfe: Mike, maybe two more questions and then I'm done.
Telpner: Sorry for the interruption.

Q. One of the things and correct me if I'm wrong, Mr. Telpner, please correct me if I'm wrong, one of the things that I understood your testimony to be, with respect to your opinion concerning whether or not Boles Trucking was entitled to any relief under Section 530 of the Revenue Act of 1978, you testified that you had, in addition to some documents, you also had looked at a number of depositions; is that correct?

A. Yes. Yes, I had looked at depositions.

Q. As an expert witness can you tell me if that is the type of information which is relied upon by experts in your field in giving their opinions?

A. Yes, but I can't speak for other experts, just myself. I've testified many times and I always start out with interrogatories, the complaint, the depositions, you know. Unless I find out what the nature of the issues are, I can't, I don't know what to look for. That way I don't waste a lot of time.

Q. In the other cases in which you've testified have you read or relied upon depositions in order to form your expert opinion?

A. I certainly have. Yes, I have.

Q. Could you tell me — well, the last question I have is could you tell me with respect to either your opinion as to whether or not Boles Trucking was liable as an employer for the payment of these federal employment taxes, or whether it was entitled to relief under Section 530 of the Revenue Act of 1978, how your expert opinion in those two areas differs in any way from any legal conclusions that a Judge might draw?

A. I don't think I can tell what a Judge might draw.

Q. That's all right. But, basically, would it be fair to say that you have arrived at a legal conclusion concerning whether or not Boles Trucking, Inc., is entitled to relief under Section 530 of the Revenue Act of 1978?

Mostek: I object on the basis of foundation. He's a CPA I don't think he's qualified to say what's a legal conclusion, what's a factual conclusion, what's an inference. You know those are all matters for lawyers. If he can answer it, that's fine, but I object.

Telpner: My niece and my brother and my son are lawyers and they would tell me if I thought I could draw a legal conclusion that I was weird. No, I can't decide what a legal conclusion is. I can say I gave you an expert opinion. Whether it's legal or not I wouldn't know.

Q. In order to arrive at your opinion you said that you had to look at statutes and court cases and so on and so forth; isn't that right?

A. To find out what the trends were, what the issues were. When I read the cases it helps me determine what I have to look at, what the issues are, what type of evidence I might need to present to people with legal minds so they can make a legal decision.

Metcalfe: That's all I have. Please answer whatever questions Mr. Mostek may have for you.

Mostek: I have no questions. Mr. Telpner will exercise his right to read and sign.

(Whereupon, this deposition was concluded at the hour of 10:50 a.m.)

The Effect of the Attorney–Client Privilege and Work Product Doctrine

7

MICHAEL M. MOSTEK, JD

7.1 Preface to the Attorney Reading This Chapter

If you are an attorney, the subject of this chapter is nothing new to you. You will already have a working knowledge of the attorney–client prvilege and the work product doctrine. However, these concepts are more or less foreign to the accounting profession and, to work effectively, your expert needs to have some exposure to these rules. This is by no means an exhaustive treatment of the subject, but this chapter will provide the attorney with a brief "refresher" course on the basics of the privilege and the doctrine, and focus on the issues that may arise as you prepare the case with your accounting expert. The attorney should be ready and willing to help the expert by sharing this information with him if he does not already have it or needs to refresh his memory. You should also be ready to help your expert by explaining or expanding upon the information presented in this chapter as needed.

7.2 The Attorney–Client Privilege

7.2.1 The Search for the Truth and the Law of Privileges

Generally, the judicial process is regarded as a "search for the truth" or a survey of all of the available information that is then used to arrive at a conclusion — guilt or innocence, liability or exoneration. Logic dictates that the search is best served by having all relevant information brought to light for consideration by the person or persons responsible for making the conclusion, such as the judge, jury, arbitrator or hearing officer. However, under certain circumstances we, as a society, deem the protection of certain relationships and information to be more important than the search for the truth. When this is the case, we say the information is *privileged*.

For centuries, the law has recognized a variety of privileges. In the course of judicial process and many cases, the courts created privileges through well-reasoned opinions that justified the need to protect information from public or judicial scrutiny. The opinions or case law recognizing the privileges have become precedent, i.e., a rule has been established that is to be followed in future cases. Generally, this judge or court-made law is referred to as the *common law*. While recognizing the well-established common law privileges, most courts today say the work of creating and defining new privileges should be left up to our legislative bodies. Some state legislatures have enacted statutes that codify, or put into statutory form, the common law privileges. However, a proposal to codify the federal law of privileges was rejected by congress. In the federal courts, and in particular with regard to questions of federal law, recognized privileges are still a matter of common law, that is, judge-made case law. (See Rule 501 of the Federal Rules of Evidence.)

Whether made by courts or legislatures, the recognized privileges are always subject to consideration of the courts. There are many cases that discuss, limit or otherwise address the scope of these privileges. If a privilege is asserted in legal proceedings, the courts or other tribunals are called upon to determine the applicability of the privilege and explain the rationale of their decisions. Generally, therefore, the primary source of law on the recognition and detailed rules of privileges are the cases that have been handed down over the years.

7.2.2   General Requirements for any Privilege

Generally, legal scholars and the courts recognize that four conditions must be present to justify the creation of any privilege, whether it be the attorney–client privilege or one of the other recognized privileges. One legal scholar has posited the following generally accepted requirements:

1. "The communication must originate in an *expectation* that it will not be disclosed.
2. The element of *confidentiality* must be essential to the full and satisfactory maintenance of the relationship between the parties.
3. The *relationship* must be one that, in the opinion of the community, ought to be sedulously *fostered*.
4. The *injury* that would inure to the relationship by the disclosure of the communications must be *greater* than the *benefit* that would be gained for the correct disposal of litigation by virtue of the disclosure." (8 J. Wigmore, Evidence §2285, at 527 (McNaughton rev. 1961).)

The recognized privileges include, for example, the privilege for marital communications, the privilege for confidential information obtained in the course of the physician–patient relationship, the privilege for governmental secrets and, of course, the privilege for communications between a lawyer and client. With the possible exception of the privilege for governmental secrets, all of these privileges are founded on the policy of promoting and protecting the free flow of information between the parties to a communication. As a society, we have determined that the need for confidentiality in these settings outweighs the potential harm to the judicial process — the search for the truth — that could be produced by cloaking the communications and information in secrecy. The underlying premise holds that the parties to the communication must be free of the fear that someone could be forced, through judicial process, to publicly disclose the confidences that are the subject of the communication. Otherwise, the parties may not provide complete and accurate information in the course of their communications. As a result, the relationship would suffer and, in the case of the attorney and client, dependable advice may not be given or received.

7.2.3 Requirements for Application of the Attorney–Client Privilege

7.2.3.1 *The Elements of the Privilege*

Although it has been stated in various ways by the courts, the consensus generally requires four elements to exist before the attorney–client privilege will apply:

> The privilege applies only if (1) the asserted holder of the privilege is or sought to become a client; (2) the person to whom the communication was made (a) is a member of the bar of a court, or his subordinate and (b) in connection with this communication is acting as a lawyer; (3) the communication relates to a fact of which the attorney was informed (a) by his client (b) without the presence of strangers (c) for the purpose of securing primarily either (i) an opinion on law or (ii) legal service or (iii) assistance in some legal proceeding, and not (d) for the purpose of committing a crime or tort; and (4) the privilege has been (a) claimed and (b) not waived by the client. *United States v. United Shoe Mach. Corp,* 89 F. Supp. 357, 358-59 (D. Mass 1950).

This is a very accurate but technical statement of the privilege. In more basic terms, the privilege may be found to apply if the following elements exist:

- Communication
- Between a lawyer and a client
- For the purpose of obtaining legal advice or services
- Which is intended to be confidential
- The privilege has not been waived

Each of these elements seems to be readily understandable. However, as discussed below, some detailed rules must be observed for the privilege to attach.

7.2.3.2   The Meaning of "Communication"

Although it is commonly referred to as the "attorney–client privilege," the rights associated with the privilege are generally viewed as belonging to the client. For this reason, it could be more aptly named the "client–attorney privilege." Because the law recognizes the privilege as properly belonging to the client rather than the attorney, the client is the one who must waive the privilege if it is to be waived. Because the lawyer generally acts as an agent of the client, this rule and the distinction of the person acting to waive the privilege can become blurred. Waiver by the client is discussed in greater detail below.

When considering the communications to which the privilege applies, the first matter to be determined is whether the privilege covers statements made by the client, by the lawyer or both. Beginning with the rule that the rights associated with the privilege belong to the client, some courts take a narrow view of the term "communication," holding that the term applies primarily to communications from the client to the lawyer. Some courts hold that the lawyer's response, including advice and opinions communicated to the client, are privileged because their disclosure would provide insight or allow inferences to be drawn regarding the facts communicated by the client. Other courts hold that the communications from the attorney to the client are automatically privileged, based on a view that the purpose of the privilege is always to promote good two-way communications.

Because these intricate rules regarding the privilege are based on case law and the result cannot be predicted with absolute certainty, lawyers generally act with great care to fashion their communications to clients in a way that would promote the application and enforcement of the privilege. For example, when writing opinion letters, the careful attorney will include a recitation of facts provided by the client. This serves to form the factual basis for the attorney's opinion, and to record the precise information provided to him by the client. This habit protects the attorney and the integrity of his opinion in the event any facts were either omitted or not accurately communicated by the client. More importantly, it also ties the opinion and the lawyer's communication to the client to the facts communicated to the lawyer by the client. In this way, the communications from the client, which are clearly within the ambit of the privilege, are linked to the opinions or advice that he sought. Given this, even the courts that narrowly construe the privilege are more likely to find that the lawyer's statements to the client are privileged.

As a practical matter, litigation over these fine points of the privilege is somewhat rare. In practice, most lawyers would accept and proceed on the assumption that any statements made by either the client or the lawyer are privileged, given the existence of all other elements of the privilege. Generally, communications between the lawyer and the client take the form of written or oral statements. Of course it may also include such non-verbal statements as a nod of the head, a wink or a "thumbs-up." These are all forms of communication. But, for the most part, the communications that are the subject of the privilege are statements made through personal meetings and letters or other correspondence. They occur when the lawyer gives a written opinion in response to written or verbal statements made to him by the client. Also, they regularly occur in face-to-face meetings in which the client recites facts and receives a verbal opinion from the lawyer. Assuming all of the other elements of the privilege are satisfied, most lawyers would consider the statements that occur during the course of these ordinary communications to be privileged.

It should be noted that communication must be made in confidence and with an expectation of privacy. This is important in the context of electronic mail and other forms of communication that are not necessarily private. The requirement of confidentiality is discussed in detail below.

However, it should be noted that the privilege does not extend to business documents and similar information simply by virtue of the fact that they have been given to an attorney. For example, the act of delivering financial statements, accounting or tax information to the lawyer and having it stored in the lawyer's files will not make the information privileged. If the information would have been discoverable in the hands of the client, it remains discoverable after being transmitted to the attorney. In contrast, statements made by the client to the attorney with regard to the documents, for example, a letter that explains or expands upon information contained in the documents, should be protected.

Another question arises with regard to memoranda prepared by the lawyer for his file. For example, suppose the lawyer and client hold a phone conference or meeting and the lawyer then dictates a memorandum to the file concerning the meeting. To the extent that these documents memorialize communications from the client to the lawyer, or *vice versa*, the better-reasoned decisions would hold that the matter is privilege. In practice, most attorneys would consider these memoranda to be privileged, but would be careful to see that they include the statements made by the client and information that ties the lawyers advice to the client's statements. Also, to the extent these memoranda contain the mental impressions of the lawyer, they may also be protected by the work product doctrine. This doctrine is discussed in detail below.

7.2.3.3 The Meaning of "Lawyer"

7.2.3.3.1 The Attorney–Client Relationship. Fundamentally, the privilege applies to a communication only when it involves a duly licensed attorney at law. The attorney at law must have a relationship or prospective relationship with the client. This means that the client must have sought out the attorney for the purpose of receiving legal advice with the intention of forming an attorney–client relationship. Statements made and advice given to relatives or acquaintances at gatherings or social occasions generally would not be protected by the privilege. However, as long as the individual seeking advice or services from the attorney has an intention to form a relationship, initial meetings and interviews will be subject to the privilege regardless of whether a relationship is eventually formed.

7.2.3.3.2 Those Who May Speak for the Lawyer.

Given the existence of a *bona fide* relationship or prospective relationship, the terms "lawyer" or "attorney" generally include in-house counsel regularly employed by corporations and other forms of business organizations. They also include specially retained counsel working outside of the client company in private practice. For purposes of the privilege, the courts generally agree that the term "lawyer" includes his employees or agents over whom he has regular direct supervision and control. This would include junior lawyers, law clerks, legal assistants and secretaries.

More difficult questions arise when the attorney specially retains employees, contractors or other agents to assist in the preparation of a case or other legal matter. This occurs when the lawyer retains an investigator, for example, who then communicates with the client. In this case, it is very important for the attorney to be certain that such agents are acting under his direct supervision and control, even though they are specially retained. If any facts indicate that the client, or some third party such as an insurance company, has employed the investigator, the privilege may be in jeopardy.

The most difficult questions arise when the agents are not directly retained or supervised by the attorney. At this point, most courts would hold that the privilege has reached its limits. For example, if an insurance company retains an investigator or similar agent, the communications between that agent and the company's attorney probably would not be privileged. This would occur because the agent would be supervised and paid by the client, the insurance company. The attorney would have no direct supervision or control. For this reason, careful attorneys will directly retain and supervise all agents who may be asked to assist with the preparation of a case or other legal matters.

7.2.3.3.3 The Forensic Accounting Witness as an Agent of the Attorney.

The requirement for the attorney to have direct supervision and control over the agent has obvious implications for the relationship between the attorney and the forensic accounting expert witness. The attorney should directly retain the expert witness to make the accounting expert his agent and subject to his supervision and control. Evidence concerning the nature of the relationship should be maintained in the form of the expert's consulting agreement, and the agreement should be one between the attorney or his law firm and the expert witness. Also, care must be taken to ensure that the expert obtains his facts through, or at the direction of, the attorney rather than the client. Any investigations done by the expert should be undertaken at the written request of the attorney and any meetings that the expert attends should be attended at the request of the attorney. The attorney should be present at any meetings at which the expert is requested to be present.

7.2.3.3.4 The Expert Witness Engagement Letter and Agreement. A detailed discussion of the expert witness's engagement letter is presented in Chapter 3. The purpose of the engagement letter or agreement, and the direct supervision and control of the attorney are to fashion the relationship to provide the best possible opportunity for application and enforcement of the attorney–client privilege, should the need arise. For example, if the attorney meets with the client in the presence of the expert witness, the privilege can be maintained if the court finds that the expert was acting as an agent of the attorney during the meeting. The goal is to structure the relationship in such a way that the presence of the expert at the meeting is no different from the presence of the attorney's legal assistant or junior attorney. All of these agents act under the direct supervision and control of the attorney, and it should be the same with the expert witness if the privilege is to be preserved.

By carefully structuring the relationship between the attorney and the accounting expert witness, they will also increase the chances that much of their work will be protected under the work product doctrine, subject to certain exceptions that are built into the rules of civil procedure. This doctrine is discussed in detail below.

7.2.3.4 The Meaning of "Client"

7.2.3.4.1 Those Who Speak for the Client.   Once again, the privilege assumes the existence of a relationship or potential relationship between a client and an attorney. The term "client" seems to be simple enough, and has a clear meaning in the case of an individual client. Business organizations can be more difficult. It is well accepted that corporations are entitled to claim the attorney–client privilege. Questions arise, however, as to who speaks on behalf of the corporation for purposes of communicating with the lawyer. If corporate maintenance managers or janitors speak with the lawyer are their statements privileged? If the president or a vice-president writes a letter or memorandum to the lawyer, are the statements in those documents privileged?

7.2.3.4.2 Determining Who Speaks for the Corporate Client.   Generally, two tests have been developed to determine whose statements can be privileged. One line of cases generally adopts a test called the "control group" test. This focuses on whether the communication is being made by someone within the corporation or other business organization that has the authority to act upon advice given by the lawyer. Generally, if he does, his statements to the attorney would be privileged. The other common test is called the "subject matter" test. This test focuses on the communication itself, to determine whether it was authorized by someone in a position of authority, made for the purpose of seeking legal advice or whether the subject of the communication was within the scope of the corporate employee's duties. If so, the communication would be privileged under this test. These tests have been adopted and followed by various federal and state courts. Some courts have adopted a combination of the two.

The two tests may yield different results. Using the control group test, it is difficult to imagine a situation where statements made to the corporate attorney by a janitor or bookkeeper in a large corporation would be privileged. While each performs an important function within the company, neither would generally be considered a member of the control group and probably would not have authority to act on the advice of the attorney without authorization from a superior. Therefore, under this test, statements made by these people to the attorney would not be certain to qualify for protection by the attorney–client privilege. In contrast, the subject matter test would probably allow for protection of the statements. For example, if the bookkeeper or accounting clerk were directed or authorized to make statements to the corporate attorney regarding accounting matters, and if this authority were granted for the purpose of receiving legal advice on tax or accounting matters that are the subject of the attorney's legal services, the privilege would probably apply.

The question of which test should be applied has been settled in the federal courts, where the subject matter test is the rule. However, the question is not resolved on the state level by rulings of the federal courts. Therefore, the rule may vary from state to state. A survey of all of the state rules is beyond the scope of this work. Suffice it to say that the question of who may speak for a corporation or other business organization can be complicated and must be carefully analyzed to determine when the privilege will apply.

7.2.3.4.3 Communications through Authorized Agents of the Client.
Regardless of which test is applied and who within the corporation is authorized to make privileged communications with the attorney, it is well recognized that the authorized person should be allowed to make statements through an agent or assistant. For example, the company president would generally be authorized to deal with the corporate attorney, but most likely would not type her own correspondence to the attorney. She would use her

secretary to perform this clerical function, or she may ask an executive assistant to write a letter to the attorney on her behalf. Just as the attorney is allowed to communicate to the client through agents over whom the attorney has direct authority and control, so too may the client, using her agents and representatives. This holds true so long as the client intends the communication to remain confidential and does not take actions that would appear to be contrary to this intention.

There may be circumstances where the client must use outside agents or consultants to communicate information to the attorney. This would occur in the case of the company's regular insurance agent or accountant who was called to a meeting to help explain or deliver information to the attorney that will assist him in rendering legal advice to the client. If this is the purpose of the communication and if it is clear that the client intends the information to remain confidential, it is arguable that the statements of the insurance agent or accountant, or the like, should be privileged. However, as was the case with the attorney's outside agents, it is less clear that the outside agent is acting under the direct supervision and control of the client. Therefore, the applicability of the privilege is less certain and great caution must be exercised.

7.2.3.5   *The Meaning of "Obtaining Legal Advice or Services"*

7.2.3.5.1   The Lawyer May Wear Many Hats.   To ensure the application and enforcement of the attorney–client privilege, the attorney must be acting in the capacity of a lawyer when the communication is made. Attorneys often "wear different hats." Attorneys provide legal advice or services. But attorneys also act in other capacities on behalf of their clients. For example, an in-house attorney who is also an officer of a company may perform many activities in the course of his duties. Some may be unrelated to the practice of law. Therefore, in-house counsel who works on negotiating a business deal such as acquisition or merger may not be acting in his capacity as an attorney when doing so. His work is more akin to that of a business executive. The same can be said of private practice attorneys who become involved in their clients' business affairs or who conduct an internal investigation on behalf of a corporate client. Likewise, an attorney who prepares tax returns is not necessarily engaged in the act of rendering legal advice. His task may involve the simple act of compiling the tax information provided by the client and filling out a return. An individual who holds dual licenses as both attorney and accountant may not be engaged in rendering legal advice when he is practicing accounting. Under all of the circumstances, the attorney–client privilege is of questionable applicability because the attorney may not be engaged in the act of rendering legal advice or services.

7.2.3.5.2 The Purpose of Communicating. Likewise, as discussed above with regard to the matter of corporate communications, the client must make the communication with the intention of seeking legal advice. If the statement is made to the attorney for the purpose of obtaining business advice, the privilege will not apply. Perhaps the client has contacted the attorney to share financial information and the question is whether the company should file bankruptcy. While legal advice concerning the options and potential consequences might involve legal advice, the question may be considered one that essentially involves a business decision. Unauthorized or random comments made by corporate employees to the attorney will probably not be privileged. However, it is likely that the statements can be kept out of evidence on some other basis such as hearsay.

7.2.3.6 The Meaning of "Intended to Be Confidential"

7.2.3.6.1 The Expectation of Confidentiality. Confidential communications are those that the client reasonably expects and intends will not be passed along to third parties outside of the attorney–client relationship. For example, assume the client sends a memorandum clearly marked "confidential" to the attorney that details the circumstances under which an employee was discharged and includes information concerning the employee's age, race, religion and sexual orientation, states the client's fear that he may be sued for some type of discrimination and requests advice on what to do next. This would be an example of a communication that is likely to be found privileged by the courts. In contrast, consider a situation in which information, such as income or expense records to be used in preparing a tax return, is included. When this information is given to the attorney, the client knows or expects it to be sent along to a government agency or another third party. Here, the courts would be unlikely to find the requisite intent of confidentiality. Under such circumstances, it is apparent that the client has no expectation that the information will remain confidential within the attorney–client relationship. Between these two extremes lie many closer cases.

A problem frequently arises when a confidential communication is sent to the attorney with a copy to some third party such as an accountant or other interested business advisor. The client may intend and expect that both the attorney and the accountant keep the information confidential, and they may honor his intention, but the privilege will usually not apply because information has been communicated to a third party who is outside the attorney–client relationship. This is a common trap for the unsuspecting client who trusts his accountant as much as, if not more than, his attorney. An exception to this general rule may apply when the accountant is present at a meeting with the client or sends information to the attorney, and the accountant's presentation is needed to convey technical information concerning a legal matter under consideration by the attorney. As discussed in section 7.2.3.3.3 of this chapter, the accountant may be considered to be a communicating agent of the client for purposes of the privilege. However, given the uncertainty created by this situation, many attorneys will presume that the conversation is not privileged and will advise their clients to act with caution.

7.2.3.6.2   A Modern Dilemma.   Today, clients and their attorneys can choose among many means of communicating, including meetings, letters, telephone, mobile phone, facsimile and e-mail. With regard to each of these methods of communication, consideration must be given to the attorney–client privilege. Can the client reasonably expect privacy in using the chosen means of communication? If not, caution must be exercised with statements made because the communication may not be privileged.

Traditional meetings, letters, telephone conversations over hard lines and even facsimiles would not seem to pose a problem. However, there may be little, if any, expectation of privacy in ordinary mobile phone conversations or e-mail correspondence. It is well known that both of these means of communications can be readily intercepted in their usual form. Given this, if the issue is squarely raised in a court proceeding, judges may have difficulty in finding that there was ever a reasonable expectation of privacy or an intention that the communication made through these means was ever intended to be confidential. Without this finding, the communication would probably not be privileged. Therefore, the client and his attorney are forced to choose between the ease and convenience of these modern forms of communication and the desire to keep their communications confidential. Because of the concern over lack of privacy, both would be well advised to use older but more private means of communication when they truly desire their communications to be privileged.

7.2.3.7   *Waiver of the Privilege*

7.2.3.7.1   Attachment and Waiver.   Assuming all of the elements of the privilege are found to exist, a given communication between the client and the attorney may be considered privileged. Some confusion exists between a finding that the privilege has attached to a communication in the first place and a finding that the privilege has been waived. In other words, a waiver cannot logically occur unless the privilege is first found to exist. However, if one of the requisite elements is lacking, some courts will say the privilege has been waived. This may occur, for example, if the court finds that the element of confidentiality is lacking because the client copied a third party on his correspondence to his attorney. This would be evidence of a lack of intention for the communication to remain confidential between the client and the attorney. Other courts would say the privilege never attached. It is probably a distinction that makes little difference. In either case, the privilege would not apply and the client could be compelled to disclose the communication to his adversary.

7.2.3.7.2   Voluntary and Inadvertent Waivers.   Because the privilege and the rights associated with it belong to the client, he can choose to voluntarily relinquish the privilege. This would occur, for example, if the client obtained an opinion from a lawyer and later sued the lawyer for malpractice. The client may choose to introduce the lawyer's opinion letter into evidence in the case against the attorney. Here, the client is affirmatively relying on the privileged information to prove his case against the attorney. Most courts would find this to be a voluntary waiver of the privilege.

Although the waiver of the privilege must be voluntary, generally the waiver need not be knowing and intentional. The courts have found that the privilege may be waived through inadvertent disclosure of the privileged communication to an adversary or other third parties. This might occur, for example, if documents are being produced in response to an adversary's request or a subpoena. If a privileged document were mistakenly included among other nonprivileged information that is delivered to the opposition, many, if not most, courts would find that a waiver had occurred. They reason that the burden is on the party claiming the privilege to see that it is maintained. The search for the truth demands all evidence and therefore, most courts will narrowly construe the privilege. Some courts have been less harsh. However, because the courts are divided and the outcome is less than certain, clients and their attorneys must once again exercise caution to prevent inadvertent waiver of the privilege.

7.2.3.7.3   Extent of Waiver.   Generally, if the client waives the privilege with respect to a communication, the waiver is considered to be permanent. Also, the privilege cannot be waived for some purposes, but reserved for others. For example, if the client introduces the lawyer's opinion letter into evidence in the malpractice case against his former attorney, the client cannot seek to maintain the privilege against other parties or matters with regard to which the opinion was originally written. Again, the privilege is most likely to be narrowly construed and the client and his lawyer must exercise great care when choosing to waive the privilege.

7.2.3.7.4   Refreshing Recollection.   Often, before testifying or during his testimony, a witness will need to review documents to refresh his recollection. This is allowed under the rules of evidence, but it is a critical and dangerous area for lawyers and their expert witnesses, including forensic accounting experts. If the expert witness uses a privileged document to refresh his recollection, this may lead to a waiver of the attorney–client privilege. This potential exists because Rule 612 of the Federal Rules of Evidence and similar rules in the state courts allow the adversary to have the document produced so the witness can be properly cross-examined. The applicable part of the rule provides:

> [I]f a witness uses a writing to refresh memory for the purpose of testifying, either – (1) while testifying, or (2) before testifying, if the court in its discretion determines it is necessary in the interests of justice, and adverse party is entitled to have the writing produced at the hearing, to inspect it, to cross-examine the witness thereon, and to introduce in evidence those portions which relate to the testimony of the witness. If it is claimed that the writing contains matters not related to the subject matter of the testimony the court shall examine the writing in camera, excise any portions not so related, and order delivery of the remainder to the party entitled thereto. (Fed. R. Evid. 612.)

The rule is based on a sense of fairness; if the witness is using the document to testify, the adverse party cannot be expected to adequately cross-examine the witness without being able to examine the document. For example, if the expert witness has made notes, the writing may include information that the expert omitted from his testimony. The omitted information may provide grounds for impeaching or questioning the assumptions or credibility of the expert. However, the adversary has no way of knowing whether this is true unless he is allowed to examine the document. Therefore, out of a sense of fairness and in the interest of justice, the court may require the writing to be made available to the adversary.

When the witness reviews a writing while giving testimony, the rule can lead to at least two types of problems for the expert and the attorney. First, assume that the writing consists of nothing more than nonprivileged notes made by the expert to help him remember details he needs to bring out in his testimony. Although the notes may not include privileged information, they may include apparent inconsistencies that, if disclosed to the adversary, could damage the expert's credibility or otherwise weaken his testimony. Second, assuming the notes do contain some privileged information — say a reference to discussions that the expert had with the client — the use of the notes could lead to a waiver of the privilege. At a minimum, the production of the writings reviewed by the expert to refresh his memory will probably lead to an extended deposition examination or cross-examination during the trial. For all of these reasons, most attorneys prefer that the expert testify without the use of notes, if at all possible. If notes must be used, the attorney should review them prior to the deposition or court testimony to determine what harm, if any, might befall his client if they are disclosed to the adversary. If the expert believes he must refer to other "writings" besides notes during his testimony, these documents should be reviewed and approved by the attorney in advance of the testimony.

The rule also applies to writings reviewed by the witness *before* testifying. This part of the rule is more likely to be applied in the course of the witnesses' deposition. Questions will usually be asked during witnesses' deposition concerning what information the witness reviewed to prepare for giving his testimony. In the case of an expert, these questions are designed to elicit two types of information. The first is information that will help the adversary understand whether there are any documents used by the expert to refresh his recollection within the meaning of Rule 612. If so, the adversary will want to have the documents produced during the course of the deposition, assuming they have not already been delivered. The second type is information that the expert is relying on to form the basis for his opinions to be given in the matter. Again, the adversary will be seeking to determine whether those "writings" have been produced during the course of discovery. The discovery of documents and other information upon which the expert's opinion is based is discussed in detail below in connection with the work product doctrine. The expert's deposition and trial testimony is discussed in detail in Chapter 10.

Both the expert and the attorney must guard against waiver of the privilege. If the expert reviews a privileged document to refresh his recollection either before or during his deposition or trial testimony, and the adversary learns that such a document was reviewed, the client may be forced to turn over the document to the adversary. Because of Rule 612 and similar rules that apply in state court, attorneys are very careful when providing documents to an expert. Even though the expert may be retained by and working under the direct supervision and control of the attorney, the most careful procedure would be to refrain from providing privileged documents to the expert whenever possible.

7.3 The Work Product Doctrine

7.3.1 The Discovery Process

The work product doctrine cannot be fully understood without first having some understanding of the rules of discovery. Discovery is a process used in modern civil litigation that allows each adversary to request from the other all relevant evidence or other information that might lead to the discovery of relevant evidence on the matter in dispute. If either fails to comply, the court can order production of the evidence. In federal court, some discovery is now automatic and certain information must be exchanged without any need for a request from the opposing party. The rules that embody this discovery process are generally called the rules of civil procedure. Similar, but more limited rules concerning discovery are also provided for in the rules of criminal procedure. These rules generally exist in both federal and state court. The rules in general and, in particular, the discovery process, are intended to promote justice, as well as the prompt, efficient and correct determination of civil and criminal matters.

At least in civil cases, adversaries are not supposed to be permitted to withhold relevant evidence that could help their opponent's case. They are not supposed to "ambush" their opponents by waiting until trial to bring forth their most devastating evidence. To the extent that an adversarial proceeding can be likened to a poker game, the discovery process provides a procedure by which each player must show his cards to each of his opponents before the hand is played. In this sense, the discovery process promotes justice and judicial economy by bringing cases to an early resolution. If all of the parties are privy to all of the evidence, the ultimate outcome may be more predictable. As a result, many cases are settled before trial, adding efficiency to the judicial process.

The basic discovery rule for federal court is provided in Rule 26 (b) (1) of the Federal Rules of Civil Procedure. A similar rule exists in state court. The general rule in federal court provides:

(1) *In General.* Parties may obtain discovery regarding any matter, not privileged, that is relevant to the claim or defense of any party, including the existence, description, nature, custody, condition, and location of any books, documents, or other tangible things and the identity and location of persons having knowledge of any discoverable matter. For good cause, the court may order discovery of any matter relevant to the subject matter involved in the action. Relevant information need not be admissible at the trial if the discovery appears reasonably calculated to lead to the discovery of admissible evidence. All discovery is subject to the limitations imposed [by subsequent sections of the rule]. (Fed. R. Civ. P. 26 (b) (1).)

In addition to setting out the type of information that is discoverable, the rules provide that discovery may be obtained "by one or more" of several methods, including depositions, written interrogatories (questions), requests for production of documents and requests for admissions. (Fed. R. Civ. P. 26 (a) (5).) These common discovery tools are employed in nearly every case. As stated previously, the objective of discovery is to have each side show the other all relevant evidence in its possession that might bear on the legal or factual questions presented in any given case. Given the breadth of the general rule of discovery and the many tools provided to accomplish the task, questions arise concerning the working papers or work product prepared by the attorney as he gets the case ready for trial, and whether these materials are subject to discovery by the adversary.

7.3.2 The Attorney's Preparation of the Case

While the attorney–client privilege focuses on facilitating the attorney–client relationship, the work product doctrine is intended to allow the attorney the ability to prepare his client's case without fear that his mental impressions and case strategies may be subject to discovery by his client's adversaries. These mental impressions and strategies are generally referred to as the attorney's "work product." Like the attorney–client privilege, the work product doctrine is intended to keep certain information confidential. But, in the case of work product, the information does not necessarily take the form of a communication; it is any information that includes the attorney's mental impressions regarding the case or that includes other information that may provide the adversary with an insight into the attorney's thought processes on preparation of the case. Without the protection of the doctrine, the attorney would be hampered in his efforts to represent his client to the best of his ability. What if the attorney's file notes, including research and the attorney's impressions concerning the credibility of witnesses in the case could be discovered and reviewed by the adversary? What if the adversary could obtain copies of the statements the attorney spent hours obtaining from potential witnesses in the case?

The rules that protect the attorney's work product are referred to sometimes as the "work product privilege" or "immunity." However, as discussed below, the application of the word "privilege" to these rules is somewhat misleading. In the case of work product, there are routine exceptions to the privacy afforded to the information, and the privacy or protection is far from absolute. Most courts and commentators, therefore, have come to refer to the rules as a "doctrine" rather than "privilege."

7.3.3 The Work Product Rule as Stated by the Federal Courts

Like the attorney–client privilege and other privileges, the work product doctrine finds it roots in the cases that have been decided over the years — the common law. The essential principle underlying the work product doctrine is that the attorney's mental processes and case impressions must be protected from disclosure to the opposition if the attorney is to adequately perform his role in the judicial system. In a landmark case, *Hickman v. Taylor*, 329 U.S. 495 (1947) the United States Supreme Court firmly established the work product doctrine as a rule of federal courts. In *Hickman*, the plaintiff's attorney sought discovery of written statements and records of any oral statements made by survivors and witnesses of a tugboat accident. While admitting that statements had been taken, the defendant refused to produce the information, asserting that the information was "privileged." The trial court did not agree and ordered the defendant to produce the requested information. On appeal, however, both the Court of Appeals and ultimately, the Supreme Court, found that the information should be protected from disclosure. The Court of Appeals observed that the information was not protected by the attorney–client privilege because it did not contain communications between a client and his attorney. However, the appellate court held that it should be privileged from disclosure under the rules of civil procedure, as the "work product of an attorney." In affirming this position, the United States Supreme Court wrote:

Historically, a lawyer is an officer of the court and is bound to work for the advancement of justice while faithfully protecting the rightful interest of his clients. In performing his various duties, however, it is essential that a lawyer work with a certain degree of privacy, free from unnecessary intrusion by opposing parties and their counsel. Proper preparation of a client's case demands that he assemble information, sift what he considers to be the relevant from the irrelevant facts, prepare his legal theories and plan his strategy without undue and needless interference. That is the historical and the necessary way in which lawyers act within the framework of our system of jurisprudence to promote justice and to protect their client's interests. (*Hickman v. Taylor*, 329 U.S. 495, 510-11 (1947).)

While recognizing the attorney's need to prepare his cases without unnecessary intrusion from his adversaries, the court also recognized that there might be situations when the opposition would be legitimately entitled to examine certain information in the attorney's files. "Where relevant and nonprivileged facts remain hidden in an attorney's file and where production of those facts is essential to the preparation of one's case, discovery may properly be had." (*Ibid.* at 511.) However, the court placed the burden on the adversary to show that the information was "essential to the preparation" of his case.

Were such materials open to opposing counsel on mere demand, much of what is now put down in writing would remain unwritten. An attorney's thoughts, heretofore inviolate, would not be his own. Inefficiency, unfairness, and sharp practices would inevitably develop in the giving of legal advice and in the preparation of cases for trial. The effect on the legal profession would be demoralizing and the interest of the clients and the cause of justice would be poorly served. (329 U.S. at 511.)

In summary, the *Hickman* case stands for the proposition that materials gathered by the attorney, such as witness statements taken in preparation of the case, are not subject to discovery by his adversary unless the adversary is able to show that the information held by the attorney is "essential" to the preparation of his case. As a practical matter, this not only protects the attorney's thought processes, but also prevents the adversary from obtaining a "free ride" by benefiting from the fruits of the attorney's labor. These principles were later carried into the formal rules of the federal courts, known as the Federal Rules of Civil Procedure and the Federal Rules of Criminal Procedure. For purposes of illustrating the discovery of work product, our primary focus will be the rules as applied in civil cases.

7.3.4 Discovery of Work Product

7.3.4.1 Discovery of Trial Preparation Materials

As previously quoted, the general rule of discovery provides that "[p]arties may obtain discovery regarding any matter, not privileged, that is relevant to the claim or defense of any party." (Fed. R. Civ. P. 26 (b) (1).) However, a specific rule that limits the discovery of work product is also included. This rule provides, in pertinent part:

> (3) Trial Preparation: Materials.
>
> Subject to the provisions of subdivision (b) (4) of this rule [concerning expert witnesses] *a party may obtain discovery of documents and tangible things* otherwise discoverable under subdivision (b) (1) of this rule and *prepared in anticipation of litigation or for trial by or for another party or by or for that other party's representative (including the other party's attorney, consultant, surety, indemnitor, insurer, or agent) only upon a showing that the party seeking discovery has a substantial need of the materials in the preparation of the party's case and that the party is unable without undue hardship to obtain the substantial equivalent of the materials by other means.* In ordering discovery of such materials when the required showing has been made, the court shall protect against disclosure of the mental impressions, conclusions, opinions, or legal theories of an attorney or other representative of the party concerning the litigation. (Fed. R. Civ. P. 26 (b) (3) (emphasis added).)

This rule carries the principles of the *Hickman v. Taylor* case into the rules of civil procedure.

In summary, the procedural rules started with a general rule that essentially provides that all relevant information is discoverable. However, when it comes to work product, the availability of certain information is restricted. Under the rule, protection from discovery is provided to:

- Documents and tangible things which are otherwise discoverable.
- Prepared in anticipation of litigation or for trial.

- By or for another party or by or for that other party's representative (including the other party's attorney, consultant, surety, indemnitor, insurer, or agent).

Furthermore, to overcome the limited protection and obtain discovery of the documents or tangible things, the party-seeking discovery must show:

- A substantial need of the materials in the preparation of the party's case.
- That the party is unable without undue hardship to obtain the substantial equivalent of the materials by other means.

The rule goes on to provide that the court, if it orders discovery of the materials, "shall protect against disclosure of the mental impressions, conclusions, opinions, or legal theories of an attorney or other representative of the party concerning the litigation. ..."

7.3.4.2   *Discovery of Ordinary Work Product and Opinion Work Product*

The courts have generally divided work product into two types: "ordinary work product," which consists of the documents and tangible things the attorney or other representative has prepared, and "opinion work product," which consists of the "mental impressions, conclusions, opinions, or legal theories of an attorney or other representative of the party." With regard to ordinary work product, the rule specifies the showing that must be made for an opposing party to discover the materials and tangible things that have been prepared. However, with regard to opinion work product, the rule is silent except to say that the court "shall" protect against its disclosure. The protection granted to opinion work product is said to be absolute, or nearly so, whereas the protection of ordinary work product is more limited and may even be eliminated upon a proper showing.

As stated previously, this rule states an exception to the broad general rule of discovery. If the materials are prepared "in anticipation of litigation or for trial" they may be discovered only upon a showing of special need. The working papers and opinions of an expert witness, who is a "representative of a party" would seem to fall within the ambit of this exception to the general rule. If so, the discovery of materials prepared by the expert witness and his opinions would only be allowed upon special showing. However, the discovery rules go on to provide special rules concerning the discovery of experts. These rules may be viewed as an exception to the exception, allowing for somewhat more liberal discovery of expert witnesses under certain circumstances.

7.3.4.3 *Discovery of Trial Preparation: Experts*

Although the work of expert witnesses is usually done in anticipation of litigation or for trial, the rules recognize that the discovery of expert opinions to be presented at trial is essential to a proper preparation of the case. This stems primarily from the need to prepare for the cross-examination of the opposing expert. Therefore, although the expert's work may be considered work product, the rules generally allow free discovery of an expert witness who will be testifying at trial.

At the outset, the rules require all parties to disclose to all other parties the identity of any person who may be called to present expert testimony at trial. (Fed. R. Civ. P. 26 (a) (2) (A).) In addition, any expert who is retained or specially employed to provide expert testimony is required to prepare and submit a detailed report for disclosure to all other parties in the case. (Fed. R. Civ. P. 26 (a) (2) (B).) This rule provides for routine discovery of every expert who will be called to testify at trial. This requirement and the testifying expert's report are discussed in detail in Chapter 9.

However, in practice, the testifying expert's report is usually not sufficient to allow opposing counsel to fully understand and prepare for the examination of the expert witness. Therefore, the rules also provide for further discovery from testifying experts through deposition. The same rule also helps describe the discovery that will be allowed with regard to other types of experts. The rule provides, in pertinent part:

(4) Trial Preparation: Experts

(A) A party may depose any person who has been identified as an expert *whose opinions may be presented at trial.* If a report from the expert is required under subdivision (a) (2) (B), the deposition shall not be conducted until after the report is provided.

(B) A party may, through interrogatories or by deposition, discover facts known or opinions held by an expert who has been *retained or specially employed* by another party in anticipation of litigation or preparation for trial and *who is not expected to be called as a witness at trial* only ... upon showing of exceptional circumstances under which it is impracticable for the party seeking discovery to obtain facts or opinions on the same subject by other means. (Fed. R. Civ. P. 26 (b) (4) (A), (B) (emphasis added).)

Through direct reference and by implication, this rule specifies three types of experts and the discovery that will be allowed with regard to each. Each is discussed in turn below.

7.3.4.3.1 Experts Who Will Be Presenting Opinions at Trial. These experts must be identified to all parties as a matter of rule and must prepare a report that includes their opinions and other detailed information for disclosure to all other parties. Also, the opposition is allowed to depose these experts as a matter of course, but only after their reports have been disclosed to the opposing parties. These are the experts who will be presenting opinions in support of the client's case at trial and rebutting the testimony of opposing experts. Fairness and justice dictate that their opinions and other proposed testimony be freely discoverable. As demonstrated by the broad discovery allowed for the testifying experts, their work receives the least protection under the work product rules.

7.3.4.3.2 Experts Retained or Specially Employed in Anticipation of Litigation or for Trial, But Are Not Expected to be Called as Witnesses. These experts are frequently referred to as "consulting experts." They may assist in the investigation or preparation of the case, but are not called upon to testify at trial. This type of expert may be, for example, an accountant with a specialty in the certain issues that are unique to the claims involved in the client's case. He may perform studies or prepare financial data for consideration by the client's attorney. He may also assist the attorney in preparing the claims or framing discovery requests to be served on the opposing parties. In the course of this work, he would become privy to facts concerning the client's claims and may even form opinions concerning the issues in the case. The opposing parties may use interrogatories to require these experts to be identified and may use depositions to discover facts known or opinions held by them, but only upon a "showing of exceptional circumstances under which it is impracticable for the party seeking discovery to obtain facts or opinions on the same subject by other means." Here, a special form of the work product rule is being applied. It is similar to, but somewhat less stringent than, the regular test that must be satisfied to allow discovery of work product materials because a "substantial need" for the information need not be shown.

7.3.4.3.3 By Implication, Experts Who Were Not Retained or Specially Employed. These experts are not mentioned in the rule, but they are included by implication when other experts who were specially retained are mentioned. These experts are often persons who are actually parties to the case, such as an accountant who is a defendant in a malpractice action, or an accountant who is regularly employed by a party to a case. These experts will be familiar with the facts of the case and may have made special investigations concerning the claims in the case to assist the attorney in preparing for discovery or trial. They may even form opinions with regard to the questions presented by the case. The extent of discovery permitted with regard to these experts is not specified by the rule that specifically addresses experts. Assuming they will not be called to present expert opinions at trial, these experts apparently will receive the full protection of the work product rules. The party seeking discovery must show "a substantial need of the materials in the preparation of the party's case and that the party is unable without undue hardship to obtain the substantial equivalent of the materials by other means."

7.3.4.4   *Waiver of the Work Product Protection*

7.3.4.4.1   Waiver by Disclosure.   While the two concepts are related, it is possible that the attorney–client privilege may be waived without affecting the work product protection afforded to a document or other tangible thing. The attorney–client privilege is concerned with preserving the confidential relationship between the client and his attorney. Therefore, disclosure to a third party is inconsistent with the claim of privilege and waiver will occur. The work product doctrine is concerned with allowing the attorney and other client representatives to prepare the case without unwarranted intrusion from the client's adversaries, thereby promoting the adversary process. Therefore, although the attorney–client privilege is waived when a privileged document is disclosed to a third person outside of the attorney–client relationship, the work product protection may still be preserved. The courts recognize that the adversarial process may require the disclosure of the information to third parties to aid in the preparation of the case and such a disclosure can be consistent with the purposes of work product protection. For example, the third party may be a co-defendant with whom it is acceptable to share mental impressions and materials produced in preparation for trial. However, if the work product material is disclosed to an adversary through use at a trial or pretrial proceedings, the work product protection will be waived.

7.3.4.4.2   Waiver through Witness Preparation.   As with the attorney–client privilege, this area of waiver is critical to the attorney and the expert witness. If a witness is shown work product material in preparation for deposition or trial testimony, courts are likely to find the protection has been waived. This could occur; for example, if the attorney has prepared a summary of the case that includes his impressions of all the claims and other feelings he may have about the case. This might take the form of a letter or memorandum to the expert to introduce him to the case or provide a summary of the pleadings or discovery obtained from the oppositions. In ordering disclosure of this type of work product, the court may rely on its discretion under Rule 612 of the Federal Rules of Evidence. Under this rule, the court may require production of any writing used by the witness to refresh his memory before testifying. Likewise, this rule requires production, without discretion of the court, if the witness uses a writing to refresh his recollection while testifying.

The court may also rely on Rule 26 (a) (2) (B) of the Federal Rules of Civil Procedure, also discussed earlier in this chapter. This rule requires the expert to prepare a report that, among other things, includes all his opinions that are expected to be presented at trial, including the bases for all the opinions and all data or other information used in forming the opinions. If the expert has relied on work product in formulating his opinions, the work product will be subject to being produced for opposing parties.

To the extent that the work product shown to the expert contains any mental impressions or opinions of the attorney, a court may find that information should be protected. However, because of the uncertainty of this result, most attorneys will avoid showing any work product to the expert unless they feel comfortable with the fact that it may have to be disclosed to the opposition. If the material is truly work product, this comfort is probably not easy to attain. Attorneys should avoid providing summaries of the claims or evidence to their expert witnesses. Instead, the attorney should provide his expert with the pleadings, discovery documents and all of the other actual case materials. Let the expert review this information himself and form his own mental impressions regarding the issues. The expert is then free to discuss this information with the attorney verbally, and if they share their respective impressions of the case, their views need not be committed to writing.

7.4   How Privilege and Work Product Protection Can Affect the Decisions and Work of the Expert

BY ZEPH TELPNER

The privilege and work product protection is of vital and long-standing interest to attorneys and their clients. Many attorneys open their files to their experts, while others are overly protective and unwilling to share much of their work (at least in an expert's eyes) for reasons discussed by Mike Mostek in the preceding paragraphs.

Because of different treatment by different attorneys of information they are willing to share with their experts, the forensic accounting expert has a duty to discuss such restrictions on information in depth with the engaging attorney.

Once the forensic accounting expert has determined with the attorney what he has been hired to resolve, he must determine what he needs to resolve it. On one case, the attorneys wanted three expert witnesses: a forensic CPA, an economist and a freight-billing clerk. The attorneys held a joint conference with us and the client's personnel to summarize what the case was about and their preliminary expectations of each expert.

I had requested the usual information, complaint, depositions, interrogatories and other related documents. Additionally, because of the nature of the issues and the few facts provided to us, I asked for access to certain accounting records. Several times I asked, and the lawyers ignored my request. Finally, they grew weary of my requests, and asked why would I want to look at the accounting records. "Because I'm a CPA," I said. "I don't always review the same information that an economist or a billing clerk might need."

I offered to resign and asked them who to bill for my time at this indoctrination meeting. They agreed to allow me to see the accounting records.

During a divorce, I was asked to place a value on a business that both husband and wife had worked to develop. The law firm was unwilling to divulge so much information that I needed that I withdrew from the engagement. An accounting expert witness must always respect the requirements of the attorney in his goal to protect his client. But we alone must decide whether our work has too many restrictions placed upon it for us to reach valid and professional opinions.

Attorneys are in charge of a legal dispute whether it is headed for trial or not. The accounting expert will defer to the leadership of the attorney, but we must retain our independence. The trier of fact, the juries, and the parties to the dispute must be able to rely on our independence and the objectivity of our expert testimony. If we cannot get the information we need, then we must discuss with the attorney why we are unable to arrive at rational conclusions.

At an appropriate time, and early enough in his work, the expert must decide to complete the job if he can or to withdraw if his hands are tied by the rules of the particular attorney. If we exercise integrity, honesty, objectivity and rational thinking in arriving at our valid opinions, then no one will mistake us for "hired guns. Instead, they will recognize us as unique professionals who seek truth, logic, facts and justice for a litigant in our march to an expert opinion.

Mike has covered the technical and legal reasons for the protection of the client by the attorney. Accountants need to learn only to discuss differences of opinion with the attorneys and to decide for themselves what they require to reach an opinion.

Research Sources
for the Expert

8

8.1 Introduction

In this age of ever-faster communication speeds and ever-more-powerful computers on our desks, sometimes we suffer from an embarrassment of riches. We have too many research materials available to us. Filed on compact disks are legal, accounting, and tax libraries that will transfer the researcher immediately to an online library when the disks themselves do not contain the answers. One of my engaging attorneys told me that a lawyer or a CPA who failed to use electronic research materials could be accused of malpractice. I'm not an attorney, but I didn't agree for the following reason: a loose-leaf subscription service can never provide as much information so quickly as an electronic library. And that is precisely one of the many problems with electronic research — too much, too soon. In a loose-leaf service, a researcher gets as much feedback as his brain can safely handle. Sometimes when I request a topic or word search in my electronic library, I can receive from one to 1,000 or more hits. My mind cannot handle more than five to ten hits at a time.

A computer searches too far, too wide, and often finds too many minor variations of the request. I use electronic research or search the Internet to get a general idea of the subject and to find available resources. A few expensive electronic research services are equipped with citators to narrow the bounds of the research and to allow the researcher to home in on more precise answers. Less expensive electronic research services, especially for income tax research, are wonderfully equipped with cases, revenue rulings, treaties and treatises, but no citators. These make it more difficult for the expert to reach the heart of a problem without eventually reading too much.

Save the electronic research for last. Let it refine whatever you have already discovered. When facts alone provide the answer, then you need look no further.

8.2 Nothing But the Facts

Most public and forensic accountants and attorneys are familiar with tax research. Assume that an IRS agent has disallowed a charitable contribution of $5,000 that was reported by a taxpayer on his return. Perhaps the facts will resolve the problem. Some factual questions to ask a taxpayer are:

- Did he actually make the contribution? If the answer is no, further research is moot.
- Was the payment for a contribution or for purchase of an asset for the taxpayer? If the answer is "an asset for the taxpayer," further research is moot.
- Was the payment a contribution or a bribe? If it was for a bribe, then further research may be needed to determine if the bribe was legal or illegal.

When facts resolve the problem, research is done.

8.3 Filling in the Background

Public libraries are great sources for background research. Most libraries maintain biographical files filled with newspaper clippings filed alphabetically by individuals, or in a business section, filed alphabetically by businesses.

Here is an example of how those yellowing newspaper clipping can fill you in on a case. A bankruptcy examiner suspected fraud by the stockholder during his examination of a large company that had filed for bankruptcy. The creditors had asked for an examiner and the federal bankruptcy judge had appointed one. While researching the company and the officers in the clipping files of the local public library, he discovered other connected bankruptcies.

At least three other bankrupt corporations had had a direct and close relationship with the bankrupt or the sole stockholder (owner). The following summaries include only those bankrupt corporations and their officers, stockholders, or directors who had interlocking relationships with owner or bankrupt. This encouraged the examiner to expand his research and his working papers are filed with the FBI.

1. **Fresh Meat, Inc.** (Bankruptcy in 1974)
   Owner
   Homer Latka
   Shirley Knot Jamison
   Bill Investor, CPA
   Herman Bupkes
   Abel Cantwell
   Logan Miles (Miles is co-owner with Owner-Mile Development Co.

2. **Always Packing Co.** (closed 1983, bankruptcy in 1985)
   Owner
   Homer Latka
   Shirley Knot Jamison
   Bill Investor, CPA
   Herman Bupkes, Esq.
   Richard Nasteer, CPA
   Charles C. Meyers
   John North, Jr., Esq. as trustee for Homer Latka

3. **First Anywhere Savings Bank** (bankruptcy in 1984)
   Owner
   Homer Latka
   Shirley Knot Jamison

4. **Shaggy Dog, Inc.**
   Shirley Knot Jamison, President
   Herman Bupkes
   Roger Doughmark

8.4 Do You Yahoo?

You do not need a search engine to find research tools on the Web, although most Internet providers list many search engines. Yahoo! for example lists four or five additional search engines to try after you have exhausted Yahoo! Without a search engine, you need only perform a topical search. If you need libraries, begin with the "Library of Congress" as the topic to locate items in that library. You can try "law libraries" for legal research.

8.5 Don't Do It Yourself

Many county historical societies will perform research services for a small fee. The Douglas County, Nebraska Historical Society subscribes to many search systems including "Dialog," which has 5,000 or more newspapers and magazines in its library. The society also has professional librarians who can usually locate topics faster than the expert accounting witness can and download them to your floppy disks.

Chapter 4 of this book explains how to find facts, issues, and answers. Chapter 4 also confirms that a forensic accountant will find many of his answers in accounting and tax libraries. Basic accounting textbooks provide the heart of accounting theory and technical requirements. Both the American Institute of CPAs and the Financial Accounting Standards Board issue authoritative pronouncements that are needed to help substantiate solutions by a forensic accountant. Federal and state tax libraries provide guidance to and substantiation of court-approved methods of valuation; income reconstruction; calculation of damages; piercing of a corporate veil; liquidation of a partnership, corporation or trust; and illegal transactions.

Libraries and research are not cheap. Many county law libraries, county and state historical societies and public libraries subscribe to electronic services with enormous databases. Their research facilities are usually supervised by skilled researchers. For a small fee, they may be able to find information for you in minutes that might once have taken hours. The AICPA has library services for its members as well as information on litigation support and forensic accounting.

8.6 Corporate Files

Trade associations and government departments are a great source for information. For one dispute, I contacted the National Accounting and Finance Council of the American Trucking Associations for statistics and mileages for different categories of trucking companies. The Department of Labor then furnished me with driving statistics, and the Teamsters Union provided me with a copy of its relevant master contract. On another case, the National Speakers Association put me in touch with an expert who could fill me in on the earnings of professional speakers. Contact the reference librarian of your local public library for a directory of trade associations.

Nearby offices of larger accounting firms have been willing to allow me to research in their libraries and one has even performed the electronic research for me. Most state CPA associations will provide a list of experts within certain categories such as communications, transportation, exempt organizations and many other specialties. These experts will offer you some guidance to finding the answers.

The attorney you are working for usually has an extensive library or can get you access to a library. Also, other CPAs in your community may have resources available.

There are no inexpensive research sources. Unless a forensic accountant has a large accounting firm or an unusually profitable one, he must find public, free-on-line, or modest-fee library resources for his research. Resources are always available to resolve most research problems.

The Expert's Written Report

9

9.1 The Requirements for a Report

9.1.1 The Purpose of the Report

In all cases in federal court, and in many state courts, the expert must prepare and submit a written report that must be provided to opposing parties and to the court if required by the rules. The report provides relevant parties with the means to judge the expert's qualifications and to discover his opinions and the bases for those opinions. It also provides a glimpse into the expert's past court work and his opinions in previous cases.

9.1.2 The Contents of the Report

The Federal Rules of Civil Procedure prescribe the precise contents of the report and rules for delivering it to the opposing parties.

"(2) Disclosure of Expert Testimony

(A) In addition to the [other] disclosures required ... a party shall disclose to other parties the identity of any person who may be used at trial to present evidence under Rules 702 ... of the Federal Rules of Evidence.

(B) Except as otherwise stipulated or directed by the court, this disclosure shall, with respect to a witness who is retained or specially employed to provided expert testimony in the case or whose duties as an employee of the party regularly involve giving expert testimony, be accompanied by a written report prepared and signed by the witness. The report shall contain a complete statement of all opinions to be expressed and the basis and

reasons therefore, the data or other information considered by the witness
in forming the opinions; any exhibits to be used as a summary of or support
for the opinions; the qualifications of the witness, including a list of all
publications authored by the witness within the preceding ten years; the
compensation to be paid for the study and testimony; and a listing of any
other cases in which the witness has testified as an expert at trial or by
deposition within the preceding four years."

9.2 The Writing of the Expert's Report

When the expert witness issues his report, the engaging attorney will tell
him to whom he should address it. If he doesn't automatically tell you, ask.
The report might be addressed to the court, the attorney or the client.
Eventually, it will be filed with the court by the attorney and presented to
the opposition attorneys.

The report must comply with *Daubert* (See Chapter 2). *Daubert* neither
adds to nor subtracts from the information that would have been included
in any expert report prepared by all competent, qualified and professional
forensic accounting consultants and expert witnesses. They would have complied with *Daubert* even before that decision was handed down. In the past,
too many experts expressed opinions based only on the fact that they were
CPAs, economist-Ph.D.s or degreed in some professional science. The expert
needs more than proficiency in his profession; he needs expert knowledge in
the subject on which he will report. If we are not computer experts, we should
help an attorney to find one. The dispute between the truck manufacturer
and its dealer who sued it for price fixing did not require an accountant who
was an expert in antitrust disputes. It required an expert on how over-the-
road trucks are bought and sold among truck manufacturers, truck sales
dealers, and trucking companies.

The expert's report will be designed to support the client and rebut his
opponent if the facts, issues, answers and authorities will lead to these conclusions. You may be asked to rebut information in the petition or complaint
and your report should list the claims made in the petition or complaint.
You should also report what you have been asked to do, and the views and
reports of the opposition. You must prepare a brief summary of your qualifications. Most important, you must report your conclusions, the authoritative support for them and how and why you interpreted the facts and relate
them to your conclusions. The following reports were issued before the
Daubert and subsequent related decisions. The most important guideline for
your report is to let your engaging attorney review your report to determine
whether it qualifies under the Federal Rules of Evidence, *Daubert* and subsequent cases. When a forensic accounting expert witnesses testifies, it is not

as a lawyer. Accountants will interpret accounting and lawyers will interpret law. In tax cases, most attorneys will work with the accountant's explanation of the tax laws. Whether the CPA testifies, writes a report or both, his job is to write a report or to testify in a manner that will explain accounting in layman terms. If the judge, the jury, your attorney and the opposing attorney do not understand what you are telling them, they will cease to listen.

The purpose of our testimony or our report is to support our conclusions and to have listeners or readers agree with us. We want our conclusions to be right. We also want the reader to accept our opinions, follow our advice or to concede to our judgment. To win acceptance of the decision makers, they must be able to understand what we have said or written. There is no other reason to testify or write our expert's report except to convince the decision makers of our opinions. We must not be shy, but we must explain forcefully why we are correct.

In order to be correct, we must support each of our conclusions with the right facts and supporting authorities that lead to our conclusions and only to our conclusions. If certain facts and authorities seem to lead away from our conclusions, we must prove that these facts and authorities are either wrong or differ from our situation. We must also prove that the facts, authorities and conclusions of our opposition are wrong. To prove ourselves right is not enough. We must always prove that our opponents are wrong. If we do not do this, we may end up with a conclusion that indicates that both experts are right, causing the jury and judge to possibly render a decision that gives us an unfavorable standoff.

We must consider all sides to our issues and answer all of them — even those that are unfavorable. This leaves little room for anyone to rebut our opinions. By answering all opposing opinions during the preparation of our report, when we issue it, we are prepared to rebut all challenges as they arise.

Even though beautiful prose may thrill a reader, we do not need beautiful prose — only proper grammar within limits. Stiffness and formality do not always win. Someone once said, "A preposition is a good word to end a sentence with." Believe that person. You do not need to write a perfect report. But it is important for you to be able to spell. Misspelled words will chill a reader — but accidents happen and the readers will accept an occasional error.

Seeking perfection usually slows down our writing and spoils our spontaneity. We often want our writing to be perfect because we do not want to be wrong. We do not want to make a mistake in what we are trying to tell our reader. We want the reader to understand us and to think we did a good job.

Not everyone will understand what we have written. Understanding of what we have written is subjective. Each of our readers interprets the facts in his own way based on his individual beliefs. It makes no difference how hard we try. Someone is bound to misunderstand what we have written or said. He may be a client, a judge, a juror, an appeals officer, an attorney or another expert witness. He might be our superior or our subordinate.

Some readers or listeners have the will to misunderstand. This happens when the reader or listener begins with an opinion that differs from ours. He has a firm conviction that he is right and we are wrong. We may not be able to change his opinion. Therefore, we must document our conclusions with authorities and strong evidence so that our opponents cannot rebut our conclusions.

Because readers or listeners often have beliefs that have hardened into convictions, when we issue a report or testify, we must support each conclusion with facts and authorities that lead directly to it. Our opposition may squirm and attempt to destroy our reasoning, but, if we have infallible facts and accepted authorities, we should win. I use "should" because to be right does not mean that we will always win.

We can take a secure thought from the courts, which have said many times that facts presented by a layperson are superior to unsupported opinions of experts.

When we write, we must be ourselves. I often wish that my writing was as inspired and as dramatic as the writing of Edgar Allan Poe, but it is not, and it will never be. So, I write the way I write, because that is the way I write.

Technical writing or speaking doesn't have to be dry. If it's dry, it will lose the reader — chase him away — ruin our intentions. If our reports require dialogue, then we should insert dialogue. If they require color and description, we should use color and description.

Humor isn't forbidden in a technical response when it is applied in the right place. If we use humor easily, if we are comfortable with it, if it fits, then use it. If we are not humorists, we shouldn't fake it. Pretending to be what we are not will harm the contents of our reports.

Repetition can strengthen writing or speaking. Repetition often puts force into what we have to say. Repetition often jars our audience into wakefulness. Repetition often can be used to our advantage. However, too much repetition can alienate the reader, who might be bored or annoyed by the assumption that he is so dim that he needs to be constantly hit over the head with the same old, same old.

By reading good fiction, we can improve our writing or speaking. Read a lot of it. Even during our busiest times, we must read it. Good fiction begins with facts and then raises issues that require more facts. When the additional facts are discovered, the entire story leads inexorably to the logical conclusion. If it doesn't, the reader is annoyed. There are exceptions. A story might have a surprise ending, which, when it is humorous, may delight the reader. When it is serious, it may make the reader feel cheated and deceived. It wasn't fun to have his logic fooled. The ending or conclusion of a technical report is as important as a reasonable ending in a novel. It must not deceive the logic of the reader. We must be certain to provide only facts, authorities and logical reasoning in our report. Someone who needs to read it and make a decision based on it will not be bothered by our inability to compete with Hemingway. The reader wants conclusions that flow logically from our facts. If he doesn't receive that, even great prose will leave him cold.

Even so, substance without form can be cold and dead. If our facts and issues are bland; if there is no color, if our factual story is not interesting, then we may bore our reader. If he is bored, he will not care to understand what we have to say.

Fiction is not the only written material that tells a story. Newspaper articles tell a story. Articles and essays in general circulation magazines tell a story. Only in technical writing do authors often neglect to tell a story.

When we write of facts, we must explain where they were found or how they arose. Explain that the taxpayer or his advisor, for example, could have found the right facts but didn't, but we recognized them as soon as we saw them.

The most important and basic step required to begin writing a technical paper is to organize ourselves before we write. We must be sure to understand the facts and issues before writing. We can use either mental or written notes to organize our thoughts before beginning. Written notes are the most useful manner of organization because they allow us to retain more facts. Some experts prefer to organize in their minds, but I suggest that you record research and outline notes in great detail and write them in complete thoughts and sentences. On occasion, we may be unable to complete our work, and someone else may have to finish it. This will save them time if your notes are complete, and if you have prepared a detailed outline listed in the sequence that you had planned for your report.

9.3 Analyses of Reports

Chapter 6 analyzes a deposition taken from Michael E. James testifying in *Conseki v. Conseki*. The following report was issued to the respondent in that case, Howard W. Conseki, on the instructions of his lawyer. Conseki's attorney filed the report with an Iowa District Court to assist the district court judge to render a decision. The report was issued before *Daubert* and related decisions were handed down to mandate requirements for expert testimony that went beyond the Rules of Federal Evidence. However, this report complies with *Daubert, et seq.*

The following cover page serves to identify the report to the court, the attorneys and the parties in the dispute: Not much commentary is needed for this report. Compare it with James' deposition in Chapter 6 and it will explain itself.

Valuation on Behalf of Howard William Conseki, Respondent

Estimated Value of the Conseki Drive-In (a Proprietorship)
4003 South Fifth Avenue
Any City, Iowa
November 27, 1985
In the Iowa District Court for any County
At Any City, Iowa
Shirley Ann Conseki, Petitioner,
and concerning,
Howard William Conseki, Respondent
Equity DM No. 6X-61X

(The text of the report begins below, but would actually be page two, following the cover page.)

9.3.1 Expert's Report to Howard William Conseki on Valuation of the Conseki Drive-In

Reason for Report

You had asked me to arrive at an estimated value of Conseki Drive-In (CDI) in the Matter of Shirley Ann Conseki, Petitioner, concerning Howard William Conseki (Howard), Respondent. Previously, in a January 3, 1986 deposition by Michael E. James on behalf of the Petitioner, Mr. James stated that the value of CDI was $80,544.

You have asked me to value CDI as of November 27, 1985, the date of the trial of Conseki v. Conseki.

Conclusion

I have performed research and made calculations to determine the value of CDI as of November 27, 1985. I prepared valuations in accordance with the Market Data Method, the Cost Method, and the Income Method (capitalization of earnings). Additionally, I made an alternative permissible calculation.

In my opinion, the value of the CDI as of November 27, 1985 is less than its net assets. Accordingly, CDI has no value.

(The expert's opinion is personal to him. He may work for a large firm, and his report may have been issued on that firm's letterhead, but the report expresses the opinion of the expert. Unlike an audit report that states, "We have examined,"

an expert's report recites what he did or had others do under his supervision. Expert opinions are not "in our opinion," they are "in my opinion." The report consists of the expert's work, his observations, his conclusions, and his opinions).

Qualifications of Zeph Telpner

I graduated from the Creighton University, Omaha, Nebraska on January 29, 1958 and was awarded a Bachelor of Science in Business Administration. I majored in accounting. The State of Nebraska issued me a certificate as a Certified Public Accountant (CPA) on February 5, 1962. The State of Iowa issued me a certificate as a CPA on January 4, 1963.

I have worked in public accounting since 1956, and had been employed by two separate big eight (*now big-five*) accounting firms. Since 1965, I have practiced accounting nationally as a CPA from my offices in Council Bluffs, Iowa. My experience has included auditing, tax, and other matters that CPAs usually perform in their practices, with the exception of computer services. Beginning in 1966, I limited my professional practice to forensic accounting in federal and state income and other tax disputes, and in general accounting disputes.

During the past 2 years, I have testified in either a federal or state court twice and have been deposed six times. Over this 2-year period, I have been either a consultant or expert witness for five defendants and four plaintiffs. My *curriculum vitae* is attached as Report Exhibit 1.

(Because states may differ in how much they require about the expert witness in his report, the expert must ask the attorney for guidance.)

Additionally, from 1955 through 1958, I owned and operated a soft ice cream drive-in that offered hot and cold sandwiches.

(My client's attorney believed that this would attribute me with more authority than my CPA certificate and my forensic experience alone when I expressed an opinion on a drive-in.)

History of CDI

Before Howard bought CDI, he had owned and operated the B&X Family Restaurant (B&X), 211 West Street, Any City, Iowa. Howard signed a real estate contract on May 31, 1979 to purchase B&X from Morris Y. Jones for $95,000. The purchase price was $72,000 for the land, and $23,000 for the building, equipment, and the license contract (franchise) upon transfer from B&X International, Inc.

After Howard operated B&X for a few months, he determined that it was too difficult to work at it full time and continue his employment with the Any City Community Schools, where he is still employed. On October 10, 1979, he listed B&X for sale with James M. Land, real estate broker in Any City. The sales price on the listing was $110,000. On about June 2, 1980, Harry A. Vest bought B&X from Howard. Howard believes that the final selling price was $95,000. On the acceptance that I saw, the selling price was $97,500, but it refers to a final acceptance to be submitted in writing. This final acceptance was not available to me. However, the closing statement from Land Realty showed a selling price of $95,000. This is the same price that Howard bought it for.

(*The expert must support his statements of fact and conclusions with documentary or authoritative evidence. In this valuation, it will distinguish his supported facts and conclusions from those expressed by Michael James in his deposition.*)

John S. Simpson, Accountant, prepared the financial statements for 14 of the months that B&X was operated by Howard. They show a net income for the total period of $17,248 or $1,437 a month. These financial statements end at April 30, 1980. The sale to Vest was in progress then, but the bulk sales transfer was not to take place until June 2, 1980.

On July 22, 1981, Howard signed a Uniform Purchase Agreement to purchase CDI from Joan A. Abey (Abey). Howard has stated that Abey had owned CDI for about a year before Howard bought it. Abey had bought it from the previous owner, who had closed it about 2 years before Abey bought it.

The Uniform Purchase Agreement shows that Howard agreed to buy CDI from Abey for $50,000. The purchase price was to be paid as follows:

Cash Down Payment	$11,000
Assumption of lease with Refrigeration Co., Inc.	3,700
Real estate mortgage to Abey	35,300
	$50,000

The purchase price was for the building and equipment only. The land it sits on is owned by Redwood Investment Co., Inc. (landlord), and is leased from it. Mr. Conseki does not have an interest in landlord.

On August 14, 1981, CDI was transferred to Howard after he executed a security agreement and a real estate mortgage. The final agreement required a down payment of $15,000, so the real estate mortgage and security agreement were for $31,300. ($31,300 plus $15,000 down plus assumed equipment mortgage of $3,700 equals $50,000.)

Although the final purchase agreement executed on August 13, 1981 showed a purchase price of $46,300, the closing statement from Gates Realtors shows the purchase price to be $50,000. The $3,700 difference is for the lease assumed for refrigeration equipment from Refrigeration Co., Inc. This lease was recorded in Howard's name on August 14, 1981. It actually called for total payments of $208 for 20 months for an amount of $4,160. Although the equipment lease provides for the equipment to return to the lessor at its expiration, Howard contends that he was granted title to the equipment at the end of the lease. Howard paid Abey an additional $2,000 for inventory.

According to Howard, when Abey owned CDI, she opened and closed CDI 7 days a week during its open months. Because Howard is a full-time employee of the Any City Schools, he could not work as many hours. CDI is now open from March until October 15 of each year and remains closed during the other months. Howard has supplied a calculation of the hours he works in CDI. They amounted to 1,669 hours annually. Even though he is the proprietor and, consequently, the manager of CDI, I have estimated an hourly wage for him at part time of only $5 an hour for a total assumed annual wage of $8,345 for use in my calculations. I have based the $5 on information supplied by my son Michael, who worked during college in the Brown Bottle Restaurant in Iowa City and who now works there full time, and by my son David, who is the assistant manager of the Howard Johnson Restaurant in Omaha, Nebraska.

Financial Statements and Accounting Records

After Howard bought CDI, its accounting records were recorded by Smith & Smith, P.C., successors to John S. Simpson, or by Jones, James and Associates (JJA), successors to Smith & Smith, P.C.

Each month, JJA provides CDI with a balance sheet and an income statement. These statements also serve as CDI's general ledger. At the end of each year, JJA prepares Howard's joint federal and state income tax returns. The returns include a schedule of CDI's taxable net income. Howard provided me with the balance sheets, income statements and tax returns for 1981, 1982, 1983, and 1984. He also gave me the balance sheet and income statement for the 11 months ended November 30, 1985. JJA provided me with records that showed no transactions for CDI after November 14, 1985. I have, therefore, accepted the November 30, 1985 balances as being the same balances that were recorded as of November 27, 1985, the date for my evaluation.

JJA let me review their working paper files for CDI. There was insufficient information in the files to review.

After I read the financial statements, I concluded that I would have to adjust them to record the correct income or loss. I reached this conclusion for the following reasons:

1. Until 1985, the SSJ report letter for CDI stated in part that the statements were prepared on the cash receipts and disbursements basis of accounting, and that, consequently, revenues are recognized when earned, and expenses and purchases of assets are recognized when cash is disbursed rather than when the obligation is incurred. However, I noted that certain non-cash items were recorded.
2. In 1985, the report stated that the statements were prepared on a tax accounting basis. This was a different method from the previously reported method.
3. The 1983 balance sheet did not include the purchase price of $3,700 for the lease assumption.
4. The 1981 balance sheet recorded goodwill of $8,797. None of the negotiations or documents for the purchase of CDI allocated any of the purchase price to goodwill. However, JJA provided me with a schedule of Abey's gain on sale of CDI to Howard. Because JJA also represented Abey, I have noted that his gain was $9,681. I believe that JJA arbitrarily recorded goodwill on CDI to include most of Abey's gain. Howard said that he did not know anything about it.
5. Accounting Principles Board Opinion (APB) 17 requires Goodwill to be amortized over a period not exceeding 40 years. Financial Accounting Standards Board (FASB) Statements 44, 72, and Interpretation 9 reaffirm APB 17. In 1981, JJA did not amortize goodwill. In 1982, they did. In 1983, they did not. In 1984, they did. In 1985, they reversed the previous amortization, but did not disclose it on the income statement.
6. In 1981, the statements did not record the recording fees on the purchases of CDI.
7. In 1985, a bank reconciliation was provided to support the cash-in-bank amount on the balance sheet. The reconciled balance differed by $231.
8. In 1980, the income tax return recorded $2,225 more in depreciation than the financial statements, in addition to an additional $273 of expenses.
9. In 1982, the return recorded $1,892 more in expenses than the financial statements showed. Amortization of goodwill of $1,759 was deducted on the income tax return. This is not a deductible expense for income tax purposes.
10. In 1983, the inventory increase, which would normally increase net income, was reported on the tax return but not on the financial statements.

11. In 1984, an income item recorded on the financial statements was omitted from the income tax return.
12. The above discrepancies were later adjusted on the financial statements by restating capital without disclosure.
13. In 1985, the statements contained a reconciliation of the proprietor's capital account. However, the beginning balance was greater than the ending balance at the end of the preceding year by about $3,500.

To attempt to determine the correct income or loss, I reconciled the beginning proprietor's capital of $17,000 (the original cash contribution by Howard to the purchase of CDI) to the ending capital based on the income reported. This showed an overstatement of capital of $7,347. I then reconciled the cash provided from reported operations since the beginning cash balance. This showed an overstatement of cash of $8,910. The net effect of these reconciliations is either an understatement of investment by the proprietor, an understatement of reported income or an error from the several restatements of the financial statements from year to year. I do not know what it is. The net amount is too small to affect my calculations, so I have eliminated it from my considerations. It would require an analysis of the transactions from inception to determine the problem.

To correct the statements, I recorded the lease assumption of $3,700 and amortized it over 60 months. I could not identify it with a specific asset and have treated it as an intangible asset. I amortized goodwill as required by APB 17 for an adjustment of $7,547 and adjusted cash in bank to the reconciliation and also recorded the recording fees.

The net effect of my adjustments was to reduce proprietor's capital at November 27, 1985 from $7,205 to $2,300.

The total combined loss since inception, reported on the income tax returns of CDI was $16, 664. I accepted this as my beginning loss before my adjustments, because the financial statements cumulatively show this amount. However, the tax return losses include nondeductible amortization.

I calculated the total net loss for the CDI from inception to November 27, 1985 as follows:

Net loss reported on the income tax returns	$16,664
Net loss reported on statements at at November 27, 1985	272
Additional loss from my adjustments 4,	905
Reduction of loss from unallowable amortization on tax return included as expense in my adjustments	(1,759)
Cumulative net loss from inception	$20,082
Add allowance for proprietor's salary	36,162
Cumulative losses after proprietor's salary	$56,244

CDI Ground Rental Lease

Howard entered into a lease on August 13, 1981 with landlord to lease ground at 4003 South Fifth Avenue, Any City, Iowa. This is the land the CDI building sits on. The lease provides, among other things, that the lease shall expire upon expiration of the demised term on December 31, 1986. If the tenant wishes to extend or renew the lease, landlord shall negotiate with tenant to that end. Tenant may remove the building and fixtures at the expiration of the lease, but is not required to. Tenant may not assign the lease.

I phoned David Allen, realtor, who represented Abey on the sale of CDI to Howard. Allen said that all previous leases were month to month and that it took 2 weeks to convince landlord to execute a written 5-year lease to expire on December 31, 1986.

The security interest granted to Abey by Howard includes an interest in Howard's lease with landlord.

Accordingly, I have concluded that the lease has no transferable value to CDI and have ignored it in my calculations.

CDI Menu

CDI serves Mexican fast foods, so it is similar to Taco Bell. It serves French fries and onion rings, so it is similar to Wendy's, McDonalds, Burger King or other burger fast-food restaurants. It serves cole slaw, so it is similar to a Kentucky Fried Chicken. It serves shrimp and chicken planks, so it is similar to a Long John Silver's. It serves tenderloin, fish, chicken and pizza burger sandwiches, so it is similar to the Bungalow Bar & Grill, and it serves cones, floats, sundaes, malts, and shakes, so it is similar to a Dairy Queen.

Additionally, CDI has no inside service. Carhops serve its food orders on trays to customers in automobiles.

Therefore, CDI is not similar to a fast-food restaurant.

Valuation

When valuing property or a business, three basic methods are dictated by reason and common sense and are accepted by the courts. These three basic and general methods of valuation are:

1. Market Data Method, in which value is determined by comparison with sales of Similar property.

2. Cost Method, in which value is based upon the cost of reproducing the property.
3. Income Method, in which the earnings from the property are capitalized to determine value.

A review of court decisions on valuations shows that most are based on one or more of these methods. According to George R. Blum, M.A.I., Omaha, Nebraska, all three methods are required to appraise most property and businesses. See also "Appraising Fundamentals" (Exhibit 2), and "What to Look for in an Appraisal." (Exhibit 3). Both are pamphlets of the American Institute of Real Estate Appraisers of the National Association of Real Estate Boards. Appraisal reports of the Federal National Mortgage Association (Exhibit 4), the Federal Home Loan Mortgage Corporation (Exhibit 5), the Federal Housing Administration (Exhibit 6) and Avco Finance (Exhibit 7), among others, require appraisers to take all three methods into account.

Fair market value is the price that a purchaser willing to buy, but not compelled to buy, would pay for the business, and a seller willing to sell, but not compelled to sell, would accept for the business. Usually, the price is established by comparative sales of similar property in the area. [*Cornish v. U.S., 221 F. Supp. 658* (D. Ore. 1963)] and Internal Revenue Estate Regulations 20.2031-1(b).

Other courts have modified the definition of fair market value. In *Lavene v. Lavene, 392 A.2d 6221* (N.J. 1978), the court said that valuation of a closely held company is an attempt to determine the fair market value of an asset that by definition does not have a fair market value. The court concluded that a market wherein a willing buyer will meet a willing seller, neither under any compulsion, generally does not exist.

One of the most frequently cited guides for the valuation of a business is Rev. Rul. 59-60, 1959-1 C. B. 237. It provides in part that the person who values a business should maintain a reasonable attitude in recognition of the fact that valuation is not an exact science. A sound valuation will be based upon all the relevant facts. However, the elements of common sense, informed judgment and reasonableness must enter into the process of weighing those facts and determining their aggregate significance.

Among the factors to be considered are:

1. Nature of the business and its history
2. Economic outlook in general, and the outlook of the industry
3. Net book value and financial condition of the business
4. Earning capacity of the business
5. Return to the owner

6. Whether or not there is goodwill, or other intangible values
7. Sales generated by the business
8. Market price of similar businesses that are actively sold

I have made my calculations of fair market value based upon many court decisions and Rev. Rul. 59-60, *supra*.

Market Data Method of Valuation

The market data method does not apply to CDI. It is unlike fast-food restaurants in Any City. It serves a more varied menu, does not have a franchise to attract customers loyal to the franchise, and does not have the heavy flow of traffic required by a fast-food restaurant. Additionally, it is housed in an old frame building, with no inside seating. It is also unlike the other restaurants, because it has carhop service, and not self-service.

I phoned David Allen, real estate broker. He knew of only one restaurant for sale recently that might be comparable. Allen said the Crystal Whip across from Central School had been listed for sale for about 6 months for $65,000. This price included the one-half-acre lot and the concrete block building on it. There were no buyers for it, and it is no longer listed for sale. It was unlike CDI, as it was mainly a soft-ice-cream stand that served an occasional hamburger according to Allen. Also, CDI does not own the land on which it stands.

In my opinion, the Market Data Method does not apply to CDI. There are no comparable sales and there may never be.

Cost Method

To determine the cost to reproduce, I had to determine what the value of the property was, and what it might cost to reproduce. If the lease is not renewed, Howard stated that he would abandon the building but dispose of the equipment.

Reproduction cost cannot be determined unless the cost of land and the cost of demolishing or moving the building are determined. I phoned Jack Anders, president of Anders Construction Co., Any City, Iowa. He said that he was familiar with the property. He does not engage in demolition work, but he estimated that it would cost about $3,000 to demolish.

Next, I phoned Arnold Rishel, owner of Rishel Construction, a demolition contractor. Mr. Rishel stated that he was familiar with CDI. He estimated demolition costs to be $2,000 with salvage retained by the demolition company. I used Rishel's estimate because he is in the demolition business and would be more accurate than Jack Anders.

I phoned Harry Muskie, House Mover, Any City, Iowa several times for an estimate to move the building. I could not get an answer, but because of other information I obtained, I believed that I would not need Muskie's estimate.

The only comparable lot that I noted in the vicinity was land for sale on the west side of the Expressway. I measured its distance from CDI with my automobile odometer. It was one-tenth of a mile away. However, it was not a corner lot. The land for sale consisted of 7 acres with frontage on the Expressway, and it was adjacent to Jack's Grocery on its south line. BHG Realtors had it listed for sale. When I called them, they told me that it had just been sold for $250,000 or about $35,714 an acre.

Howard told me that his leased lot was 200 by 200 feet. This is 400,000 square feet or about 4,445 square yards. An acre is 4,840 square yards. Accordingly, a portion of the nearby land equal to CDI's present land size would be $32,799.

Based on the net losses of CDI, it would not be economical for anyone to reproduce it. In my opinion, the Cost Method will not apply to CDI.

Income Method

The income method is the last of the three major evaluation methods to be applied to CDI. It is based upon capitalization of earnings and is an approved method.

Earnings may be the most important criterion of value in some cases whereas asset value will be the most important in others. More consideration is given to earnings for companies that sell products or services to the public. More value is given to assets for investment or holding companies. (Rev. Rul. 59-60, *supra*). Mr. James stated in his deposition that he had used the income method to arrive at a value for CDI.

A business consists of many assets. These include tangible assets such as real estate, machinery and equipment, inventories and other physical assets. It also consists of intangible assets such as copyrights, trademarks, franchises, leasehold costs and unidentifiable intangible assets such as goodwill. (See W.B. Meigs, A.N. Mosich, C.E. Johnson & T.F. Keller, *Intermediate Accounting* (3rd ed. 1974) (Meigs). The FASB Statements and APB Opinions confirm Meigs' explanations of intangibles.

Mr. James had determined that the assets of CDI are worth $80,544. He had arrived at this amount with a two-step process. First, he capitalized earnings at a rate of 15% to arrive at $42,056 in capitalized earnings. Next, he assumed that the tangible assets were worth $38,488. He added these amounts together to arrive at his total valuation of $80,544.

If we, for a moment, assume that James' value is correct, then he should have deducted the real estate mortgage balance from it. He did not do that. That balance at November 27, 1985 was $25,153. This would leave an adjusted value based on James' calculation of $55,391. However, that amount is substantially overstated.

To correctly capitalize earnings, we must determine many things. Why are assets worth more than net value as shown on the balance sheet as prepared by JJA or as adjusted to $2,300 by me? Assets may be worth more than net book value if they produce a rate of return on assets in excess of what assets are worth. When they produce such a rate of return, they have the ability to earn a superior rate of return (or excess earnings as stated by James).

When earnings are capitalized, if the capitalized value exceeds the net book value, the difference is an intangible asset called goodwill.

In *Staab v. Commissioner*, 20 T.C. 834(1953), the court stated in part that whether a company business had any value greater than the value of its physical assets depends upon the earning power of the business. If the business had any excess earning power, that is the basis for computing goodwill.

The court continued that "goodwill may be defined by the following formula: Goodwill equals a – b, where "a" is capitalized earning power and "b" is the value of assets used in the business. Goodwill, then, is an intangible consisting of the excess earning power of a business. A normal earning power is expected of the business assets, and if the business has greater earnings, then the business may be said to have goodwill. This excess in earning power may be due to any one or more of several reasons, and usually this extra value exists only because the business is a going concern, being successful and profitable."

According to all authoritative pronouncements (whether those of the courts, the Internal Revenue Service, or Generally Accepted Accounting Principles), when earnings are capitalized, the resulting amount is the total value of the business, both of tangible and intangible assets.

In Meigs, *supra*, goodwill is defined as the intangible value of a business in excess of tangible asset value. It is similarly defined in Niswonger and Fess, *Accounting Principles*, Fourth ed., South-Western Publishing Co., page 377.

Accordingly, when James capitalized earnings, he arrived at a total value of the business of $42,506. There is no basis, authoritative, or otherwise, for his addition of his assumed and separately calculated value of physical (tangible) assets to the capitalized value. When the mortgage balance is subtracted from James's capitalized value, the result is $16,909. This is still a substantial overstatement.

James has used a capitalization rate of 15%. He has offered no authoritative support for its determination or correctness. From a reading of his deposition, it is obvious that he based it upon his experience. He mentioned a range of rates from 15 to 20%. He chose the low end of the rates to increase value more than the high end would have, but he offered no external proof to justify his choice. In similar circumstances, the court stated that "without evidence, we should not base an opinion on theories of value that lack support in the record, demonstrated market reliability, or general acceptance." (*Bowen v. Bowen* 473 A.25 73, N.J. 1984).

Mr. James did not express a general and specific knowledge of the subject matter that was sufficient to enable him to speak with authority. I cannot accept his evaluation.

In discussing capitalization rates, Rev. Rul 59-60, *supra*, states that to apply certain fundamental valuation factors such as earnings, it is necessary to capitalize the average or current earnings at some appropriate rate. That there is no ready or simple solution becomes apparent by a cursory check of the rates of return and yields in terms of the selling prices of stock shares listed on the major exchanges. Wide variations will be found even for companies in the same industry. The rate will fluctuate from year to year, depending upon economic conditions. Thus, no standard tables of capitalization rates that apply to closely held companies can be formulated. Among the more important factors to be taken into consideration in deciding upon a capitalization rate in a particular case are: (1) the nature of the business; (2) the risk involved; and (3) the stability or irregularity of earnings. James offered no evidence that he used approved methods to determine a capitalization rate. In my opinion, there is no support for his capitalization rate, and it is not acceptable.

I have disclosed that CDI has had continuing losses since inception. Even without a deduction for a salary for Howard, there has been an unrelenting series of annual losses. CDI could not survive unless Howard continued to subsidize it by his free labor.

Because there are no earnings, there is nothing to capitalize and James' valuation is wrong.

It is well established that in determining intangible value, the earning power of the business is an important factor. [*Estate of Walter A. Kraft v. Commissioner*, 61,035 P-H Memo TC (1961).] CDI has no earnings.

The ability to earn a superior rate of return on net assets that do not include goodwill is evidence that goodwill exists; the ability to earn a normal rate of return on assets that include the goodwill is evidence of the existence of goodwill in the amount computed. (Meigs, *supra*). CDI does not have the ability to earn a superior rate of return nor a normal rate of return. It has earned only losses.

In my opinion, James has overstated the value of CDI with no basis for his valuation. "No one has the right or authority to arbitrarily inflate the fair market value of the property in question." (*C.I.R. v. Tower*, 327 U. S. 280).

Other Comments on Valuation

Although goodwill can be based on earnings, primarily such factors as the prestige and renown of the business, the ownership of a trade or brand name and a record of successful operations over a prolonged period in a particular locality also may furnish support for the inclusion of intangible value. (Rev. Rul. 59-60, *supra*). None of these factors apply to CDI.

Is there going concern value as opposed to goodwill? No. "Generally, a going concern, from a businessman's viewpoint, is a healthy, vigorous and prosperous venture operated by aggressive, ordinary, prudent personnel in line with established customs and practices in the industry." (*Cornish, supra*). There is no basis for CDI to fit within this going-concern concept.

In *Matter of Brown*, 242 N. Y. 1.6, (1926), Mr. Justice Cardoza called goodwill "a reasonable expectance of preference ... (which) may come from succession in place or name or otherwise to a business that has won the favor of its customers."

The income statements of CDI show a decline in sales for each full year of operations. Sales from the income tax returns are somewhat higher than those shown on the financial statements. The following tabulation of sales is taken from Howard's income tax returns.

1982	$106,004
1983	$97,675
1984	$92,803

It is apparent that there is no "reasonable expectance of preference" for CDI.

In *Menendez v. Holt*, 128 U.S. 514 (1888), the Court defined goodwill to mean that "every positive advantage that has been acquired by the old firm in the progress of its business, whether connected with the premises in which the business was previously carried on, or with the name of the late firm, or with any other matter carrying with it the benefit of the business."

CDI has no positive advantage as disclosed by the facts.

In *Providence Mill Supply Co.*, 2 BTA 791, the Court held that "ability, skill, experience, acquaintanceship, or other personal characteristics or qualifications do not constitute goodwill as an item of property; nor do they exist in such form that they could be the subject of transfer."

Over and over, the courts have held that personability of the owner or manager does not create goodwill or any intangible that can be transferred. If it cannot be transferred, it has no value. (See *Eisner v. Macomber*, 252 U. S. 189 and *Walls V. Commissioner*, 60 F. 2d 347.)

For other decisions that personal efforts do not create an intangible asset or goodwill that can be transferred see, *Grace Bros. Inc. vs. Commissioner*, 173 F. 2d 170. Similarly, where the commissioner used the income method, the court held that personal efforts do not constitute an intangible value. See *Northwestern Steel & Iron Corporation*, 6 BTA 119, *S.H. Bryden*, T.C. Memo 1959–184, *Stillwagen*, T.C. Memo 1979–174, *Richard A. Hopping*, T.C. Memo 1947–162, Joseph Mansback, T.C. Memo 1946–239, *Howard B. Lawton*, 6 T.C. 1093, reversed on another issue, 164 F. 2d 380.

CDI has no earnings. James' capitalization rate is not supported and personal efforts do not constitute goodwill. In my opinion, the income method does not apply to CDI.

What, Then, Does Apply?

(After your report has rebutted the facts and conclusions of the opposing expert, you now must prove that your opinions are the correct ones for the court to accept, and why they are correct.)

Can a business be worth less than its underlying net book value? Of course it can. Uncertainty as to the stability or continuity of the future income from a property decreases its value by increasing the risk of loss of earnings and value in the future. (Rev. Rul. 59-60, *supra*).

Generally accepted accounting principles provide for a value less than the net book value. See *Meigs* for the following discussion of negative goodwill. If book value of the net assets exceeds the value of the company as a whole, the deficit is negative goodwill.

When the earning potential is such that the business is worth less than its net assets, the owners would be better off to dispose of the assets piecemeal, pay the liabilities, and terminate. In reality, this may not be done because of concern for the welfare of employees, willingness of the owners to operate an unprofitable business, optimism about future prospects, etc. Although negative goodwill exists in many unsuccessful businesses, it is not isolated and reported in the balance sheet. The only evidence of its existence is a low rate of return on net assets.

What, then is the value of the CDI? I calculated its value based upon the authorities that I have previously cited.

Refrigeration, Inc. appraised the equipment of CDI at $5,200. It reviewed the equipment on site. It has maintained it for CDI since inception, and has prepared a listing of the equipment to value it individually.

The building value was estimated by David Allen to be worth $10,000. He is familiar with the property because he represented the seller when it was sold to Howard. These outside valuations of building and equipment are greater than the net book value of these assets on CDI's balance sheet and increase the value of CDI.

Accordingly, I have calculated the value of CDI as follows:

Net Book value of CDI as reported earlier by me	$2,300
Add:	
Increase to buildings and equipment from estimates by outside sources	566
Deduct:	
Balance of recorded goodwill in accordance with authorities cited	(1,250)
Balance of amount from failure to record assumed lease. Lease	
Payments were expensed	(2,379)
Cash (explained below)	(8,522)
Prepaid payroll (expense item)	(5)
Returned checks	(13)
Balance, negative goodwill	$(9,303)

Is there excess cash as stated by James in his deposition? There can be no excess cash.

In a corporation, there can be cash in excess of operating needs. Because a corporation is an entity separate from its owners, the only way it can divest itself of the excess cash is by distribution to the stockholders either as a dividend or as a loan. The stockholders may not mingle it with their own funds, nor can they receive it without official action by the corporate entity.

A partnership can also have excess cash. Because of restrictions in the partnership agreement, a partner may not be allowed to take excess cash without permission of the agreement, or of his partners.

However, in a proprietorship, there can be no excess cash except in narrow accounting theory. A proprietorship is not an entity separate from its proprietor. The proprietor is the proprietorship — the proprietorship is the proprietor.

Howard is entitled to withdraw CDI cash at any time without permission from others. Had he withdrawn it and transferred it to different checking or savings accounts, it would not have been listed on the CDI balance sheet.

Howard, or any proprietor, can keep his cash in any bank account he chooses. Regardless of the title of the account, it is all his. He is free to use it for business or personal expenditure.

In addition, cash can have no value in excess of face. With today's inflation, it is rapidly declining in value. Who would buy cash? Any buyer of CDI's cash would pay face for it. Thus, if CDI sold the $8,522, CDI would receive $8,522 of cash for it. Accordingly, CDI would be in the same position after the transaction.

Therefore, I have removed cash from my calculations of the value. Cash is cash regardless of where it is recorded and it neither adds to nor detracts from my calculation. The Plaintiff has a record of the amount of the cash. Therefore, it is immaterial to my calculations.

Even if the cash is not deducted, there will still be a negative goodwill.

In my opinion, the value of CDI is less than its net book value.

A final question arose in my mind. I asked Howard why he paid $50,000 for CDI in the first place. He said that he had been optimistic when he bought it based on his experience with B&X.

CDI is not comparable to a franchised famous brand. Unfortunately, this was not considered when CDI was purchased in 1981.

Zeph Telpner

When I presented this report and its related deposition to a forensic accounting CPE class 2 years ago, several in the class objected to the citations of court cases that explained issues and settled precedent. One said that I was practicing law. He said that one judge in Texas said that the citations would create the unauthorized practice of law. This accountant did not understand the concept of substance vs. form explained in Chapter 6, which discussed that the person with decision-making authority will decide what is substance and what is form. Luckily, I have never appeared before that "one judge." You should always prepare your reports and cite whatever authority you believe is needed to support your conclusions. The attorney that you are working for will decide whether your report is acceptable. The lawyer will interpret the Rules of Civil Evidence and related decisions for you. If you are both a CPA and a lawyer, but practice accounting and not law, then you are in the same position as a CPA who is not a lawyer.

9.4 Using Experience from Previous Cases

The following report is on the value of an over-the-road truck repair shop in the dissolution of marriage dispute of *Becher v. Becher*. In that respect, it addresses issues similar to the issues in the Conseki Drive-In litigation. If issues are similar, but for different litigation, you can cannibalize from some of your previous reports.

In the Conseki Drive-In dispute, the report served to rebut the value of the Drive-In calculated by Mrs. Conseki's expert accounting witness. That witness offered no authoritative or substantive proof of his valuation methods. His testimony expressed in vague terms only how he had arrived at his value. My rebuttal report offers a zero value for the respondent, which was accepted by the judge ,who ruled that the Conseki Drive-In had no value.

The purpose of the *Becher v. Becher* report differs somewhat from the Conseki report. It is similar in that it uses most of the same authorities to support its valuation. (On similar issues for different litigants, you can use some of your previous reports.)

Its purpose for explaining its valuation is to rebut the value in the report of the petitioner's expert accounting witness. In Conseki, the expert for the respondent rebuts the higher value of the petitioner's expert and proves a lower value. In *Becher*, the following report disposes of the opposition's lower value and reaches a higher value. The explanation of the methods of computing value serve here to dispute the method used by the petitioner's expert. Its other purpose is to discredit the petitioner's expert witness. He issued a report that violates the canons of an expert witness. An expert witness, of course, owes a duty to his client, to his client's opponent, to his profession, to his regulating state boards of accountancy and to the trier of fact.

He owes his client the duty to be convinced of the client's position and to do all within his ability to help the client resolve the accounting dispute. He owes the opposing side, his profession and his accounting regulatory agencies his professional knowledge, honesty and integrity. And he owes the trier of fact the duty to be independent to the extent that he presents honest, intelligent and comprehensible statements of accounting issues, facts and his professional opinions. Armed with authoritative substantive opinions from the accounting expert witness, the trier of fact should reach a just decision or assist the jury to make one. At times, one of the parties believes that the decision is not just, and then the appeals process begins.

After reading the report of the respondent's expert accounting witness, the petitioner's accounting witness reached the opinion that the report of the respondent's witness was prepared solely to ensure that the unsupported valuation of the petitioner would be accepted by the trier of fact. The petitioner's expert witness was also the auditor of the company he was valuing and had prepared the joint income tax returns of the litigants. His report tends to confirm that he was not independent.

Expert accounting witnesses must temper and distinguish their expert witness independence from their independence when they audit a company and issue certified financial statements. A CPA expresses his opinion in general that the financial statements "present fairly." An expert's opinion and testimony requires more than a "presents fairly." It requires an unambiguous opinion such as: "my value is right, and his value is wrong," or "she stole the cash," or "they did not use the clothing labels that the petitioner claims were used, thus causing his company damages, or the corporate veil is pierced and therefore, the corporate stockholder is liable for the $1 million dollars." The report commences, in part:

Valuation in Behalf of Respondent

Estimated Value of Missouri HDT Repair, Inc. (an S Corporation)
Any City, Iowa
December 31, 199X
In the Iowa District Court for Norse County
At Any City
In re: the Marriage of Henry Louis Becher, Petitioner, and concerning
Mary Ann Becher, Respondent.

Reason for Report

You had asked me to arrive at an estimated value of Missouri HDT Repair, Inc. (HDT) in the Matter of Henry Louis Becher, Petitioner (Henry or Petitioner), concerning Mary Ann Becher, Respondent (Mary or Respondent). You have provided me with a report prepared by Joseph X. Jeater, CPA (Jeater) on behalf of the Petitioner. Jeater states in his report that the December 31, 1993 fair market value of HDT is $119,000.

You had also asked me to value HDT as close as possible to the trial date of April 21, 1994. However, the only financial statements furnished to me after December 31, 1993 were for the month of January 1994. They had not been reviewed by the company's outside accountants, and they were not adequate to consider in the context of an evaluation. Accordingly, to prepare a valuation of HDT based on the most complete information, and to compare the valuation with that of Jeater, I also used a valuation date of December 31, 1993.

Conclusion

I have performed research, interviews, and prepared calculations as I considered necessary to determine the value of HDT as of December 31, 1993. I have considered evaluations in accordance with the Market Data Method, the Cost Method, and the Income Method (capitalization of earnings) and modifications of the Income Method.

In my opinion, the value of HDT as of December 31, 1993 is not less than $200,000 and is probably more.

(*Professional qualifications of Zeph Telpner would appear here.*)

History of Missouri HDT Repair, Inc. (furnished by Respondent):

Henry had previously been a car and truck mechanic and, immediately before forming HDT, Henry had been the service manager of Cinder Motors (a division of Gold City Implement), Gold City, IA (Cinder).

Cinder was going out of business and Henry saw this as an opportunity to begin HDT. Personal funds of Henry and Mary (collectively, the parties) together with a loan from the Eagle's Savings Bank were used to purchase certain assets of Cinder.

The parties entered into a lease with Maynard and Harriet Perry (lessor) who agreed to build a shop in Gold City (the present location) and lease it to the parties for $1,550 a month until April 30, 1992.

On March 4, 1987, HDT was incorporated. Its beginning inventory was purchased from Cinder, and it operated out of the Cinder facilities until the lessor completed the new shop. The shop was completed and HDT moved to it in May or June, 1987.

The initial employees except for Mary had all worked at Cinder. They were Henry, mechanics David Allan and Joel Stephens, and parts manager Robert Mavis. David Allan is the current service manager for HDT.

The leased shop was destroyed by fire on December 10, 1987. HDT leased temporary space from the lessor and from Big Properties, Inc. until lessor constructed a new shop on the site of the destroyed shop. The new shop was completed and a new lease signed by the parties on August 31, 1990.

Terms of lease: The new rent was $2,000 monthly for a building of 11,000 square feet and parking areas of 45,000 square feet.

The lease was executed by the parties for a corporation called OTR Repair, Inc. (OTR) instead of in the name of HDT. (For purposes of continuity only of this report, HDT will be used to identify the corporation and not OTR.) However, the lease is for the previous HDT location. The lease expires on June 30, 1995 with an option to renew for another 5-year period at a negotiated rental.

In addition to credit terms received from vendors, HDT has borrowed floor plan funds from the Big City State Bank and operating funds from an individual named Jonathon Wills-Ross.

HDT has become an associate dealer of a Volvo Truck franchised dealer. An associate dealer has an agreement with the franchised dealer and not with the manufacturer.

As of December 31, 1993, HDT employed ten persons in addition to the two children of the parties. Mary said that the children have been receiving monthly salaries of $200 each from HDT. However, neither one has worked for HDT for some time.

HDT sales consist mainly of repair labor, parts, and truck sales.

Financial Statements, Income Tax Returns and Accounting Records

Accounting records were not furnished to me. However, HDT's income tax returns for the years ended December 31, 1987 to December 31, 1993 were provided to me. Also, all available financial statements were furnished to me. I considered these records, among others I used, to be adequate to reach a valid conclusion.

The corporation filed an election on March 4, 1987 with the IRS to report its income as an "S" corporation. An S corporation is one that elects to be exempt from corporate income taxes, and therefore, the income of the corporation is reported on the individual income tax returns of the stock-holders in a manner similar to that of a partnership or a proprietorship. (Internal Revenue Code Section(s) (IRS sec.) 1362, 1363 and 1366.)

The returns report that Henry and Mary each own one half of the capital stock of the corporation.

All of the corporation returns except for the year 1993 were prepared by Becker, Dale & Co., PC, (Becker) Gold City, IA. Swagman & Billabong P.C., Big Sioux, IA prepared the 1993 return. I was told that Stanley Billabong (Stanley) was asked to prepare the 1993 returns because Jeater, an employee of Becker who had previously prepared the returns, would serve as the expert witness for the Respondent.

The corporation's income tax returns and the financial statements have recorded a paid-in-capital account that is first reported on the 1988 financial statements. It has been as high as about $6,000 and as low as about $10,000. The December 31, 1993 balance was $33,767. There was no explanation for the changes between years. Stanley, who prepared the 1993 return, investigated this with Jeater. This account has been charged with such items as Henry's income tax estimates, and Par None Golf Club payments. It has been credited with items identified only as "report."

Paid-in-capital is money or property paid to a corporation for its capital stock. (*Black's Law Dictionary* 998 (rev. 5th ed. 1979) (Black's). HDT is accounting for the paid-in-capital as if it were a liability to petitioner.

Physical Inspection

Respondent's attorney (and I have assumed the same for petitioner) said that respondent finds it necessary to conserve funds, and could not afford especially large amounts for this valuation. Therefore, certain steps were omitted.

I had asked for a physical inventory count and to have the inventory priced at fair market value by vendors. I also asked for an appraisal of all of the fixed assets of HDT. We decided that we should use the same basis as petitioner for valuation — the values reported on the financial statements. This will make Respondent's valuation comparable to the Petitioner's.

Ordinarily, I make a physical inspection of the property. Respondent instead prepared a two-hour videotape of the property, both inside and outside, which was satisfactory in lieu of an in-person inspection. The attorneys for the parties agreed that the videotape provided to me was a true videotape of HDT.

The videotape recorded the outside of the building, the parking lot and the truck inventory. The tour inside began with Henry's office, followed by the offices of the service manager and the bookkeeper. Next, the parts counter was shown. The tape then moves to the showroom floor and its related displays, and the used truck inventory board.

Several minutes were devoted to the parts inventory, followed by a view of the trucks being serviced, the north bay with used parts, the inventory and equipment on the north wall, a view of the same on the east and west walls, the loft area, and the south wall of the lower level. I was satisfied that this video was an adequate substitute for a physical inspection.

(Here would follow the description of the three methods of valuation, as described in the Conseki case. What follows is my application of each to this particular case.)

Market Data Method of Valuation

On February 21, 1994, I wrote to Jay Jay Jackson (Jay), attorney for Respondent and requested that he determine if recent sales of similar businesses had been made within the trading area of HDT. He phoned to tell me that he could find no record of comparable sales. Because the Market Data Method determines value by comparison with sales of similar property, I could not calculate the value of HDT under the market data method.

Cost Method

To determine the cost to reproduce, I had to determine what the value of the property was and what it might cost to reproduce. However, HDT does not own real property, but leases it under a 5-year lease with a 5-year renewal.

Article 15 of the lease provides that the lease will terminate at the expiration of its demised term or at the expiration of the exercised option. It does not automatically renew after the option term expires.

Therefore, I did not assign a value to the lease. Although it undoubtedly is valuable until it expires, I had no basis to calculate a value.

The value of the net inventory and equipment alone does not begin to measure the value of the service type business of HDT. (See further commentary under Income Method below).

In my opinion, the Cost Method will not apply to HDT for a determination of its value.

Income Method

The Income Method is the last of the three major valuation methods to be applied to HDT. It is based upon capitalization of earnings and is an approved method. Earnings may be the most important criterion of value in some cases, whereas asset value will be the most important in others.

More consideration is given to earnings for companies that sell products or services to the public. More value is given to assets for investment or holding companies. (Rev. Rul. 59-60, supra). Mr. Jeater indicates in his schedule labeled "*Valuation*" that he had used some variation of the Income Method to arrive at a value for HDT.

(*Here, insert the information on Income Method as it appeared in the Conseki case.*)

In discussing capitalization rates, Rev. Rul. 59-60, *supra* states that to apply certain fundamental valuation factors such as earnings, it is necessary to capitalize the average or current earnings at some appropriate rate. That there is no ready or simple solution becomes apparent by a cursory check of the rates of return and yields in terms of the selling prices of stock shares listed on the major exchanges. Wide variations will be found even for companies in the same industry. The rate will fluctuate from year to year depending upon economic conditions. Thus no standard tables of capitalization rates that apply to closely held companies can be formulated. Among the more important factors to be taken into consideration in deciding upon a capitalization rate in a particular case are: (1) the nature of the business; (2) the risk involved; and (3) the stability or irregularity of earnings. Jay told me that Jeater arrived at a capitalization rate of 17.5% by asking an officer of the Gold City State Bank what he thought a fair rate of return should be.

It is well established that, in determining intangible value, the earning power of the business is an important factor. (*Estate of Walter A. Krafft v. Commissioner*, 61,305 P-H Memo TC 1961). In my commentary concerning the attached computation schedules, we will discuss the adjusted income.

The ability to earn a superior rate of return on net assets that do not include goodwill is evidence that goodwill exists; the ability to earn a normal rate of return on assets that include the goodwill is evidence of the existence of goodwill in the amount computed. (Meigs, *supra*). HDT has the ability to earn a superior rate of return after the adjustments discussed in the commentary on my schedules.

In my opinion, Jeater has understated the value of HDT and has not used an acceptable basis for his calculation.

Other Comments on Valuation

Although goodwill may be based on earnings, primarily such factors as the prestige and renown of the business, the ownership of a trade or brand name and a record of successful operations over a prolonged period in a particular locality, also may furnish support for the inclusion of intangible value. (Rev. Rul. 59-60, supra). Most of these factors apply to HDT.

When Henry bought the inventory from Cinder and continued to operate from that location with former Cinder mechanics and the parts manager, the goodwill of Cinder and the employees inured to HDT. Also, the location without close competition provides an advantage. In *Menendez v. Holt*, 1228 U. S. 514, 522 (1888), the Court defined goodwill to mean that "every positive advantage that has been acquired by the old firm in the progress of its business, whether connected with the premises in which the business was previously carried on, or with the name of the late firm, or with any other matter carrying with it the benefit of the business."

Is there going-concern value also? "Generally, a going concern, from a businessman's viewpoint, is a healthy vigorous and prosperous venture operated by aggressive, ordinary, prudent personnel in line with established customs and practices in the industry." (*Cornish, supra*). HDT's revenues have grown respectfully and Henry's salary has correspondingly increased.

In Matter of Brown, 242 N. Y. 1.6 (1926), Mr. Justice Cardoza called goodwill "a reasonable expectance of preference ... (which) may come from succession in place or name or otherwise to a business that has won the favor of its customers." The income statements of HDT show increases in sales for each full year of operation. These increases are identified on the accompanying schedules. It is apparent then, that there is a "reasonable expectance of preference" for HDT.

What are we to make of Providence Mill Supply Co., 2 BTA 791, that the "ability, skill, experience, acquaintanceship, or other personal characteristics or qualifications" of the owner "do not constitute goodwill as an item of property that could be the subject of transfer"? What also of *Eisner v. Macomber*, 252 U. S. 189 and *Walls v. Commissioner*, 60 F.2d 347? These courts held that personability of the owner does not create goodwill that can be transferred. These are different issues. The IRS wanted to tax non-taxable transfers. In *Becher v. Becher*, we are making a determination of the earning capacity of the petitioner from HDT in dissolution of marriage.

Valuation Commentary and Computations

The accompanying schedules 1 through 6 are the schedules of my calculations and assumptions to allow me to determine the fair market value of HDT. The schedules are discussed according to use and not according to a numerical order.

My schedules record the 5 calendar years of HDT from 1989 to 1993. Jeater had omitted the year 1987 because it was a start-up year, and 1988 because a fire destroyed the business site. I agree with this omission to prevent distortion of our calculations. Abnormal years should be eliminated. (*White & Wells Co.*, (CA-2) 50 F. 2d 120) (*The authors did not include the schedule exhibits of either party. The explanations in the report are important. The schedules are important to lay persons, but accountants will understand them from the commentary.*)

Schedule 5

Jeater has prepared two schedules to arrive at net income. These are the amounts reported as "net income per books" on HDT's corporation income tax returns (1120S). My Schedule 5 is a reconciliation of the sales net of any returns and allowances to the net book income on the 1120S and on Jeater's schedules. Schedule 5 reclassifies the other income and expenses to arrive at net income before other income and expenses. This net income is operating income, which must serve as a basis to compute a potential value from operating the business. HDT is not, for example, in the business of earning interest. Section 179 expense will be discussed later. This schedule also serves to set out Henry's salary.

Schedule 4

To use the Income Method, we must arrive at an adjusted or "Net Valuation Income." This is shown on Schedule 4. The first line of the schedule, "net book income," can be traced directly to the last line of Schedule 4. Certain adjustments must be made to net book income to arrive at a valuation income for capitalization of earnings.

The first two adjustments are for depreciation. However, Section 179 deductions are not depreciation, but such deductions before repeal and reenactment were defined as additional first year depreciation. After reenactment, the term depreciation was traditionally misused. IRC sec. 179(a) provides that a taxpayer may elect to treat the cost of certain depreciable property as an expense to deduct up to a limit of $10,000.

The adjustment to add one half of regular depreciation is made also based on a change in the law. IRC sec. 167 provided for a depreciation deduction of a reasonable allowance for exhaustion and wear and tear of certain assets. Depreciation was deducted over the useful life of the asset. For the years on Schedule 4, actual book depreciation was computed under the modified accelerated cost-recovery system provided by IRC sec. 168. It is a double declining method that deducts depreciation over half the time as straight-line. Both IRC sec. 179 and 168 were passed into law to provide incentive to business to invest in machinery and equipment. It has no basis in a computation of value, which should use the straight-line method to match costs with revenues in the years to which they relate.

The life of an asset for depreciation may be shorter on an income tax return than its actual useful life. (*Black's*, 397).

Depreciation is a consistent, gradual process of estimating and allocating cost of capital investments over the estimated useful life of an asset in order to match cost against earnings. *Coca-cola Bottling Co. of Baltimore v. U.S.*, 203 Ct. Cl. 18, 487 F. 2d 528, 534.

The term "depreciation" as used in accounting is frequently misunderstood because the same term is also commonly used to connote a decline in the market value of an asset. Any similarity between the amount of unexpired cost of assets reported in the balance sheet and the amount that could be realized from their sale is merely coincidental. Plant assets are held for use rather than for sale, and their current market values are irrelevant. C.R. Niswonger & P.E. Fess, *Accounting Principles* (10th ed. 1969).

I have added the salary of Henry and the related taxes on them for several reasons. In theory, one can compute the value of an S corporation by computing income taxes on it as if it were a regular corporation. However, Henry raises his salary without formal approval as income increases. (See Schedule 6). Also, because income flows one half to each shareholder and is reported on their individual returns, equity demands that it be recorded for this computation as if it were a partnership or proprietorship. Indeed, as discussed earlier in this report, Henry takes distributions from capital and ignores the corporate form. Similarly, I have added the salary of his children because, according to Mary, they are not actually entitled to a deductible salary.

The deductions for Sec. 179 are made to deduct the 179 expense on the straight-line method of depreciation to match costs with revenues.

Schedule 6

Schedule 6 demonstrates that, except for the period 1989 to 1990, Henry's salary had increased substantially and disproportionately to the increase in income. Because valuation income is greater than the income reported by Jeater, the disparity between the valuation income and salary increase is not as dramatic as it would be with the income in Jeater's report.

Schedule 3

Schedule 3 serves to compute the December 31, 1993 equity that is used in the calculation on Schedule 2. Further, it serves to set out certain asset and liability classifications that were omitted from Jeater's report.

Schedule 2

Schedule 2 is a computation of value based on the approximate method used by Jeater. Notice that in the excess earnings computation, the total net valuation income of $346,489 from Schedule 4 is used. Because it is for a 5-year period, I have used the same method as Jeater to compute a simple average by dividing the $346,489 by 5 to arrive at an average of $69,297. I have used this average because it is comparable to the same type of average computed by Jeater. However, this is an arithmetic mean (mean) and has the tendency to distort the computed amount. The median seems the most appropriate method of arriving at an average, but it is only slightly higher than the mean. The mode does not appear to be a satisfactory average.

I had reviewed Jeater's calculation valuation and I am not sure what method he has used. He is apparently attempting to compute value by using the "excess earnings method." The *IRS Valuation Manual* explains that this "method is based on the theory that the value of net tangible assets plus the capitalized value of the excess earnings (the goodwill factor) equals the value of the business." The computation begins with the net tangible assets computed in the adjusted book value method. The adjusted book value method requires more adjustments than Jeater has made.

"The next adjustment is to remove from earnings all unusual items. This will generally include items, such as investment income (interest, dividends, etc.) that are derived from other than operations. This amount is called the 'adjusted earnings.'" Normal earnings are then subtracted from adjusted earnings to arrive at excess earnings or, as Jeater has labeled them, "net capitalized earnings."

"The amount that is considered 'normal earnings' based on the industry standards is then subtracted from the adjusted earnings resulting in 'excessive earnings.' This amount is then capitalized (most often at 20% in the real world) and results in 'goodwill,' which is then added to net intangible assets for the total value." (*IRS Valuation Guide for Income Estate and Gift Taxes, Valuation Training for Appeals Officers*, 7–15, 7–16).

This excess earnings method was originally set out in IRS A.R.M. 34, CB 2, 31 (1920). It calculated industry earnings at 8 to 10% of net tangible asset when the industry percentage was not available. I have used 8% on Schedule 2. The IRS has ruled that this method should not be used if there is better evidence available to determine the intangible values. It repeats that this method "may be used for determining the fair market value of intangible assets of a business only if there is not better basis, therefore, available." This also modified Rev. Rul. 59-60, *supra*. The ruling also superseded A.R.M. 34, and Rev. Rul. 65-192, which had restated A.R.M. 34. (Rev. Rul. 68–609, 1968-2 CB 327).

Jeater's calculation does not subtract average industry earnings but subtracts HDT's actual average equity. I am not familiar with this method and believe that it is not an acceptable method. Even if it were, it would have been unacceptable in relation to a better method.

My calculation on Schedule 2 has accepted Jeater's capitalization rate of 17.5 for this method, and has calculated average industry earnings at 8%. (Rev. Rul. 68-609, *supra*).

By basing the valuation on the acceptable method, the value on Schedule 2 amounts to $396,304. I believe that this value is excessive and disproportionate to the earnings of HDT. It is one of the reasons that this method is accepted only with great reluctance by the IRS and it is to their advantage to reach a high valuation.

For this reason, I do not believe that Jeater's value of $119,000 is correct, nor do I believe that the value on my Schedule 2 is correct.

Schedule 1: Schedule 1 uses the capitalization of earnings method. (Rev. Rul. 59–60, *supra*). I phoned Ethan Axel (Ethan), a trailer manufacturer in Council Bluffs. Until last year, he had been the president for many years of Midwest International Truck, Inc. (Midwest) in Council Bluffs. Midwest sells new and used International trucks and provides repair services and parts sales to its customers. Ethan considered the different profit factors for fleet sales, individual and small quantity truck sales, used truck sales, parts sales and service revenues. He derived a capitalization rate of 31.17% to compute a fair market value of $222,319.

Additionally, I once more refer you to Schedule 6. Since 1991, Henry has raised his salary in larger amounts. The total was $14,400. Additionally, his children receive $4,800 annually from HDT. Mary also revealed that Henry's personal automobile is owned by HDT and auto expenses are paid by HDT. Henry's increase from 1992 to 1993 before fringes was $9,422. Revenues and profits have increased each year. HDT should be able to put a lid on Henry's salary to pay one half the value of $222,319 calculated on Schedule 1 to Mary over a period of no more than 10 years together with interest. However, in my opinion, I have stated that the value is not less than $200,000 to explain that computing the value of a business is not an exact science.

The petitioner's attorneys decided that the lower value computed by their expert was not correct and accepted the report and valuation of the respondent's expert. Depositions were not taken and a trial was not held. The litigation was ended with an expert's report. Always prepare a complete report and explain, explain, explain facts, issues, and conclusions so the reader will understand what you mean. If we do our jobs right as experts, we may be able to save time and money for the attorneys and their clients.

The Expert's Testimony 10

10.1 A Brief Look at a Trial

The following trial transcript is a sequel to the deposition given by Zeph Telpner that was discussed in Chapter 6. From these trial transcripts and the depositions in other chapters, the accounting expert witness can learn what an attorney does to qualify a witness. This also gives him the opportunity to learn from direct- and cross-examination what judges, jurors, and attorneys want to know about facts and issues. Direct examination of the accounting expert witness by his engaging attorney is necessary to establish that he has the know-how, education, professional experience and certifications to testify as an expert in this dispute. It gives information to the judge so that he can accept or reject the expert as a witness. The testimony and direct- and cross-examination are sufficient to give a beginner insight on testifying, and the experienced accounting expert can learn something new.

10.1.1 Trial Tips for the Expert

1. Hand your business card to the court reporter as you pass on the way to the witness stand. Your name has a better chance of being spelled right.
2. Speak loudly enough for the judge, jury and attorneys to hear you. If they can't hear you or understand you because of sloppy speech, they may tune you out and your testimony will be worthless. If the court furnishes a microphone for the witness, then you may have to tone down your volume.
3. Ask your primary attorney what to wear. Some locations prefer browns, others blacks or grays. Don't wear shoes that squeak as you walk to the witness stand.

4. Listen to the attorney's entire question before you respond. Don't say too much. Just answer what is asked of you.

10.2 The Trial Begins

Zeph Telpner (**A**), as the plaintiff's witness, is directly examined by Mike Mostek (**Q**). They begin by establishing the basics: name, address, educational background, etc. We will pick up the examination as the witness is describing his professional experience in some detail, beginning with his time with Arthur Andersen.

A. For the first couple of years I did auditing of companies like Mutual of Omaha and Northern National Gas, Sioux City-Sioux Falls Stockyards Company, Iowa Public Service, Consumer Public Power District, a lot of regulated industries that were regulated by various governmental agencies.

Q. Did you continue working for Arthur Andersen for some period of time?

A. Yes, I did, but they transferred me into the tax department. The managing partner wanted to build a tax department and he thought that my talents would be adaptable to taxes.

Q. What is the difference between the tax department and the auditing department in a firm like that?

A. The auditing department specializes in examining and giving opinions on financial statements. CPAs have a monopoly on giving an opinion on a financial statement. You cannot sell stock and securities and register with the Securities and Exchange Commission unless a CPA examines your financial statements and expresses an opinion that it presents fairly or it does not present fairly the results of the operations and the finances of the company.

Q. Would that be an example of an audit?

A. Yes, that's an audit.

Q. What would be the tax department?

A. The tax department specializes in taxes of all kinds. They give advice to clients who have tax problems. They might ask you, how can I handle this? They represent taxpayers before the Internal Revenue Service when they are adjusted by Internal Revenue Service agents. Sometimes they go to appeals and file a protest. They also prepare income tax returns and they are responsible, on an audited client, for determining that the liability for income taxes is properly recorded at the right amount so the people who rely on those statements won't be misled about the liability.

Q. Mr. Telpner, you mentioned that Arthur Andersen wanted you to start a tax department. Did you do so?

A. They wanted me to build a tax department. They didn't have a tax manager at the time. But did I do so? Yes, I did.

Q. How long did you continue working for the Arthur Andersen Company?

A. Three more years.

Q. Are you familiar with the term big eight accounting firm?

A. Yes.

Q. What does that mean? Can you tell us?

A. Yes. Back in those years, eight of the largest accounting firms in the world were spoken of as big eight. For example, let's say even today, one accounting firm, the largest might have 70,000 employees and the 20th-largest might only have 1500 employees. There is such a large difference between these accounting firms, and yet with 1500 employees you are considered to be an international firm because most CPA firms are very small.

Q. Mr. Telpner, has Arthur Andersen Company ever been considered one of the big eight accounting firms?

A. Yes, at the time I worked for them, they and Peat, Marwick, Mitchell were considered to be neck and neck for the two biggest.

Q. I would like to ask you briefly about your other experience in public accounting. Did you continue working in accounting after your tenure with Arthur Andersen?

A. Yes.

Q. When did you leave Arthur Andersen?

A. I think it was 1963, in the fall.

Q. What did you do after you left Arthur Andersen Company?

A. I merged with an Omaha firm and started a new partnership in Council Bluffs. It was Telpner, Bernstein, Friedman and Tighe.

Q. When you say you merged, you mean you took your clients that you had and joined together with some other accountants?

A. I might say that I formed a new partnership with other accountants. When you work for a firm like Arthur Andersen, you are an individual, there is no way you are going to walk away with clients of theirs. They are very large.

Q. Now, with regard to the firm that you formed in Council Bluffs, did you continue working with that firm for a period of time?

A. For about a year. The other three partners had an opportunity to merge with Elmer Fox and Company. And Elmer Fox wanted me to move to Wichita to take charge of their tax department, and I didn't want to go to Wichita. So those three partners went with Fox and Company an I merged with Peat, Marwick, Mitchell and Company and managed their Council Bluffs office, which had been my office. They had never had one in Council Bluffs until then.

Q. Mr. Telpner, have you continued to be engaged in public accounting since that time, the 1960s through the present date, in one form or another?

A. Yes, I have.

Q. Specifically I would like to ask you about your accounting experience with regard to the trucking industry. At any point in time did you ever have any clients who were trucking companies or otherwise involved in the trucking industry?

A. Yes, I did.

Q. When did you get your first trucking client?

A. 1964.

Q. Who was that client?

A. Clarence Werner, Werner Enterprises.

Q. Would you describe for us what sort of work you did for Werner Enterprises beginning in 1964?

A. I prepared his income tax returns, set up an accounting system for him, assisted him with his payroll tax returns, assisted him with his highway use tax returns, his fuel tax returns. He was working out of his house when I started with him. I think he had one or two tractors. Whenever he needed research or a financial statement, I might prepare the financial statement, not an audit. One time, when he finally needed an audit, I recommended some other CPA firms because by then I had devoted so much of my time to taxes that I discontinued performing audits.

Q. Mr. Telpner, when you say Werner Enterprises, are you talking about the company that is currently based out of Omaha, Nebraska?

A. Yes.

Q. After 1964 in those early years, did you continue to represent Clarence Warner and Werner Enterprises?

A. Yes.

Q. Did you do other additional work through the years, other than what you have described, for Clarence Werner and Werner Enterprises?

A. Yes. He was a contract carrier at that time. In '71 he got contract authority. Before that, he didn't have authority and he used to haul exempt freight, like agricultural commodities, certain things that he didn't have to have a permit for. And in '71 he applied for a permit as a contract carrier. So he had to convert to the ICC accounting system. I converted his records to the ICC accounting system and on one occasion I wrote the proposal to one of the shippers so he could serve them as a contract carrier.

Q. You mentioned the term "contract carrier." Could you briefly describe for us what that means?

A. A contract carrier is a regulated trucking company that has a permit that allows him to dedicate himself to one or more shippers, usually — it used to be about eight at that time — and he could only haul for those shippers. But because he had authority, if he went out empty, he could bring some freight back. Whereas, without authority, he couldn't do that.

Q. That's called a contract carrier?

A. Yes, he signs a contract dedicated to a particular shipper. For example, Sears and Roebuck, years ago when I worked for Sears after high school, didn't have their own trucks. They had a contract carrier that hauled for them.

Q. Are you also familiar with the term "common carrier" as it applies in the trucking industry?

A. Yes.

Q. What would be your understanding of that term?

A. Well, at that time, common carriers didn't get a permit. They got a Certificate of Convenience and Public Necessity. That meant they had a monopoly on certain highways that they could travel on and nobody else could, and certain types of freight that they could haul and other truckers couldn't haul. But they also had an obligation to serve the public for their convenience and necessity. In other words, if you, for example, had a full trailer load or 50 trailer loads of wheat going out and I only had one to ship, they couldn't discriminate, they had take my one. They didn't want to take my one trailer load; they would rather take the 50. But, because they had that Certificate of Convenience and Public Necessity, they didn't have any choice.

Q. What period of time are you talking about?

A. Up until July of 1980.

Q. What changed at that time?

A. There was a Motor Carrier Reform Act. Originally, President Carter wanted to deregulate the industry or at least make it less regulated. That didn't happen, but they did have a reform that made it easier to get a certificate. It didn't have to be a convenience and public necessity. It had to serve a useful public purpose. There is one other test, a trucking company has to be fit, willing and able to haul the freight. So that means that there wasn't really a monopoly. Almost anybody could say, "If I haul this, it's useful, it's going to get one more truck in here to help haul freight." So it was easier to get authority. It meant there was much more competition.

Q. When did you set up Werner Trucking on the ICC accounting system?

A. That would have been '71 it was a Class 3 carrier.

Q. How big was Werner Enterprises at that time?

A. A class 3 carrier then was $300,000 in revenues.

Q. Did you continue to serve Werner Enterprises or Clarence Werner after that point in time?

A. Yes.

Q. What sort of things did you do for them?

A. I assisted him. He did some consulting up in Round Lake, Minnesota, for Sather Cookie Company to set up their private fleet, turn it into a contract carrier, and I went along with him to help handle the accounting and tax part of the consultation. Sometimes I would conduct a meeting for him for his employees about accounting and tax and finance so the employees would know more about how a business operates.

Q. How long did you continue to serve Werner Enterprises?

A. Until '81.

Q. What happened at that time?

A. I had the opportunity to sell out. I had quite a bit of trucking work by then. I had the opportunity to sell out my ongoing trucking business to Arthur Andersen and Company. And Werner was getting so big by then, I knew that if I didn't sell out pretty soon they would be too big for me. And so I sold out to Arthur Andersen, but Clarence asked me to stay on another year throughout '81 so he could get used to the new accountants.

Q. Mr. Telpner, you have mentioned other trucking companies that you have represented. Without going into a lot of detail, could you give us an idea of some of the other companies that you have been involved with?

A. Emporia Motor Freight in Emporia, Kansas. Thompson Truck Transportation in Arlington, Texas. Chip Carriers Inc., in Omaha. Ring Brothers Transportation out of Neola, Iowa. Cargo Contract Carriers from Sioux City. BRAE Corporation Surface Transportation Group in San Francisco and Memphis, Tennessee. There are a few more.

Q. When you sold out your practice to Arthur Andersen in '81, how big was Werner Enterprises at that point in time?

A. On July 1, 1980 when we had deregulation, a lot of companies went bankrupt for a particular reason. A Certificate of Convenience and Public Necessity was no longer a monopolistic license, and some of them that had cost $200 million were suddenly worthless, so a lot of trucking companies went out of business.

But Clarence Werner — I always thought he was a marketing genius and a management genius and I knew that he would grow. He was restricted, he was held back by the monopolies, but the minute it came time to compete, he could do it. So he went from about $9 million a year as of July 1, 1980, and then I figured it out to June 30, '81, so we would get a full year, he had jumped to $21 million in annual revenue.

Q. What have you been doing in your career since you sold out your practice to Arthur Andersen?

A. I still do a lot of trucking work. For example, recently I was the examiner on the Best Refrigerated Express bankruptcy. I was the expert witness on the Mason and Dixon bankruptcy, a $200 million trucking company in Greensboro, North Carolina, but this time I was on the opposite side. My client was the Central States Pension Fund, the teamsters union.

Q. You testified as a witness for the pension fund?

A. Yes, and I also testified for them in Cleveland for the pension fund against a trucking company. And then in Pittsburgh it was to determine the value of a trucking company in the federal district court in western Pennsylvania.

Q. Have you continued to perform public accounting services as well as your work in cases and so forth?

A. Yes.

Q. Now, all the companies that you mentioned when I asked you about your clients, what sort of trucking companies were those, Mr. Telpner?

A. They were truckload carriers.

Q. Would your clients have been what you described as common carriers?

A. They would be common carriers.

Q. With ICC authority?

A. That's right.

Q. And would those companies have had trucks, I suppose that they put out on the road?

A. Yes.

Q. And those trucks would have needed drivers?

A. Yes.

Q. And you testified that you had experience with payroll matters with regard to one or more of your clients?

A. Yes.

Q. Mr. Telpner, I would like to turn our attention now to some of your activities in professional associations, so we can get a familiarity with what sorts of matters you have been involved in from that point of view. Are you a member of any professional associations involving either the trucking industry or the accounting profession?

A. Yes.

Q. What would be some of those?

A. I am a member of the American Institute of Certified Public Accountants, the organization that actually works with the Financial Accounting Standards Board to determine that financial statements and accounting is kept up to date and that CPAs are kept up to date. For example, boards of accountancy require CPAs to have continuing professional education.

Q. Are you or have you been affiliated with any state associations or societies during your career?

A. The Iowa Society of CPAs. And the Nebraska Society of CPAs.

Q. Have you been affiliated with those during your entire career?

A. Well, since 1962. That's a long time.

Q. Mr. Telpner, have you been affiliated or associated with any organizations having to do with the trucking industry?

A. The American Trucking Association, National Accounting and Finance Council.

Q. Where is that headquartered?

A. At that time it was in Washington, D.C., but it later moved to Alexandria, Virginia.

Q. Is that a national organization?

A. Yes.

Q. You mentioned that that was an Accounting and Finance Council?

A. Yes, American Trucking Association is made up of state trucking associations and then it has councils, like an operation council, sales and marketing council, accounting and finance council. So people who specialize in certain things and want to take more education in certain things and know about the developing issues, for example, if you are an accountant and you would want to know about the developing tax issues, you would get it in the National Accounting and Finance Council. And if you were interested in taxes, you would get on the taxation committee, because trucking companies have so many different kinds of taxes that you need to have people who specialize in that to help you learn about it.

Q. How long have you been a member of the National Accounting and Finance Council of the American Trucking Association?

A. I am not a member now because I am getting close to retirement.

Q. How long were you a member?

A. I was a member for 15 years.

Q. What time span would that cover?

A. Sometime in the 1970s — 1986 was the last year I was in that one nationally. It might have been longer. I think I joined in '71 or '72. I can't remember now.

Q. Did you serve on any other committees in that organization?

A. Yes. I was on the board of directors for several years until I finally retired from it.

Q. The board of directors of?

A. Of the National Accounting and Finance Council of the American Trucking Association. I served on their taxation committee. I served on their independent contractor committee. I served on their securities committee, when they used to get information about issuing securities and regulation of securities in the trucking industry.

Q. Did they have any committees having to do with small carriers or smaller carriers?

A. Yes, they had the small-carrier committee and the independent-trucker committee, both having to do with small carriers.

Q. Were you a member of those committees?

A. Yes.

Q. How long was that during your affiliation with the organization?

A. That was almost the full amount of time I was in the council. The council would have an annual meeting, and then they would have regional seminars where they would put one on in Omaha for a five-state area, and on accounting and taxation in the trucking industry. And then the committees would have special meetings, too. Sometimes one, two or three times a year.

Q. You mentioned that that national organization was made up of state associations; is that correct?

A. The American Trucking Association is an association of state trucking associations.

Q. And the Accounting and Finance Council that you described for us was part of the American Trucking Association?

A. Yes, it was a council. The American Trucking Association has 13 councils. They have a sales and marketing council. I used to be involved in that, too, because I had to know about some of the methods they use to bill freight and to get freight coming in.

Q. Were you ever involved in any state associations having to do with the trucking industry?

A. The Nebraska Motor Carriers Association.

Q. What was, briefly, the extent of your involvement with that organization?

A. I was on its board of directors. I also gave many programs at the annual meetings and at monthly meetings on taxes and accounting problems in the industry and about new tax laws that were passed. I would be one of the speakers who would usually interpret it.

Q. Did the state association also have an accounting and finance council?

A. They did after I founded it, but I can't remember what year that was, sometime in the '70s. I organized it. I went to the board of directors of the Nebraska Motor Carriers and asked them if they would sponsor us as a council of the Nebraska Motor Carriers and we would affiliate with the national Accounting and Finance Council. We did get the outstanding council award from the national one year.

Q. Who did?

A. The Nebraska Accounting and Finance Council of the Nebraska Motor Carriers. It took a long time for a small outfit.

Q. How long were you a member or otherwise associated with the Nebraska Motor Carriers Association and what period of time did it cover?

A. I think that was from about '72 or '74 to about 1986.

Q. You mentioned that the state organization received an award. Have you personally ever received an award for accounting within the trucking industry?

A. Yes, I received the meritorious service award to trucking from the National Accounting and Finance Council. From the Nebraska Accounting and Finance Council, I got the outstanding trucking accountant twice and the professional service award in accounting twice.

Q. What were those awards given for?

A. For competence in and knowledge of the accounting industry, for giving continuing professional-education courses to the accountants and other financial people in the trucking industry, for setting up regional conferences every year and getting speakers on continuing professional education that specialized in trucking for the trucking industry.

Q. You have mentioned a term a couple of times, "continuing professional education." Would you please describe for us what that is?

A. Certified public accountants must have 120 hours of continuing professional education in certain seminars and courses and topics like Subchapter S corporations, estate and gift planning, (if you do that, I don't do any estate and gift planning), auditing, if you are doing auditing. Whatever your specialty is. You have to attend seminars in, let's say a certain part of taxation, like Section 351 of the Internal Revenue Code. That's when you form a corporation.

Q. Are those intended to keep you up to date on what is changing with regard to the tax laws and what is going on in the industry?

A. Yes. You can't get a permit to practice every year without the continuing education. You have to turn in a report and then the board can check this report to make sure you do have these. For example, Nebraska requires me to get at least 16 hours a year on accounting and auditing. Iowa doesn't require that. The boards of accountancy have different requirements. So I have to get 16 hours in Nebraska, which takes away from my ordinary time that I want to spend on taxation. So I would take some extra hours to make up so I wouldn't miss my full time in taxation.

Q. You mentioned that you received some rewards with regard to setting up seminars and so forth. What has been your experience with teaching seminars, for example?

A. I have written and taught seminars for 26 state CPA associations. And on the trucking industry, that was the first one I put out.

Q. When was that?

A. The first one I wrote was in '72 for the American Institute of Certified Public Accountants.

Q. That was on the trucking industry?

A. Yes, it was limited to contract carriers, because at that time Werner was a contract carrier.

Q. Would that be a book or some sort of materials that you wrote?

A. It was a book of about 200 pages, single spaced, with case studies and discussion leader's lecture outline. Sometimes the state society would have their own discussion leader. For example, in Pennsylvania, a man named Tom Tinsley from Wilkes-Barre, the Pennsylvania society wanted him. And in Georgia I taught a few times, but they also wanted one of their own people, Paul Harris from Stone Mountain, who did a lot of trucking work down there.

Q. So you designed and taught a course to the state associations, or some of them, regarding the trucking industry?

A. Yes. They had to qualify under the rules of continuing professional education that were promulgated by the American Institute of CPAs and adopted by the state boards of accountancy. If you didn't comply with the requirements for training, the people who took it wouldn't get credit for it.

Q. Have you done any other writing or speaking with regard to the trucking industry?

A. I had another course out after contract carriers. I had demand for a more advanced course. So I put out an advanced course in accounting for the trucking industry. It was distributed by the Iowa Society of CPAs for many years, and finally they changed their organization and I had to distribute it myself. And that went to the same CPA societies that the American Institute had been selling to, although I sold few on my own that they had not gone through. I think for about 12 years I taught in Los Angeles and San Francisco and Anaheim for the California Foundation on Accounting Education. I taught in Oregon, in Georgia, in North Carolina, in Nebraska, Iowa, Maryland.

Q. What course are you speaking about now?

A. The advanced trucking course.

Q. Have you done any other teaching or speaking in relation to the trucking industry in particular?

A. Yes, at the National Accounting and Finance Council annual convention I was the first person who was not from a big eight firm, a public accountant, who was asked to speak for them.

I spoke in San Francisco in 1979 at their national convention on their continuing education. And also again in 1982 in St. Louis. And then I gave seminars for the Iowa Motor Truck Association on trucking and taxes. The Nebraska Motor Carriers Association. New York–New Jersey Metropolitan Accounting Council of the New York–New Jersey Trucking Association. I gave a seminar for the American Institute of CPAs on trucking. And one for DeLoitte, Haskins and Sells.

Q. You mentioned that you were the only one who was not from a big eight accounting firm. When was that? Was that after you had left Arthur Andersen?

A. Yes, 1979, 1982. All the others were either from huge trucking companies like Consolidated Freightways, Yellow Freight, UPS and Roadway. The big eight accounting firms (which are now the big six), always supplied the speaker year after year. And I was the first one — not just the big eight, but international firms. For example, Grant Thornton was the ninth largest and it was international, and Seidman and Seidman was also an international firm.

Q. When you did this teaching and speaking, what types of people would attend your courses?

A. Well, I had presidents of smaller trucking companies and financial vice presidents of Consolidated Freightways and their tax department managers. Commercial Carriers, that was the largest automobile hauler. Peat, Marwick, Mitchell. Arthur Andersen. Coopers and Lybrand. Touche-Ross. The Internal Revenue Service. The FBI. The United States Postal Service.

Q. As part of your career and as part of your profession, have you or do you subscribe to any professional publications and periodicals?

A. Yes, although not as many as I did.

Q. During the period of time, say from when you got you CPA license through 1986, did you subscribe to any periodicals or publications specifically for accountants for example?

A. Yes, I did, specifically for accountants.

Q. Did you subscribe to any having to do with the trucking industry?

A. Yes, I did.

Q. Why would you subscribe to ones from the trucking industry, Mr. Telpner?

A. Because much of my work was in the trucking industry I had to keep up my courses, so I had to know about the most current developments all the time. Sometimes I would have to revise my course every month. In 1979–1980 when the Motor Carrier Act was coming out, it was almost a daily change. You can't spend 365 days a year in a class and get any work done. So you have to use periodicals, too, and study. You have to go to continuing education.

Q. Would it be fair to say that you did all those things to help you keep up with what was changing in the industry?

A. Absolutely, just so I could serve my clients.

Q. What sort of trucking publications did you subscribe to?

A. *Commercial Car Journal* — originally it was called *Commercial Carrier Journal* — a special magazine on the trucking industry. *Transport Topics*, a special weekly newspaper of the trucking industry. *Motor Freight Controller*, which is a trucking industry — it specializes in taxes and finance. I also was on the ICC Regulated Carrier Subcommittee of the American Institute of Certified Public Accountants, a national committee that promulgated the accounting and tax requirements for trucking companies, for CPAs to follow, and they sent me bulletins from the national office on trucking and on the railroads, too, regulated transportation industries.

Q. I would like to briefly turn our attention to some more terms having to do with the trucking industry. Have you heard of the term "ICC authority"?

A. Yes, I have.

Q. What does that mean?

A. Well, the Interstate Commerce Commission was a regulatory body over economics and finance of the trucking industry.

Q. ICC stands for … ?

A. Interstate Commerce Commission.

Q. That's part of the federal government?

A. Yes. It's a — the Motor Carrier Act, Part 2, was passed in 1935. The Interstate Commerce Commission has been around since 1898 to regulate the railroads.

Q. What does it mean to say a company has ICC authority?

A. It meant they either had a Certificate of Convenience and Public Necessity or a permit as a contract carrier to haul regulated freight. You see, the trucks weren't really regulated by them. The freight was regulated and the routes they could travel over were regulated. There was some freight that was not regulated, agricultural commodities.

Q. Have you an understanding of the term "truckload carrier"?

A. Yes.

Q. What does that mean?

A. A truckload carrier is a carrier that — let's say Campbell's Soup Company wants to fill a trailer with soup to send it to California. So a truckload carrier would take an entire trailer load of one product from one shipper to one consignee.

Q. Do truckload carriers always carry just one product? Is there ever any exception to that?

A. This was an exception in ICC. When deregulation came about, ICC was loosening up and one truckload carrier was allowed to put two or three types of items on one trailer. If you had three small shippers, they could each pull a third of a trailer. But it was very restrictive on what they could do. And before 1980 they couldn't do that at all.

Q. Do you have an understanding of the term "less than truckload carrier"?

A. Yes.

Q. What does that mean?

A. Well, it's a carrier that picks up a lot of smaller packages and consolidates them until they have a trailer load. I could give an example, if you wanted.

Q. Can you give us a brief one?

A. Yes. If you ever fly, you know what a truckload carrier is, because you walk into the terminal at the airport, and maybe you are all from Omaha, but you are all going to different destinations. So some of you go to the United gate, some to the TransWorld gate. So you start together into the lobby and then you are shuffled around and reconsolidated by gate. Within that gate they have different flights. So they will consolidate all the passengers going to San Francisco on one flight, consolidate others that are going to New York on another. So theoretically they have a plane load. And that's what you do with an LTL carrier; it has to consolidate this freight.

Q. According to the destination?

A. Yes.

Q. Have you heard the term "independent trucker"?

A. Yes, I have.

Q. What is your understanding of that term?

A. That is a trucking company that is in the leasing segment of the industry. It does not have ICC authority.

Q. Do you have an understanding of the term "owner–operator"?

A. Yes, I do.

Q. What is your understanding of that term?

A. That's usually, in general, a driver who owns a tractor and drives it.

Q. Have you ever heard other meanings applied to that term?

A. Yes.

Q. What sort of meanings?

A. Subhauler, subcontractor, contractor. You mean of one person? And also independent contractor, contractor independent trucker.

Q. To clarify an independent trucker, how is that different?

A. An independent trucker actually is leasing a lot of trucks, more than one. He is usually not the driver, but he can be.

Q. He owns trucks and leases them?

A. Yes. He leases tractors to — usually it's tractors that he leases to a regulated carrier, or a private carrier like Campbell's Soup Company.

Q. Mr. Telpner, during the course of your career, have you had the opportunity to take courses on trucking, as well as teach them?

A. Yes, I have.

Q. What sort of courses did you take?

A. I took courses on taxation, finance, operating taxes — these are taxes other than income taxes, on how freight bills operate, the weigh bills and the bills of lading, what they are.

Q. Where did you take these courses?

A. At the National Accounting and Finance Council national and regional seminars.

Q. Did you take more than one?

A. I used to get about 24 to 40 hours a year just in trucking topics alone. Sometimes, I had — you had to have 40 hours a year, 120 hours every 3 years. But there were years when I had 238 hours of continuing education. That cut into my work. It was very hard to get my work done.

Q. You attended all those meetings and seminars on a regular basis?

A. Yes, I did.

Q. Mr. Telpner, have you ever had an ownership interest in a trucking company?

A. Yes, I have.

Q. When was that, sir?

A. That was between about 1976 and 1980.

Q. What sort of trucking company was that?

A. That was a contract carrier that hauled for a furniture manufacturer out of Eldora, Iowa.

Q. Where is that located?

A. It's in northern Iowa, not too far from Ames or Grinnell.

Q. Mr. Telpner, you have mentioned in your testimony companies that lease tractors to other companies. Can you describe for us generally why a company would lease a tractor rather than go out and buy a tractor, and by that I mean a semi tractor truck?

A. Yes. Prices keep going up. A tractor might cost between $80 and $100,000 today. That's a lot of money to finance. Initially, truckers couldn't get financing and banks didn't normally finance trucking companies. Usually equipment manufacturing companies financed trucking companies. And they had to pay a substantial down payment and a substantial add-on interest. It was quite high. So sometimes, in order to finance growth, they would have to lease equipment from someone else.

Q. I would like to ask you questions regarding your specific experience with independent trucking issues and employment taxes. During the course of your career, have you become familiar with the laws and regulations concerning payroll taxes and the payment of such taxes?

A. Yes.

Q. How did you become familiar with those, briefly?

A. Continuing professional education, preparing income tax returns, and assisting with payroll tax returns. And I also was involved in some payroll tax return audits, examinations by the Internal Revenue Service.

Q. Are you familiar with these forms that Mr. Metcalfe has been asking about, forms 940 and 941, the employer's quarterly federal tax returns?

A. Yes.

Q. During the course of your career have you had an opportunity to study issues concerning independent truckers, including payroll tax questions and concerns as they relate to independent truckers?

A. Yes, I have.

Q. How did you have an opportunity to study those issues?

A. In 1974, Neil Larsen, who was financial vice president of Little Audrey's, asked me to take a look at some of the payroll tax problems of drivers.

Q. What was Little Audrey's?

A. Little Audrey's was a refrigerated meat hauler, about $25 million in revenue, and they were a subsidiary of Midwest Emery. At the time, Midwest Emery and its other trucking fleets Navajo, Safeway and some others, were in the top ten largest motor carriers in the United States.

Q. How did that Little Audrey's company compare in 1974 to another company you knew about, Werner Trucking?

A. Little Audrey's was about $20 to $25 million in revenue. In 1974, Werner's might have been $1 million by then, I don't know for sure.

Q. Do you have any idea how many trucks Little Audrey's operated in 1974?

A. I think it was around 200.

Q. What was the problem with the drivers' payroll taxes that Neal Larson asked you to look at?

A. Little Audrey's did not own any tractors and did not hire any drivers at all. They told me that their fleet operators or the independent truckers that were leasing to them were not withholding on the drivers.

Q. Did you have an opportunity to review that situation with Mr. Larson?

A. Yes.

Q. Who was Mr. Larson? You said he was an officer of the company?

A. He was the financial vice president of Little Audrey's.

Q. Did he call you to consult with you and visit with you on that issue?

A. Yes.

(Note how some testimony differs from the deposition. The deposition questions were not those intended to jog my memory. If you make changes to your testimony, you must notify the other side.)

Q. Did you actually do so?

A. Yes.

Q. Have you had any other opportunity during the course of your career to study issues concerning independent truckers and payroll tax questions as they relate to independent truckers?

A. Yes. Between 1978 and 1982 Nebraska Motor Carriers asked me to prepare a course for the Nebraska Accounting and Finance Council and for the Motor Carriers on owner–operator — I mean independent contractor versus employee.

Q. When you say versus, do you mean comparing the two?

A. Yes, comparing to see which one is — how to tell which is which.

Q. Did you prepare such a course?

A. Yes, I did.

Q. What did you have to do to prepare it? Did you do any research?

A. I had to research the Internal Revenue Code, the regulations written by the Internal Revenue Service. Some revenue rulings — these are decisions, interpretation of law by the Internal Revenue Service. Some of the tax court decisions on the issues. Some of the district court decisions on the issues. I don't recall whether I had any appeals court or claims court decisions on it.

Q. Are all those things the type of things that people in your field normally rely upon when they are doing their research on issues?

A. Yes, they are.

Q. As part of your research, did you come across any issues concerning moratoriums on classification of truckers or other independent contractors as employees?

A. Yes, I did.

Q. What sort of moratoriums would those be?

A. There is a moratorium that —congress said, for example, that the Internal Revenue Service hasn't been enforcing some of these interpretations consistently, so we want you to stop making adjustments between owner–operator — between independent contractor and employee, making a determination of what they are, until we finally pass a law.

Q. Who said that?

A. That was the congress, but one of them I remember was Dole, Robert Dole, that was about — in 1982 he wanted to pass a new law of his own, because congress had put a moratorium on it in about 1978. Some of the decisions that I researched, some said they were this, some said they were that, and nobody really knew who was what or what was who.

Q. So congress put a moratorium on reclassification of such people?

A. Yes.

Q. As part of your research in preparing your course and your seminar that you wrote and taught on independent contractor versus employee, did you have an opportunity to familiarize yourself with the practices of different companies in the industry through your research or your course teaching?

A. Yes.

Q. How did that come about through your course teaching?

A. Well, I made a case study. I gave a program for the Nebraska Motor Carriers on this and then, in 1982 in St. Louis, that was part of my program at the National Accounting and Finance Council.
     But in my classes and the courses I had, we would have case studies. I took them from actual transactions that happened with real trucking companies. So the information, the textbook and the case studies would go out a month in advance and the truckers who came would have a chance to study it and then we would discuss it. And during my classes,

I would have other trucking companies that said hey, we do the same thing as this, we had the same problem or they don't withhold on our drivers either, et cetera. But this type of reaction and response I would get from the students.

Q. Mr. Telpner, during the course of your career, did you gain an understanding through your personal knowledge, your contacts in the industry, and your education and teaching experience, as to the customs and practices of trucking companies in treating drivers as independent contractors and employees?

A. Yes.

Q. How did your personal contacts in the industry help you gain that understanding?

Metcalfe: Your Honor, at this time we are going to ask the court to give a limiting instruction, that what the witness is testifying to can be received as understanding the basis for his opinion, but not for the truth of the matter asserted. Either that or we would ask the court to require the plaintiff to lay a foundation for his personal knowledge of these matters.

(A bench conference is held and the witness is allowed to answer the question.)

A. How did my personal contact help me gain an understanding? Is that the question?

Q. Would you like me to rephrase the question?

A. Yes, could you?

Q. What sort of contacts did your career give you in the industry, Mr. Telpner?

A. It gave me contacts with the president of Yellow Freight. For example, if I had a tax problem I couldn't solve — one time I called him, his tax department couldn't solve it, so he arranged for the tax manager of Clorox Corporation to solve it for me. Sometimes, there are certain answers that just aren't in the textbooks yet or aren't in your experience. I had contact with the National Directors of Transportation, with Touche-Ross, Arthur Andersen, Peat-Marwick, Price Waterhouse. I had people in my classes that I met at the accounting council from smaller trucking companies, from Cooper-Jarret, from Santini Brothers in the Bronx, and these were people who would ask me to speak at their meetings or would talk to me about their problems. I used to get a lot of phone calls from trucking companies throughout the country asking me how to solve this or that.

Q. I assume that some of these contacts and conversations and meetings would involve employment taxes and driver compensation issues and so forth?

A. Quite frequently, because these type of taxes, other than income taxes, have been a big issue in this industry for many years.

Q. During the course of your career did you gain this understanding regarding how trucking companies treated drivers as independent contractors or employees through serving on the National Accounting and Finance Council of the American Trucking Association that you described earlier?

A. Yes, I did. Especially with the small carrier committees and the independent contractor committees.

Q. Did you discuss issues on those committees with your peers?

A. Yes.

Q. Did you discuss issues concerning payroll taxes and compensation of drivers?

A. Yes, and they also had continuing professional education programs on it.

Q. As part of your association with that group?

A. Yes.

Q. Did you gain this understanding as to how — as to the practices of trucking companies in treating drivers as independent contractors or employees through experience in serving as a member and board member of the Nebraska Motor Carriers Association?

A. Yes, I did. They even asked me to give a program on it.

Q. That's the program you described for us earlier?

A. Yes.

Q. Did you also gain this understanding of practices in the trucking industry with regard to payroll taxes through articles, treatises, texts and
professional publications, which you have read and subscribed to during
the course of your career?

A. Yes.

*(Direct examination continued in the same vein. All questions were repeated
in many variations to establish the professional knowledge of the expert.)*

Q. How did those help you gain an understanding in this area?

A. For example, the *Journal of Taxation* would have a technical article
about it. A tax lawyer or somebody who really specializes in that area
would write a very technical article and they would have footnotes
referring to the revenue rulings and the court decisions on these issues.
It might just take one Internal Revenue ruling about this issue. I
remember one in particular that they said had changed a little bit, and
so the whole magazine article was on that. The New York University
Annual Institute on Taxation every year puts on a 3-week program with
people anywhere from the commissioner of the Internal Revenue to
renowned tax attorneys to speak. They publish these and I subscribe
to that and used to read them. *Major Tax Planning* by the University
of Southern California Tax Institute did the same thing. And *Taxation
for Accountants* I used to get. *Journal of Accountancy, Tax Ideas* from
Prentice-Hall. And CCH also had a magazine called *Taxes* that I would
— used to read the articles.

Q. Let me ask you this. Prior to your involvement as a witness in this case,
did you know Bruce Boles or have anything to do with Boles Trucking?

A. No, I didn't. I had never heard of him.

Q. Now, I would like to ask you about the matters that you reviewed. Do
you recall that I asked you to render an opinion in this case regarding
the industry practice and the treatment of truck drivers for payroll
tax purposes?

A. Yes.

Q. In relation to my request, have you done some analysis of the issues
involved in the preparation of your opinions?

A. Yes.

Q. Since becoming involved in this case have you had an opportunity to study the business of Boles Trucking, Inc., and familiarize yourself with its financial and business operations as they existed from the time the corporation was founded through the present time?

A. Yes.

Q. Is that the type of information that would normally be relied upon by a person like you in the work that you do?

A. Yes.

Q. Since I contacted you regarding the case, have you had an opportunity to read depositions that have been taken from witnesses in this case and the testimony that witnesses gave in other depositions?

A. Yes.

Q. Is that the type of information that you normally rely on in your other experience in rendering opinions?

A. Yes.

Q. Since I contacted you, have you had an opportunity to listen to the testimony of Mr. Boles, Mr. Clifford, Mr. Flavell, the depositions of Mr. Shrdlu and Mrs. Roberts in this case?

A. Yes.

Q. Is that the type of information that you normally rely upon in formulating opinions, sir?

A. Yes.

Q. Since I contacted you, have you had an opportunity to review your personal records, courses you have written, course materials from courses you have attended and taught, and notes, correspondence and memoranda regarding your courses, and students in those courses and people involved in the industry?

A. Yes.

Q. And is that the type of information that is normally relied upon by people like you in rendering your opinions?

A. Yes.

(Direct examination continued with several more "since I contacted you" questions.)

> **Q.** Mr. Telpner, based on your education, training, all of your years and experience working, teaching, speaking and all of your associations and contacts in the trucking industry, all of the matters you have reviewed in relation to this case, your review of the Boles Trucking Inc., business from its beginning in 1982 through the present date, and all the information regarding the trucking industry that came to your attention during your years of working in the industry, do you have an opinion, within a reasonable degree of certainty, as to what area of the trucking industry Boles Trucking, Inc., has operated in since 1982?

The Court: Answer that yes or no, please.

A. Yes.

Q. What is your opinion?

Metcalfe: Your Honor, at this time I have several objections I would like to make to the court. First of all, we would object to the court receiving opinion testimony from Mr. Telpner on the subject because we submit that he is not qualified to the Rule 702 to provide expert testimony on this issue.

We further submit that his expert testimony will not assist or be helpful to the trier of fact in this case, because neither the question nor his response is phrased in terms of adequately explored legal criteria. More specifically, it is not bounded with respect to any geographical limitation as to industry practice as required by the case law. We submit that the basis for his opinions, which consist of matters that include hearsay statements made by others to Mr. Telpner, are not of the type reasonably relied upon by experts in his particular field in forming opinions. We believe that the subject matter of Mr. Telpner's testimony and his opinions are not appropriate for expert testimony in this case, because the trier of fact is fully capable of drawing the inferences that he will be providing through his expert testimony.

And lastly, we submit that under Rule 403, because Mr. Telpner's opinion testimony will go to an ultimate issue in this case, that the prejudicial effect of his testimony will substantially outweigh its probative value.

The Court: I am going to overrule your objections, Mr. Metcalfe, and I am going to permit him to express an opinion. But I am going to give a cautionary instruction to the jury at this time. What Mr. Telpner is about to testify to with respect to his opinions will not be taken by you as establishing whether as a matter of fact the employees of Boles Trucking, or the drivers, I should say, who worked for Boles Trucking Company were independent contractors or employees. This testimony is received for the sole purpose of establishing, or as it goes to the issue of establishing whether or not there was an industry practice, whether it was correct or not, whether there was such an industry practice in the period 1984 through 1987 upon which Mr. Boles could reasonably rely in treating the drivers in the fashion in which he treated them. I will include in the closing instructions another instruction that touches upon this so that you understand the limited purpose for which you may use this testimony.

Metcalfe: Your Honor, if I may have a continuing objection to this line of testimony?

The Court: You may. You may proceed, Mr. Mostek. Do you recall the question upon which you have been asked to give an opinion now, Mr. Telpner?

The Witness: No, sir, I don't.

The Court: I think in the interest of keeping this record straight, I'm going to have to ask Mr. Kuhlman down here to read the original question back and then have you state your opinion, Mr. Telpner.

(*Pending question is read.*)

Q. What is your opinion, Mr. Telpner?

A. Boles Trucking, Inc., has operated in the fleet leasing-independent contractor segment of the industry.

Q. Now, I would like to break down that statement. When you say "fleet leasing," would you please expand for us on what you mean?

A. He has several over-the-road tractors that he leases to a regulated truckload motor carrier.

Q. And the second word was "independent contractor," the second phrase.

A. Yes. He does not work for that motor carrier that he leases to. He is an independent leaser.

Q. Is this a regularly identifiable segment of the industry, to your understanding?

A. Yes.

Q. As you described earlier, is it a way for trucking companies to get more equipment without having to finance it?

A. Yes.

Q. Based on your education, training, all of your years in experience working, teaching, speaking, and all of your associations and contacts in the trucking industry, all of the matters you have reviewed in relation to this case, and all of the information regarding the trucking industry that came to your attention during your years of work in the industry, do you have an opinion, within a reasonable degree of certainty, as to what the practice of companies like Boles Trucking, Inc., in the fleet leasing-independent contractor segment of the trucking industry has been with regard to the treatment of drivers of their equipment for payroll tax purposes?

A. Yes.

Q. What is your opinion?

Metcalfe: Your Honor, I would like to make our objections for the record.
The Court: Yes. The same ruling and, of course, the same limiting instruction to the jury. You may proceed.

A. Some people, some of these fleet-leasers, withheld on the drivers and some didn't.

Q. All right, sir. Now, with regard to your opinion that some withheld, do you have more than one basis for your opinion?

A. Yes.

Q. If you have more than one, we will start with the first one.

A. Attending meetings at the Nebraska Motor Carriers where they discussed it, I knew that many truckers didn't withhold and many fleet operators, like Bruce, didn't withhold and many did.

Q. What other basis do you have, sir?

A. From attending the National Accounting and Finance Council meetings I learned — and the independent contractors committee and the small carrier committee, that some withheld and some didn't.

Q. Did you base your opinion on any sort of personal contact with companies, like you described earlier?

A. Yes, I did. Midwest Seaboard. Little Audrey's. Shark's Tooth Trucking.

Q. With regard to Little Audrey's, can you describe for us in more detail than you did before what the situation was that presented itself there and how … why they were asking you about the drivers' payroll taxes and the fact that those taxes were not being withheld?

Metcalfe: Your Honor, I object to this testimony as being irrelevant.

The Court: Sustained. To go into the detail, is not, I believe, necessary, Mr. Mostek. The opinion goes to what was the practice in the industry, what it may have been, and to go into individual trucking companies instances, I don't believe — since I have overruled the objections, that he has the background and experience and the expertise to issue these opinions.

Mostek: Very well, your Honor.

Q. Other than the contacts in the industry, the contacts with companies, did you base your opinion on any other matters having to do with your teaching and speaking experience?

A. Yes, the discussions in my classes that we had, were from trucking companies that had similar situations. I think there was one in Fort Dodge, Iowa, or Dubuque, Iowa, that had been a student in my class in Chicago and he called me on it.

Q. Did this issue of fleet operators not withholding on their drivers come up in your national meetings that you had?

A. Yes.

(Direct examination on definitions of lieasing companies and distinctions between types of lessors continued.)

Q. Mr. Telpner, I would like to direct your attention now to some accounting matters that I have asked you to review regarding this case. Through your experience as an accountant and working in the trucking industry for other clients, have you become familiar with the term "Sub S Corporation" or "Subchapter S Corporation" or "S Corporation"?

A. Yes.

Q. I know there are many terms used. What is the proper term?

A. Up until 1982 it was Subchapter S. After the 1982 Subchapter S Reform Act, it became S Corporation.

Q. Why did that change?

A. They reformed it a little bit to make it easier for small-business people to form a Subchapter S Corporation to get certain distributions out of it and to operate under that format.

Q. Would you please tell the court and the jury your understanding and describe for us what an S Corporation is?

A. Yes. But I will have to describe a regular corporation first. A corporation for tax purposes is an artificial person who pays an income tax, not the same as individuals pay, but it's a special corporate income tax, has special provisions in the Internal Revenue Code. This type of corporation pays income tax. They have an option, if they are very small, like now it's 35 or fewer shareholders, it used to be ten or fewer, and if there are 35 or fewer they can elect to be exempt from corporate income tax. That means the corporation will no longer pay regular income tax.

Q. When did that come into being?

A. 1958.

Q. Please continue.

A. But there still is income and someone has to pay tax on it. And so they let the shareholder of that corporation that has made the election report the income or loss on their own individual income tax return as if it were their income.

The Court: Isn't that much like the way a partnership is treated under the tax law, that the partnership as such does not pay any taxes, it makes a report to the IRS, but you the individual members of the partnership then, based upon their interest in the partnership, pay that proportionate share or pay taxes on their proportionate share of the income of the partnership?

A. Basically that's right. Actually taxed somewhat like a partnership, somewhat like a corporation, somewhat like neither.

The Court: One of the — and this is a question, and the reason I am asking this is that the jurors have submitted to me a question about Subchapter corporations — under a Subchapter S corporation, the income passes through the corporation to the individual shareholders, they pay the tax on it so that it's not taxed first to the corporation as income to the corporation and then to the individuals as dividends received from the corporation; is that generally correct?

A. That is generally correct.

The Court: You may proceed.

Q. When the Sub S corporation first came into being, I believe you said that was 1958?

A. Yes.

Q. How did that come about? Do you have an understanding of that?

A. Yes.

Q. Would you describe that briefly for us?

(*The witness explained S Corporations.*)

Q. Thank you, Mr. Telpner. Through your experience and training have you also become familiar with the term "fiscal year"?

A. Yes.

Q. Can you explain that to us, please?

(*The witness explained. Several questions were asked about fiscal and calendar years and who could use either one for tax reporting.*)

Q. Are you familiar with the term "self-employment taxes"?

A. Yes.

Q. Would you describe to us what that means?

(*The witness explained.*)

Q. Are you familiar with the term "employment taxes"?

A. Yes.

Q. Now, earlier you said self-employment taxes are paid by a sole proprietor?

A. Or a partner.

Q. During the course of your experience as a certified public accountant, have you had opportunity to counsel owners of S Corporations?

A. Yes.

Q. And have you had an opportunity to counsel owners or other people involved in S Corporations regarding self-employment taxes?

A. Yes.

Q. Do you know, is an owner of an S Corporation required to pay self-employment taxes?

A. On his income from the S Corporation?

Q. Yes, sir.

A. No, S Corporation income is not subject to self-employment taxes.

Q. Has that been the case since the Sub S Corporation Act was enacted in 1958?

A. The first revenue ruling that I can remember on the topic issued by the Internal Revenue Service said that Subchapter S Corporation income was not subject to self-employment tax, and that is still in effect today.

Q. Is that a good ruling yet today?

A. Yes.

Q. Now, when you counseled your clients or other people involved in S Corporations, did you tell them whether they had to pay self-employment tax?

A. Yes. I would tell them they didn't have to pay it on Subchapter S income.

(*Examination continued on statutory employees and what testimony or depositions the witness had read or heard. Additionally, the witness was asked to explain in depth S Corporation taxation.*)

Q. And since I asked you to do that, have you had an opportunity to review information, including the checks, which have been discussed in evidence here, including the tables prepared by the IRS showing amounts attributed to Bruce Boles, and other financial information that would give you a basis for rendering the opinion that I requested?

A. Yes.

Q. Have you done so?

A. Yes.

Q. And is that the type of information normally relied upon by people in your field?

A. Yes.

Q. Since I asked you to prepare this opinion, have you had an opportunity to review the tax returns of Boles corporation, and returns as they relate to the 1040's 1120-S returns that have been filed in the years in question, '84 on through '86 and '87?

A. Yes.

Q. Have you done so?

A. Yes.

Q. Is that the type of information usually relied upon by people in your field?

A. Yes.

Q. Based on your experience as a certified public accountant, all these matters that you have reviewed, and all information that has come to you and that you have become knowledgeable about regarding the case, do you have an opinion as to the amount of taxes due with respect to the adjustment made by the Internal Revenue Service to Boles Trucking, Inc., with respect to the claim status of Bruce Boles as a statutory employee of corporation?

A. Yes.

Q. What is your opinion?

A. I can't remember the exact figure on the calculation but it was approximately $34,000.

Q. Would it help if you used the overhead to illustrate how you made that calculation?

A. Yes.

(*The witness steps to the overhead.*)

Q. Mr. Telpner, I have handed you a transparency of Exhibit 109(A), which has been received into evidence. This is a chart that was compiled by the Internal Revenue Service showing the amounts of employment compensation that they attribute to Bruce Boles by virtue of their claims. I would like you to review the columns of Exhibit 109(A) and generally orient the court and jury as to what they are about.

(*The courts breaks here for noon recess and to make copies of the exhibits.*)

Q. Mr. Telpner, when we broke for lunch I had asked you to tell the jury and the court how you computed or arrived at your opinion as to the amount of taxes and interest due with respect to the adjustments made by the IRS in relation to Bruce Boles' status with the corporation. To do that, I would like you to first describe generally what steps you had to take in order to make this calculation.

(*The answer and further related questions continued for about 5 hours.*)

Mostek: Pass the witness, your Honor.
The Court: Before we do that, would counsel approach the bench?
(*Bench conference held.*)
The Court: Mr. Metcalfe, you may cross-examine

Cross-Examination by Metcalfe (Q):

Q. Mr. Telpner, I want to ask you some questions first of all about your background. Did I understand your testimony on direct to be that you had written certain articles or books or treatises on federal employment taxes; is that correct?

A. I said I wrote some programs, continuing professional-education programs for the Nebraska Motor Carriers Association, and I also delivered — I guess you just need a yes, don't you? Sorry.

Q. Mr. Telpner, I take it you have never been employed by the Internal Revenue Service as a revenue agent or revenue officer-examiner; is that correct?

A. Yes.

Q. As a certified public accountant, have you ever represented a client before the Internal Revenue Service in connection with a federal employment tax audit or examination?

A. Yes, I have.

Q. Are you sure it was not a state as opposed to a federal?

A. No. I know what you asked me in my deposition, but went back and looked through all my old records, and I can't remember everything anymore, and I did have some cases on it before the Internal Revenue Service.

Q. Approximately how long ago was that, sir?

A. I don't recall. I could tell you the name of the taxpayer, if it's all right.

Q. Please don't. Mr. Telpner, do you claim to have any familiarity or knowledge of the procedures employed by the Internal Revenue Service in conducting federal employment tax examinations?

A. To a degree, yes.

Q. Where is the source of your knowledge or familiarity from?

A. The Internal Revenue Service hired me in 1990 to teach 130 of their agents in Nebraska how to improve their examinations, and the next year in Iowa, and in that case we covered all items to be examined.

Q. Can you tell us what a revenue agent's report or 30-day letter is?

A. Yes, when a revenue agent examines a return, after correspondence back and forth and talking back and forth, finally it will go to review and they will send you a 30-day letter. And that letter says you have 30 days in which to either pay the tax or decide to file a protest against the adjustment in the regional office of appeals.

Q. Did you have the occasion to read any revenue agent report or 30-day letter issued by the Internal Revenue Service in connection with an employment tax audit or examination of Boles Trucking?

A. I don't recall whether it was a 30-day letter, but I did read a report.

Q. Can you recall when you last wrote a protest to a revenue agent's report in a case involving federal employment taxes?

A. No.

Q. Was it more than 10 years ago?

A. I don't know. Pardon me, sir. You asked me when I wrote a protest? I don't think I have said I have written a protest to the IRS on employment tax. Didn't say I had cases on employment taxes? Not all of them go to appeals.

Q. Do you ever recall writing such a protest?

A. Not on employment tax. I had a protest on one of the adjustments, but that wasn't the total adjustment

Q. Isn't it true that you haven't seen many federal employment tax adjustments in the course of your practice as a certified public accountant?

A. That's true. They are all the same, though, income, employment. It's the same Internal Revenue Code.

Q. Are you saying income taxes are the same thing as employment taxes?

A. No, I am saying that it comes from the same Internal Revenue Code, the same regulations and laws. It's all from the Internal Revenue Code, 54 code that we are still under that applies to all those taxes, except some of the treaties and stuff that aren't in the code.

Q. Within the trucking industry, sir, have you ever represented a client or taxpayer whose workers were reclassified as employees for federal employment tax purposes?

A. No, I haven't.

Q. You did not represent Boles Trucking before the Internal Revenue Service in connection with an employment tax examination or audit of Boles Trucking. Is that correct?

A. That's correct.

Q. So you did not participate in the administrative proceedings in this case involving the Internal Revenue Service and Boles Trucking; is that right?

A. That is right.

Q. Have you ever been asked in your professional career as a certified public accountant to formally determine whether a particular worker is an employee for federal employment tax purposes under what are called the usual common rules applicable to the determination of the employer-employee relationship?

A. No. I'm sorry.

Q. Sir, have you ever testified as an expert in any federal district court in any matter involving federal employment taxes?

A. No.

Q. What is your particular field of expertise in this case? By that I mean in what field do you claim to be an expert?

A. I'm considered to be an expert in how to find the answers to a revenue agent's adjustments by the Internal Revenue Service, who hired me to write a course for them called the Substance of Examinations and to teach their agents how to write up reports that can't be overturned or adjusted — that is, not to make frivolous adjustments. I had about 130-some agents in Nebraska and 200-some in Iowa. I was also asked by Chicago to teach 800 agents, but that's when I had that quadruple bypass and didn't want to take on any more. That was in '90–91.

Q. What would we call that field of expertise, sir?

A. The ability to research and analyze tax adjustments and to either rebut them or help support them. Tax adjustments of excise tax, income tax, FICA tax, FUTA tax, any kind of tax that is assessed by the Internal Revenue Service.

Q. Have you conducted any surveys or made any inquiries to determine how various trucking firms or carriers or leasing firms treated their truck drivers for federal employment tax purposes?

A. May I have that part again? Did you say have I conducted any surveys, sir?

Metcalfe: Your Honor, may I repeat the question?
The Court: You may withdraw the question and you may restate the question.

Q. Mr. Telpner, have you yourself, sir, conducted any surveys to determine how various trucking firms and carriers and leasing firms treated their truck drivers for federal employment tax purposes?

A. No, I haven't conducted any surveys.

Q. I believe, sir, you stated earlier in response to one of Mr. Mostek's questions that Boles Trucking was a fleet-leasing independent contractor; is that correct, or did I write that down wrong?

A. I'm not quite positive. That's probably what I said. It is an independent contractor or an independent trucker that leases a fleet of tractors to regulated carriers, truckload carriers.

Q. When you say that Boles Trucking is a fleet-leasing independent contractor, you are referring to the corporation itself, aren't you?

A. Yes, Boles Trucking, Inc., that's correct.

Q. You are not referring to the truck drivers, are you?

A. No, I am referring — you asked me only about Boles Trucking, Inc. I think Mr. Mostek did. I'm not sure now.

Q. I want to ask you a question concerning self-employment taxes, Mr. Telpner. Did I understand your testimony on direct to be that self-employment taxes were the equivalent of the employee and employer portion of FICA or Federal Insurance Contribution Act taxes? Was that your testimony?

A. I think I said basically — didn't I explain that the rate was a little less if the self-employed person paid it? I gave an example, like if it was 15 for FICA, both halves, then a self-employed person in those years paid

13%. But I think it's now about the same rate for both self-employed and FICA.

Q. Could you tell me the first time you ever heard of Boles Trucking?

A. When the attorneys for Mr. Boles contacted me.

Q. Can you recall when that was?

A. I think it might have been sometime in the fall or December of '92, but I'm not sure. Maybe it was '92.

Q. Was that the same time you met Mr. Bruce Boles?

A. Whenever the first time I came over to their office would have been. Remember when you and I were there? That was about the first time, I think, just a few days before that, but I don't remember when that was.

Q. Were you at some point, sir, formally retained by the plaintiff in this case, Boles Trucking, to serve as an expert witness?

A. Yes, I was.

Q. And in return for serving as an expert witness, did Boles Trucking in turn promise to compensate you for your services?

A. No, but I'm sure that they intended to. All they said was, the lawyer said we want to hire you as an expert witness, and we didn't talk over compensation, much to my regret. But I know that when I send a bill, I'm sure I will get paid.

Q. Could you tell, sir, how much you are being paid for your role as an expert witness in this case?

A. I am getting paid $100 an hour.

Q. Do you have any idea of the total amount of time you have spent on this case?

A. No, I have not. I'm sure that there are quite a few hours, but I haven't added them up yet.

Q. Mr. Telpner, as you did not hear of Boles Trucking until 1992, would it be fair to say that you don't have any firsthand knowledge as to why

Boles Trucking decided to treat its truck drivers as contract labor or independent contractors?

A. Yes.

Q. You don't have any personal or firsthand knowledge as to whether the plaintiff in this case relied on any industry practice or custom to treat its truck drivers as independent contractors, do you?

A. He told me he did. Is that firsthand knowledge?

Q. Well, you weren't around when Boles Trucking ...

A. No,

Q. ... came to the decision to do that, were you?

A. No, I wasn't.

Q. So you don't have any knowledge apart from what Mr. Boles may have told you, do you?

A. That's correct.

Q. You have testified as to the amounts of federal employment and unemployment taxes which you believe the plaintiff owes in this case; is that correct?

A. Did you say federal unemployment and — I'm sorry, I'm having a little trouble hearing.

Q. Have you testified as to the amounts of federal employment and unemployment taxes that you believe the plaintiff owes in this case?

A. Yes, I have.

Q. And would it be your opinion that the plaintiff indeed does owe these taxes to the United States of America?

A. I have reservations on that, but I'm not arguing about it. On a Subchapter S I usually don't see any adjustments like that, in all the years I have been in practice. The only Subchapter S adjustment I ever had, when the agent found out that the corporation was Subchapter S, he said I am not going to make the adjustment because it's going to end up on the taxpayer's return anyway, so it will zero out. And that's an agent from the Omaha district.

Q. Would you agree with me during the period between 1984 and 1987 that Boles Trucking should have been withholding and paying over federal employment taxes based upon the fact that Bruce Boles was an employee of Boles Trucking?

A. Yes. Bruce Boles, I have come to the conclusion that he was a statutory employee.

Q. So Boles Trucking should have been withholding and paying over federal income taxes and social security taxes based upon Mr. Boles' compensation between 1984 and 1987, isn't that correct?

A. I don't think he should have been paying over income taxes based on his compensation. The reason I don't believe he should be paying over income taxes, because had he known it was going to be called a salary, he would have been allowed to file a W-4 form that said I didn't owe any income tax last year and I don't expect to owe any next year, so I can be exempt from withholding income tax.

Q. But that's not what Mr. Boles did, is it?

A. No, Mr. Boles didn't even pay himself a salary.

Q. Instead he took money out of the corporation, isn't that right?

A. That's a distribution from Subchapter S, and even Publication 589 that the Internal Revenue Service publishes absolutely talks about distributions of Subchapter S income that's already been taxed.

Q. So it's your position, sir, when Mr. Boles sits down and writes out a check on the checking account of Boles Trucking and takes a trip to Cancun, that's a corporate distribution?

A. No, it isn't my opinion that the whole thing is, because I think he should be paid a reasonable salary and he should be allowed a reasonable dividend of his pretax income.

Q. Are you familiar with the term "experience rate" as it applies to social security or FICA or FICA taxes?

A. Experience rate is applied to FUTA taxes.

Q. What does that mean to you, sir?

A. Because on the state, for example, if you have claim against your unemployment compensation reserve — when you pay your unemployment compensation, the state keeps track of it and you build up a reserve of all these monies you have been paying in. And if somebody files a claim against it, that is, they are wrongfully discharged or something, they can draw unemployment compensation and it comes against your reserve. And so if you have no claims for a period of years, the rate keeps getting lower. It could go down to zero because you have enough reserve. But if you get a lot of claims, then the state might increase your contribution rate and say you have to pay more taxes because your reserve is getting too low.

Q. Mr. Telpner, do you agree with the recharacterization of the loans against future profits, the payments of the personal expenses of Mr. Boles, and the leasing value, leased value of the Lincoln Continental Mark VI automobile being recharacterized as income to the president of the plaintiff during the years between 1984 and 1987?

A. If the automobile is used for personal business, because I didn't see that on there, then I have no choice but to agree, because the IRS publishes charts that tell you how to figure it out and what the amount should be. So if you use your automobile in business, a portion of it that is personal is supposed to be added to your W-2. So I have to agree with that.

Q. Do you know if the taxpayer in this case actually kept any books and records as to the use of the automobile?

A. No, I don't.

Q. You never asked him?

A. No. I accepted your adjustment.

Q. Would you agree with me that during the years between 1984 and 1987 that the loans against future profits represented income to Mr. Boles in those years?

A. No. His Subchapter S income or loss represented his income or loss. Even the Internal Revenue Service, at one time on Subchapter S, if they thought the salary was too high, they would force the taxpayer to reduce it and call it a dividend. That's because when the rate before '81 was 70% on dividend income and 50% on salaries, they didn't want you to have much of a salary. So it was just the opposite of what you are seeing now.

Q. Was the same true with respect to the personal expenses of Mr. Boles which were paid by the corporation known as Boles Trucking during the years between 1984 and 1987?

A. Publication 589, I'm not talking about the code, but this is summarized by the IRS, says you may take a distribution of your previously taxed Subchapter S income, because you report on your return, you have already paid the tax on it, now you can draw it out. And then it says if you don't have any, if you have losses, first the money comes out of your capital. That's the difference between your assets that you have and — that the corporation has, corporation assets, and what the corporation owes, the difference is called capital net worth. So the IRS regulations even provide in which order the distributions will be charged. First against the current income. Second against income from the previous years that you have already paid taxes on. Third from capital. And then fourth it starts — if you use up all the capital and all that, then it becomes taxable.

Q. Mr. Telpner, do you have any knowledge for any year prior to 1988, and for any geographical area, of the total number of companies like Boles Trucking that lease tractors and drivers to a common carrier?

A. No.

Q. How many different firms or businesses that use truck drivers in their business did you look at in arriving at your opinions in this case?

A. I'm including all the companies that I had experience with over the years, you know, with my classes, with the Nebraska Motor Carriers accounting council, and it's hard for me to count. I know I had literally several hundreds of people in my classes, and it came up at every class. If I gave 100 classes over a few years, or 200 classes and attended all these meetings, let's say there was one in each class, there would be at least 200. But I can't tell you for sure, because I didn't keep track of everybody who had that problem.

Q. Were any of these firms or businesses that had truck drivers working for them and that you relied upon in forming your opinions in this case located outside the state of Nebraska?

A. Yes.

Q. Do you have any feel for, as a percentage, how many or what percentage of these firms were located outside the state of Nebraska?

A. Well, some of them were in Iowa, which is the same area. Some were in Kansas, but I don't have an idea. Some were in San Francisco. Some were in Georgia. Even here, you can have a trucking company in Omaha and your driver may live in Los Angeles and another one in Dallas. Over-the-road long-haul truckers don't necessarily live where the tractors are because they are on the road 3 and sometimes 4 weeks at a time.

Q. Sir, I was asking you about the location of the firms, not the truck drivers.

A. No. I don't know what percentage are located in Omaha or whatnot. There are a lot of trucking companies in Omaha and there are a lot of them outside of Omaha.

Q. I believe you stated on direct that you had worked with Mr. Werner up until about '81; is that correct?

A. Yes.

Q. And that's Clarence Werner you are talking about?

A. Clarence L. Werner. Now it's a corporation. Werner, according to the last SEC report, still owned 69.5% of Werner Enterprises, Inc.

Q. Did you do any work with the books and records of Werner Enterprises prior to '81?

A. Yes, I did, prior to '81.

Q. Do you have any personal knowledge as to how Werner Enterprises, prior to '81, treated its truck drivers?

A. Yes, I have personal knowledge of how they treated their truck drivers.

Q. Can you give me some estimate of how large Werner Enterprises would have been in '81, the last year you worked there?

A. I think I said that from July 1, 1980, when the Motor Carrier Act came in, until June 30, 1981, they had hit $21 million then. And you must remember that back in those days, $21 million, it's still not peanuts, but it was big for a trucking company.

Q. Did you ever develop any knowledge or understanding as to how many truck drivers worked for Werner Enterprises, say in '81?

A. Well, what I said was the revenues were $21 million. As a rule of thumb, $150,000 revenue per tractor, so you can figure between 180 and 210 drivers, trucks, trucks and drivers.

Q. Would that make Werner Enterprises the largest employer of truck drivers in the Omaha, Nebraska, area in '81, to your knowledge?

A. Oh, I don't think so. I don't know when Little Audrey's closed its doors, but — let's see, Best was about — the reason I can tell you is because they used to file their annual reports and it's public. Best was — I think maybe Hill Trucking was probably bigger. Hill or Hill Brothers, I can't remember. ATI wouldn't have been bigger yet. Best wouldn't have been bigger.

Q. Mr. Telpner, I asked you specifically with respect to Omaha, Nebraska.

A. I'm sorry. I'm thinking out loud. I'm sorry. Go ahead.

Q. Asking you, sir, with respect to Omaha, Nebraska. Is it true that Werner Enterprises would have been the largest employer of truck drivers in '81?

A. No.

Q. Because why, sir?

A. Because you had Hill Brothers here. You had — I know they were bigger. I can't think of who else was. Yellow Freight had a terminal. I know they weren't the largest. It had to be Hill Brothers back then. Maybe Hilt Trucking.

Q. Mr. Telpner, isn't it true that from its inception in the 1960s that Werner Enterprises treated its truck drivers as employees for federal employment tax purposes?

A. Its inception was 1956, sir.

Q. I stand corrected. From 1956 onward to '81, isn't it true that Werner Enterprises treated its truck drivers as employees for federal employment tax purposes?

A. Only those who drove the trucks that were owned by Werner. Those individuals that leased to Werner's, they didn't treat as company employees.

Q. Did you ever hear of a firm called American Transport, Incorporated?

A. Yes.

Q. And are you familiar with the operations of that firm?

A. They are a refrigerated meat hauler, or they were a refrigerated meat hauler.

Q. Are they still in business, to your knowledge?

A. I don't know right now. I think they are, but I don't know for sure.

Q. Did you ever gain any personal knowledge as to how American Transport, Incorporated, treated its truck drivers for federal employment tax purposes?

A. The controller, John Pester, and the systems director, John Sandersfeld, were in the Nebraska Accounting Council with me and I knew them well. But I can't remember — they would have participated in discussions, but I can't remember what they said.

Q. With respect to the firm you have identified as Yellow Freight, could you tell us approximately when you first became aware of this firm?

A. Yellow Freight? About 1962 or '61. Arthur Andersen used to audit Yellow Freight. It would have been about 1962.

Q. Is the firm still in existence?

A. Yes, takes in over $1 billion a year.

Q. Did you ever gain any personal knowledge as to how — where is Yellow Freight located?

A. Shawnee Mission, Kansas.

Q. Did you ever gain any personal knowledge as to how Yellow Freight treated its truck drivers for federal employment tax purposes?

A. Yes.

Q. Could you tell us?

A. From their company truck — remember, they are an LTL carrier, so they don't have lease operators, but their company drivers drove Yellow Freight-owned trucks and they paid payroll taxes on them.

Q. Mr. Telpner, I believe you stated in response to one of my questions that you agreed with the determination made by the Internal Revenue Service that Mr. Boles was a statutory employee of the corporation known as Boles Trucking, Inc., is that correct?

A. Yes. I agreed that he is a statutory employee.

Q. And I also believe that you agreed that, based upon that fact, that Boles Trucking was required to at least withhold social security taxes and to pay those taxes over to the Internal Revenue Service during the period between 1984 and 1987; is that correct?

A. No, I don't think it is what I intended. I said that he should have paid them over if he had paid himself a salary.

Q. He didn't pay himself a salary?

A. That's correct. He was allowed to take out previously taxed Subchapter S income by the Internal Revenue Code and your own regulations.

Q. Is that what he did in this case?

A. I don't know. I haven't studied that part of it.

Q. Do you have any opinion, sir, as to whether Boles Trucking, Inc., was required to file what are known as federal employer's quarterly tax returns or forms 941 based upon Mr. Boles being a statutory employee of Boles Trucking between 1984 and 1987?

A. If he received a salary. You know, he had losses in those years.

Q. How many times, sir, have you advised individuals to do what Mr. Boles did in this case, that is to take out funds from the corporation as loans against future profits?

A. I am going to have to go by years, if it's all right with you, sir.

Q. Let's do it for 1 year. Let's say for 1975.

A. If you had set it for 1959 it would have been easier. I am trying to think. All the Subchapter S corporations I would have had in 1975 would probably already have had a salary.

Q. Did you ever see any notes, by that I mean things such as promissory notes, that were signed by the president of Boles Trucking in connection with these loans against future profits?

A. No.

Q. How did you know that they were, in fact, loans against future profits?

A. I wouldn't have called them loans against future profits. I would have called them distributions of Subchapter S income as allowed by the Internal Revenue Code and Publication 589 regulations. I would have called them a non-taxable distribution of capital.

Q. In preparing the exhibits that you referred to here today, did you have the occasion to review the U.S. individual income tax returns of Mr. Boles?

A. Yes, I did.

Q. The fact that Mr. Boles can take a deduction for or offset any withholding tax liability that the corporation may have, in this case, as you have testified to, does that change the fact that Mr. Boles was required to withhold and pay over any social security taxes or withholding taxes to the Internal Revenue Service in the first instance?

A. I think I already said if he had a salary, then he should have paid it over. If it wasn't a salary, then he shouldn't have paid it over. Had I been arguing this from the beginning, it wouldn't have been a salary, in my opinion.

Q. Is it your opinion that, based upon Mr. Boles' receiving over $108,000 over 4 years, that no taxes are due and owing on that amount. Is that your opinion?

A. No, that's not what I said. I said that if you give him a salary of $108,000, under the law it throws the Subchapter S into a loss of $108,000, and if you take $108,000 income and subtract a $108,000 loss, under the law you get zero. It's not that unusual.

Metcalfe: Your Honor, before I end my cross-examination of Mr. Telpner, I would like to renew my objections to his expert testimony as regards industry practice in this case. I would also move to exclude that evidence based upon the fact that the government's position is that Mr. Telpner is not qualified under Rule 702 to give such opinion, that such opinion is not helpful to the trier of fact under Rule 702, and that it is, in fact, more prejudicial than probative in this case under Rule 403.

The Court: I will overrule the motion.

Metcalfe: I have no further questions, your Honor.

The Court: You may redirect.

Mostek: Thank you, your Honor. I have very few questions.

Redirect Examination by Mostek(Q):

Q. Mr. Telpner, Mr. Metcalfe asked you how many times you advised clients about taking loans against future profits, whatever terminology you want to use, and he asked you what your advice would have been in '75 and you said take a salary. What would your advice have been in 1959?

A. 1959, the Internal Revenue Service ruled that, as I mentioned, that Subchapter S income was not subject to self-employment taxes. And we just didn't — I am not saying just Zeph Telpner, I'm saying that the accounting profession said, hey, congress did this to give the small businessman and woman a break. They didn't want them to pay double taxation. And they said, you are going to have to report all this income on your individual return as if it were yours. So you report all — let's say the corporation makes $100,000. The stockholder has to pay tax on it. Since congress said we only want you to pay one tax, you can take that income out now. You have pay income tax on it, now you are like a proprietorship, it's yours, you paid the tax. We are not going to have you pay tax again when you take it out. So we had them take it out. And because it had to be out within 2.5 months, we used to charge many of the distributions to accounts receivable until we determined whether he had income or loss. You see, at a certain time in 1984, the law changed. If you owed more than $10,000 to your own corporation, you had to pay interest on it. But before 1984 the Internal Revenue Service said, we want you to pay interest on it, but the Supreme Court said no. It wasn't until congress changed the law in 1984. So they intended to have people take it out or charge it to receivables.

Q. Mr. Metcalfe was asking you about Werner Enterprises and the work you did for them. Do you recall that?

A. Yes, I do.

Q. Do you consider Werner Enterprises to be in the same industry segment as Boles Trucking?

A. No.

Q. Was Werner Enterprises what you described as a common carrier?

A. They are a common carrier, irregular route truckload.

Q. Also he questioned you about American Transport, Inc.

A. Yes.

Q. Did you consider that company to be in the same industry segment as Boles Trucking?

A. That is not the same industry segment as Boles Trucking.

Q. Was American Transport an authorized carrier?

A. It's a common carrier with refrigerated meat-hauling authority, as of the last I know.

Q. He also asked you about Yellow Freight. Would you consider that company to be in the same industry segment as Boles Trucking?

A. No, they are a common regular route LTL carrier. They are in the top five largest trucking companies in the U.S.

Q. They are ICC authorized?

A. Yes, ICC authorized.

Q. When you say LTL, what do you mean?

A. Less than a truckload, where they consolidate the freight.

Mostek: No further questions, your Honor.
The Court: Does any member of the jury have any questions?

This question from the juror, I'm going to read it to you, Mr. Telpner, as it is written, the question says, if I understood what was said, why did the tax law change every month to the point a person would be out of touch within 30 days if he did not keep up with the pace? Did you intend to testify during the course of your testimony that the tax laws changed every month?

The Witness: No, sir.

The Court: You had some testimony about change every month and I think that was in interest rates that were changed; is that right?

The Witness: Yes. Sometimes every month, sometimes every 2 months. One year they went as high as 20% and the next month they were down to 8.

The Court: This was reflected in the bulletins or the publications the IRS issued that would be used to calculate or determine the amount of interest that may be due on taxes that had not been paid on the due date; is that right?

The Witness: Yes, sir. They reflected it in those tables.

The Court: And your reference, I take it, and believe I'm correct in this, is that those would change every 30 days; is that correct?

The Witness: Sometimes the interest rate could be different within 30 days, sometimes in 60, but — I can't recall in the tables whether any changed less frequently. But it fell within a period, for example, where we had the leap year, we might do it for 30 days and the next 30 days it would be the new interest rate.

The Court: Mr. Mostek, if that prompts any questions?

Mostek: No questions.

The Court: Mr. Metcalfe?

Metcalfe: No, your Honor.

The Court: You may be excused, Mr. Telpner.

Afterword 11

Work always remains after a trial for the lawyer and his expert. The expert must prepare his final billing. In forensic engagements, an invoice stating "for services rendered," is not adequate. It should be prepared in detail, listing every step taken, who was interviewed, research done and the time and charges involved. If you read a deposition, note that in your invoice.

Sometimes the expert's fees will be challenged. Perhaps the opposing side lost and has been ordered to pay the his fees. That may create a challenge to your fees and you will need detailed work and time records to support them. When there is a court-appointed forensic engagement such as bankruptcy examiner or special master, you may need to hire an attorney to prepare the legal documents to file with the court to collect your fee. This is especially true of work for a court or a governmental agency.

I had been hired to study the costs charged by two hospitals for care for indigents. The County Board of Supervisors (Board) believed that the hospitals were overcharging the Board for indigent care. When I completed my study, I reported to the Board that the hospitals were undercharging them for the indigent care. The hospitals wanted to renegotiate the contract to increase their charges.

The Board held a public hearing to question me and to protest my fee. The Board members thought that accounting was like politics and that we would say anything to please our employer. They did not understand the concept of independence and integrity.

If the case is to be appealed by the loser, whether your side is the loser or the winner, you may be required to write opinions and memos on accounting-related matters to help your attorney to understand the accounting issues.

Sometimes the decision is unknown until the accountant makes certain calculations. Perhaps the U.S. Tax Court ruled that its decision will be entered under rule 155. Rule 155 of the Tax Court Procedures means that the court has decided on the amounts and formula needed to arrive at the ultimate amount of tax due or refundable. The court though, will not multiply, add, or subtract the numbers in the formula. The taxpayer and the Commissioner of Internal Revenue must each calculate the final amount from the formula and numbers supplied by the court. If they both arrive at the same answer, the court will agree. If their answers differ materially, the court may order them to recalculate the amount or the court may do it. If the court does it, the decision they reach is final unless appealed.

The essential argument presented in Chapter 7 is this: The lawyer who will be doing the examination and the forensic accountant who will be giving the opinions must work together very closely. Around this skeletal premise, we have fleshed out the details each needs to help accomplish this goal. For example, the lawyer must have a sound understanding of what a forensic accountant does, and what he can and cannot do for the case. Likewise, the accountant must have the benefit of some understanding of the legal process, the law of privilege and the rules and customs under which expert opinions as testimony may be presented.

Also, we believe that the parties to the dispute and everyone else concerned, including the legal system, are best served when this working relationship is built very early in the case. This is because litigation is a very inefficient means of resolving disputes. The tremendous expense involved in any proceeding, be it administrative, civil or criminal, practically mandates most disputes to be resolved on an acceptable basis as expeditiously as possible. The process of searching for the truth and having it decided by a judge or a jury is often wasted because of litigation inefficiency. Our private resources, including money, time and energy, can be put to better use when disputes can be resolved more efficiently. This is why methods of alternative dispute resolution, including binding arbitration, mediation and good-old-fashioned negotiation, have become so popular. The relationship between the lawyer and the forensic accounting expert plays a role in all means of dispute resolution, from the most informal negotiation to the most formal — a full-blown adversarial trial. The role should be reserved only for those cases that demand no less. Significant public resources, including that relationship between the lawyer and his expert, is to develop and determine which facts and circumstances support or refute the case of their client.

To an extent, modern discovery rules turn the adversary process into an exercise in fortune telling. Both sides look into their "crystal ball" (the known facts as applied to the law) and try to predict the ultimate outcome of the dispute. Both sides advise their clients based on these prognoses. The most skilled lawyers are very good at this sort of soothsaying, and they know that the integrity of their predictions is only as good as the information upon which they are based. It follows that, working closely with their experts, lawyers have a better chance of obtaining more and better information upon which to predict and even fashion the outcome of the dispute. And, the sooner they are able to develop this information, the sooner the dispute can be resolved.

Given a case that requires their skills, forensic accountants can aid lawyers and this process significantly, but only if given the information and opportunity to do their best work. If all can do their best work, the outcome can be predicted (in many cases) with greater certainty. Many cases are settled because of this exercise in prognostication, and clients, both private and public, save the expense, aggravation and delays associated with a trial and, possibly, appeal. This also serves the best interests of the judicial system, which has become clogged and overburdened with civil and criminal cases working their way through the process.

We understand that this must occur within the limits imposed by the circumstances of the case. If it is a small, private, civil matter, the amount in controversy may not justify the expense of having the lawyer and accountant spend many hours together working up the case. We also understand that some lawyers, or their clients, will not retain an expert witness until they are certain the case is going to trial, i.e., it cannot be settled. Usually they do this to save expense. This may be the correct course in some cases but, generally, we believe it is wrong. The best way to save expense in the long run is to develop the needed accounting opinions and other evidence early in the case. If the evidence is positive, it will strengthen your hand. If it is negative, it will tell you to work toward resolving the matter soon. Of course, we also understand that some cases cannot be settled. Some just have to be tried either because they are too close to call, or because one side or the other needs more "convincing."

We have witnessed the results that usually accrue when the working relationship between the lawyer and the expert forensic accountant is not close or formed early in the case. Sometimes the outcome of the case is affected. Lawyers often learn that they could have done a much better job at trial if only they had begun working with their expert sooner. Sometimes, they learn that the case could or should have been settled. The realization may be brought about by some fact that they wish they had communicated to the accountant, or it may be a total surprise statement or opinion by the opposing expert (or even their own expert) that the lawyers could have anticipated if only they had worked more closely with their expert.

We believe that the lawyer must take primary responsibility to see that the working relationship is a good one and that it is established early in the case. Some lawyers will be quick to blame the expert when cases go bad. But if a qualified expert who is able to communicate with skill and persuasion does poorly in his deposition or at trial, the lawyer must examine his own efforts to determine whether he should take some or all of the responsibility.

Accountants often feel "hung out to dry" when the only exposure they have to the facts of the case is perhaps a brief letter written to them by the attorney at the time of engagement. Then they confer a couple of times and the expert writes a report if the attorney wants one. If asked, the accountant shows up for a deposition, suffers through at least an hour of strange questions about what kind of education, training or experience he may have, what he has reviewed and what opinions he holds. Then the lawyer does not call the expert again until it's time for trial. The expert shows up at trial, gives his testimony, suffers the barbs and missiles launched at him on cross-examination, and leaves the trial wondering what just happened to him and why.

Lawyers must take responsibility for selecting a qualified expert and sharing with him all of the information needed to do his work effectively. He must also accept the fact that he may not be in the best position to judge exactly what it is the expert needs to review. Lawyers must listen to the expert and his requests for information. They must also take responsibility to learn what they need to know about the issues and rules unique to the accounting profession that will affect their expert's work and opinions. Some people say a trial lawyer is a "jack of all trades and master of none." Trial lawyers are exposed to many different disciplines, from medicine to engineering to accounting, and everything in between. They must learn about the profession and skills involved with the facts and issues of the case. The expert is invaluable as a source of this knowledge. And, if the accountant can teach the lawyer what he needs to know to understand the case, chances are it will be good practice for the education the expert must give the judge or jury in presenting understandable and persuasive opinions at trial.

Lawyers must also adequately prepare their experts for their depositions and trial testimony. This includes educating the expert about the adversarial process in general — discovery, evidence, procedure and strategy. Lawyers are the ones who are supposed to be familiar with all of the mysterious language, customs and procedures of the courtroom. They must take the lead and make sure the expert is prepared and comfortable with all that can be expected or possibly foreseen. Forensic accountants must be able to tell the lawyer whether they feel qualified to take the engagement and educate the lawyer on the important accounting issues of the case, what they need to do their job well, and what constraints they may feel in either developing their opinions or giving testimony.

After the trial is over — or the dispute is settled without a trial — or before the jury renders a decision, the expert and the lawyer should hold a last meeting. They can help one another for the next trial if they critique their work in relationship to what was written in the preceding paragraphs.

If their client lost the decision, a critique is always necessary. If they have won, the critique will help them to win the next time. No lawyer always wins, but, if the critique follows a win, it may help your lawyer to have a preponderance of positive outcomes.

Index

A